796.41
Lurie

Heart of Steel

The Dan Lurie Story

Dan Lurie with David Robson, Foreword by Regis Philbin

authorHOUSE®

AuthorHouse™
1663 Liberty Drive, Suite 200
Bloomington, IN 47403
www.authorhouse.com
Phone: 1-800-839-8640

© 2009 Dan Lurie with David Robson, Foreword by Regis Philbin. All rights reserved.

No part of this book may be reproduced, stored in a retrieval system, or transmitted by any means without the written permission of the author.

First published by AuthorHouse 9/1/2009

ISBN: 978-1-4343-8545-1 (sc)
ISBN: 978-1-4343-8546-8 (hc)

Printed in the United States of America
Bloomington, Indiana

This book is printed on acid-free paper.

Dan's website is www.DanLurie.com
Contact Dan at: DanLurie@webtv.net
Write him at:
    Dan Lurie
    Box 21
    21 Vanderbilt Park
    Valley Stream, N.Y. 11581

This book is dedicated to my brother Morris "Terry" Lurie who was killed in World War II and my sister Pearl who passed away as a very young child. In addition to my siblings, I would also like to dedicate this book to my parents Abe & Rachel Lurie who gave me everything they possibly could while I was growing up and helped make me the man I am today. To my 5 children, Mark, Andrea, Shelly, Sandy & Jill, my 15 grandchildren and my great-grandchildren, some of whom are on this earth already and those who I anticipate in the years to come… You keep me young & inspired and I love you all very much. Lastly, my loving wife Thelma…62 years of marriage and counting! She has been there for me through everything. I love you with all my heart. Thank you.

Contents

Foreward		1
Chapter One:	The Dream Begins	3
Chapter Two:	America's Most Muscular Man	29
Chapter Three:	Barbells, Contests, and Controversy	53
Chapter Four:	The Grimek Challenge	75
Chapter Five:	Television Strongman	88
Chapter Six:	Muscles and Magazines	107
Chapter Seven:	A Hulking Challenge	142
Chapter Eight:	The Arnold Years	158
Chapter Nine:	The Greatest Gift of All: Family. Everyday Life for Dan the Man	172
Chapter Ten:	People	201
Chapter Eleven:	The World's Most Physically Fit President Joins the WBBG	269
Chapter Twelve:	Bodybuilding Champions	287
Chapter Thirteen:	Dan Lurie Says, "Say no to drugs"	316
Chapter Fourteen:	Bodybuilding Pioneer	335
Chapter Fifteen:	Back, Although Never Really Gone	367
Index		409

Foreword

By Regis Philbin

I have known of Dan Lurie for almost 60 years. This extraordinary man is one of the true bodybuilding founders. In fact, when I was a 16-year-old boy living in the Bronx, my father Frank went to Brooklyn to the Dan Lurie Barbell Company to buy me a set of 110-pound barbells. In those days, when fewer Americans were into bodybuilding, there were only two barbell companies: York and Dan Lurie Barbells.

All my life I've believed in physical fitness and have always worked out - in fact, to this day I still go to the gym regularly to keep myself in great physical condition.

Back in February of 1984, I had Dan Lurie appear as a guest on my Morning Show, a few days after he arm-wrestled with President Ronald Reagan right in the Oval Office. I arm-wrestled Dan myself right on my show and, using two hands, I beat him - the former America's Most Muscular Man!

When I had my Fitness TV show, Dan appeared several times, bringing me the world's strongest men and women. I even had the Best-Built Fireman on my show. I took off my shirt to challenge this amazing specimen. This book has a picture of me with him and Dan! And we always used a Dan Lurie 310-pound Olympic Weightlifting Set on our show.

Several years ago on my Morning Show, Dan inducted me into his World Body Building Guild Hall of Fame as the Man of the Year. He presented me with a plaque as "TV's Most Physically Fit Man in Show Business," as Kathy Lee cheered him on!

Dan, I know that on April 1st, 2009, you'll be 86 years young, and that you're still going strong! God bless you for all of your pioneering work in the fitness world - and for letting me use two hands when we arm-wrestled!

Your friend,

Regis

Regis Philbin is an Emmy Award-winning American television personality who has worked in the entertainment industry for over 50 years. Regis is widely known for hosting 'Live with Regis and Kelly."

Regis Philbin

Chapter One:
The Dream Begins

Many believe we are placed on earth for a purpose and that finding this purpose is what we must do to live a meaningful, accomplished and fulfilled life. Some people find their purpose early on, for some it takes longer, for others it never happens. For me it came early and, looking back, the events that led up to it seem as though they were put in place to teach me the lessons needed to overcome the hurdles that would stand in the way of its achievement. This is my story.

As I studied the muscleman on the cover of the July 1944 edition of *Your Physique* Magazine, the most muscular bodybuilder in the world at the time, standing strong with a body as large and proportioned as could be found anywhere on earth, my mind turned to the events that placed me there. I had achieved what many in my field had not: won the AAU America's Most Muscular Man title three years consecutively and appeared on many muscle magazine covers. At age 21 I had arrived. Hot off the press, that issue symbolized to me the struggle and commitment that had taken place in the years leading up to its publication. As a child, my dreams were full of heroic and daring adventure, typical imaginings for a boy of my age. As a youngster I was determined to become a man of strength and might. In fact, it was my only wish back then: a way in which to drag myself out of the Great Depression years to become somebody. And for this, boxing became my vehicle and I worked hard to become a champion in this sport. At 16, having trained tirelessly for three years, my big chance came and I finally was given the opportunity to prove I had what it took to become such a champion. A Golden Gloves boxing tournament, where the winner would go on to fight in the finals at the iconic Madison Square Garden, came at the perfect time in my life. I felt I had the skills and toughness to make a major impact in the sport I loved, and prove to myself that I was a man of strength. At a fighting fit five feet five inches, 118lbs, I was ready. Then it ended before it even began. During the pre-fight medical examination I was told I could not compete because of a heart murmur I had had since birth. Right then my world was shattered. *What would I do?* I thought as I sat there, dejected. Upset and feeling sorry for myself, I was approached by a muscular and dignified-looking man, an ex-boxer turned bodybuilder who kindly told me not to give up on my dreams, that I would move on to bigger things. Little did I know it at the time, but this man, Terry Robinson, would be my guiding light; a mentor who would get me started in weight training and on the road to a life in bodybuilding. With Mr. Robinson's advice, fighting spirit and a generous dose of tenaciousness I began training for a little-known sport called bodybuilding; it would become a discipline I devoted every day to and teaching it to others for health and fitness, along with its worldwide promotion, was to become my passion.

Despite the financial hardships that hit hard with the Great Depression, my childhood was largely one of joy, but many challenges came with the times, some positive, and some that would have disastrous consequences for my family and I. Some of my earliest memories are of playing sporting games, both organized

The Dream Begins

and on the street after-school with my siblings and neighbourhood kids, and excelling in them all. In fact, a highlight of my younger years was the physical challenge such games, along with the typical rough and tumble antics of youth provided. It was when these games took a more serious turn that I would find my calling.

"I had arrived" - Your Physique, 1944.

The head of my family was my father Abe Lurie, a very strong man who ran a moving business, Abe Lurie Parkway Vans. He was a rock whose dependability and patience was an inspiration to those he knew. My mother Rachael (Ray for short) provided love and guidance to my five siblings and I and was a compassionate lady who would help anyone in need. My father was born in Brooklyn, New York, and his father emigrated from Poland. My grandfather was Nathan Lurie and he was also in the moving business, but rather than using trucks as my father did, he used a horse and wagon. My industrious side may even have came from Granddad Lurie as he would rent horses from a stable of over 50 to wagon peddlers in the New York City area. One of his more notable customers was John West, a respected boxer and weight trainer who had a daughter, Mae, who would herself achieve notoriety, and who, in an interesting turn of events, I would someday meet.

I was born during a raging blizzard in the East New York section of Brooklyn on April 1, 1923 and my entry into the world could be considered anything but spectacular. Moments after my birth the doctors discovered I had a hole in my heart and they promptly told my parents that I would be lucky to reach the age of five. Despite this prediction I began life the way I would continue through it: with plenty of energy. I was a rather large baby, with an even larger appetite, and the hole in my heart certainly did not slow me down during my early years. Shortly after my birth, my mother and father moved from their home on Sheffield Avenue in East New York to what would become my permanent childhood home: 1729 Rockaway Parkway in the Canarsie section of Brooklyn.

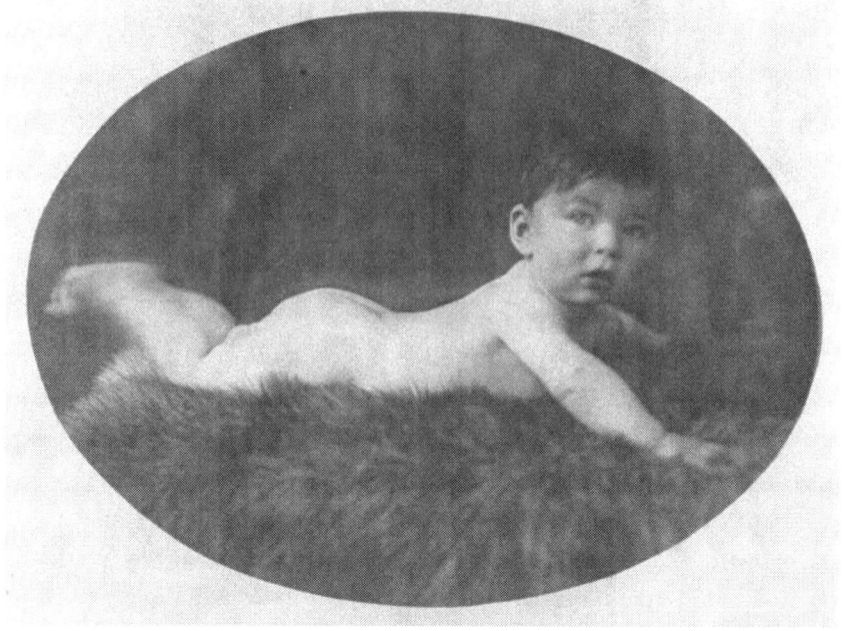

"I began life with plenty of energy." Dan: one month old.

Our family was a close-knit one. All us brothers and sisters would support one other and the love we shared got us through much of the hardship we faced during the Depression. I was second youngest and my oldest sister, Mildred, or "Molly" as I called her, would take care of me. She mothered me as if I were her baby, spoiling me with lots of food and care. She would regularly baby-sit my younger sister Pearl and I. My middle sister, Jean, also helped me, but less as a "mother", more as a teacher: she assisted me with my homework and helped me stay afloat academically during my high school years. In fact, both Jean and Molly were the most academically gifted of us kids. They were also incredibly ambitious and career minded. Molly had the most beautiful voice and dreamed of becoming a famous singer. She sang on her own radio show at age 18 and around this time received offers to go into show business. But my father said no. He was of the opinion that showgirls who traveled around the country were not the kind he wanted his daughter to mix with. Instead, she began establishing a family and has raised four lovely children with her husband Manny Cohen, a physical education teacher. Jean started her career running a dress shop, a role she was very successful in. She too married and spent much of her time traveling and enjoying life with her husband, Charlie Revzin. Jean eventually sold her dress business and retired to Miami, Florida. My brother-in-law, Charlie, who I loved very much, died unexpectedly in Florida in 1979. A real gentleman, Charlie was fantastic dresser and extremely good looking. He always passed his ties down to me and, to this day, when I wear one I think of him.

Besides my father, the strongman of the family early on was my brother Harry. Four years older than me, he was much bigger and stronger, though I would beat him at wrestling, an activity us brothers would often compete with each other in. Harry's strength was so great that he would carry large pieces of furniture on his back when helping my father in his business. My other brother was Morris, "Terry" as he liked to be called. He was two years younger than Harry but, of all my siblings, the one I looked up to the most. He had it all. An extremely good boxer and popular with the girls because of his good looks, Morris, or Moish as I called him, gave me a lot of confidence in myself. He taught me boxing skills and I became, in many respects, a better person because of the time he spent with me. He was killed at the young age of 21, at Anzio Beach, Italy, during World War II. He is sadly missed by us all - a true gentleman. He was my hero and best friend.

Dan's Sisters: Jean Revzin (left) and Mildred Cohen.

Dan and his brother Harry (left) taking a break from testing their strength against one another through engaging in Dan's other passion: checkers.

The Dream Begins

American Hero: Morris Lurie - killed in action fighting for his country during World War II. He was Dan's hero and best friend.

During our early days as kids we would always be up to some kind of mischief, always on the go and never sitting still. I think the fact we were poor caused us to create our own fun. Many times the whole family would get together and enjoy each other's company. And meal times were always special, as we would all get together and share the stories of the day. In 1936, when I was thirteen, our family rented two rooms at Rockaway Beach. This was a real novelty for me, and a wonderful time for all, which luckily became a regular event. Every summer for the next 10 years we would rent a bungalow in Rockaway Beach; my memories of these vacations are fond as, during these times, our entire family were able to completely relax and simply enjoy time together. In time I would carry on the Rockaway Beach tradition with my own family: in the summer of 1948 we rented a whole house, very large with white shingles and a red roof. It stood on 88th Street, just a block from the boardwalk. I remember the landlord could not find anyone to rent it and rather than lose a full season's rent, gave the whole place - all 10 apartments - to us for $500 for the entire summer. We were able to house all of our relatives that year as they all got an apartment or two each. They all chipped in to cover the cost. My wife Thelma, son Mark - nine months old at the time - along with my wife's parents, Izidore (Izzy) and Adell Rothman, and her sister, Sylvia and Sylvia's husband Seymour Garber had a great time on the beach and in the water with extended family including many cousins. On the first floor of that house there was a big kitchen and we would all eat together every night. Great times!

Other good times with my family during my younger years included the many picnics we went on. Rockaway Beach on the Atlantic Ocean was a regular picnic destination and our yearly vacation spot. We would all pile into my father's little Ford with a lot of food, happy that we would be spending our hot summer days swimming in the cool Atlantic waters and playing in the sand. Looking back I am so surprised we all fit into my dad's little car. But we did, and our outings were almost always pleasant. On one occasion, though, we did not make it home and it all began as we returned from Rockaway Beach. That night the pounding rain made driving next to impossible and in the 1930s ignition wires were not waterproof. Our little car just died when the water hit the wires. While many of our nights had been spent sleeping on the beach because of the heat, that night was spent in the local firehouse because of the rain. My brothers and I loved this little adventure.

My family was not what you would call overly religious. My grandmother and grandfather, who were from Poland, where my mother was born, were very orthodox people, but my mother - maiden name Rosenberg - made no big show of any religious upbringing and I was the only boy in my family to be Bar-Mitzvahed. At the time I was 13 and to prepare for the big day studied at the home of Rabbi Spector, where we used a recording and some of the Rabbi's books. Though the old Rabbi was blind, we did not get away with anything and had to study hard. For the event my mother had a little party for me where she served peanuts and I received a fountain pen. Remember, this was the Depression and such occasions were rare back then, the pen I received, an expensive gift. Today I cannot say that I am very religious, not a big believer in all the ceremony governing religion, but I have a strong faith in God and when something does go wrong I can pray with the best of them.

The Dream Begins

Diligent Student: Dan Lurie aged 13, on his Bar Mitzvah day.

As a young man I was known for my quick thinking and large appetite for food, two traits that I would often combine to my advantage, and I had many jobs as a youngster, several of them involving the selling of food. While in grammar school - at Public School 115 – I would start my day at 4.00 to begin working on a bakery truck, where I would deliver bread and rolls to many stores in the surrounding Canarsie district. Around this time I also sold ice cream at the Golden Gate Canarsie Arena, on the boardwalk at Rockaway Beach, on the Mackaway Line's boats between Rockaway and Canarsie and later at the concession at the Yiddish Theater on Irving Place and 14th Street. When I think about it, ice cream played a big part in my life even as I entered adulthood. For one thing, I have always loved its taste. Still do today. And one of my biggest breaks actually came as a result working for a famous company that made the stuff: Sealtest. But as a youth, selling it would help develop an entrepreneurial streak that would last me throughout my life. And this is where my quick thinking came in handy. At age 13, and because of my connection with, and affinity to ice cream, I was to become very popular with my friends. At this time

I was running the Bungalow Bar ice cream concession on Beach 59th Street. For children, the Bungalow name was popular at the time, as it was one of the main suppliers of ice cream for the entire district. Its trucks, looking like little bungalows on wheels, were distinctive with their peaked red shingle roofs. In 1936, Bungalow had what they called Lucky Sticks, a promotion where for every ice cream that was found to have a Lucky Stick, the owner of this treat would get another for free, and any kid who licked their ice cream stick clean to discover a Lucky Stick would gain instant popularity among their friends. My popularity came through discovering a way to identify Lucky Sticks before the ice cream was eaten: the winners had slightly more rounded edges than the others. Upon discovering this, I got to work selling my friends the lucky ones. They were happy because they got two for one. I was happy because whenever I wanted more ice cream I would help myself to an easily identified Lucky Stick. Since I had a large appetite, I would put away a fair few of these frozen treats.

My large appetite was also noticed during regular family visits to Epstein's Hotel in Spring Valley. At Epstein's they offered at the time a Sunday afternoon special: all you could eat for $1.25 (children only 75 cents). Most kids would have to be practically forced by their parents to eat and this was what the owner had in mind when he advertised the low rates for children. This would get the whole family in, along with their money. But I loved to eat and could really put it away. Three or four helpings later and I would still be ready for more, and this applied to most of the foods they served. Although my brothers and sisters ate moderately, I ate enough for all four of them, causing much consternation among the management. Exasperated, the owner had one Sunday seen enough. He complained to my mother that I was eating *too* much. She replied that I was only a little boy and really could not be eating what he claimed. The restaurant had a policy of giving the child who ate the most a free lollipop at the end of their meal. That day the owner had to present me with the lollipop, after I had eaten my fourth helping. I not only ate him out of house and home, but policy demanded that he reward me for doing so.

A less enjoyable job I had, possibly because it did not involve eating ice cream or any other food, called for a level of inventiveness of which I was blessed: household chores. Every week it was my job to scrub the kitchen floor. My mother, having gained a lot of weight after her first pregnancy, found she could no longer do this job so the duty was mine. To quickly complete this job, I developed a game plan. What I would do is divide the floor into large squares and wash the floor four feet at a time. To cover the most distance in the shortest period, because I was usually in a hurry to do something else, like eat ice cream or play street games with my friends, I would limit my squares to six large ones. To do this I had to stretch out with my brush and cloth from my position on my knees and move back and forwards. Once the linoleum was sparkling clean I would cover it with newspaper and keep it that way for at least a day.

My foresight was not limited to floor scrubbing and ice cream. When I was seven years old my uncle Abe Bender would put a penny and dime in one hand and ask me to pick one. I thought he would think of me as greedy if I took too much and figured if I chose the dime he would never let me pick again. So I always picked the penny and he would act like I was stupid for doing this. But he continued to offer me the choice every time we met and he seemed to gain enjoyment showing others how dumb I was. This went on for many years and I probably got over a dollar in total. Looking back on this, my approach was pretty smart for such a young man. Rather than take it all at once it is best to make gradual progress because in the end the results will be much greater, as quick fixes rarely work. This philosophy can be applied to business and weight training. We all know what may happen if you go too heavy too soon on a given exercise: you could suffer an injury. The same thing holds true for anything else. Slow and steady wins the race. Years later I discovered that uncle Abe was, in fact, testing me to see whether, in a fit of greed, I would take it all in one go. It seems I passed the test. A Chinese proverb says, "A coin a day makes a thousand coins in a thousand days, in time a rope may saw through a tree, and dripping water can wear away a stone". If you achieve many small goals, over time these will shape who you become and provide for you a life of riches. It has worked for me so far.

A love for the movies and entertainment is something I have always had. Throughout my life I have performed on one stage or another, but my first real break came through, you guessed it: ice cream. It was in 1938 while selling ice cream at the Yiddish Theater on Irvine Place and East 14th Street that I made my stage debut. During one of the performances the child who normally played the baby in a carriage got a stomach-ache. I happened to be there at the time so the director, out of desperation, draped a white sheet around me while two stagehands folded me to fit the carriage. At 15, I played the baby. Thereafter, they would call on me to play small parts whenever there was an emergency. Although hardly the stuff of Hollywood superstardom, it did spark an interest in performance that would last a lifetime.

Around the time of my "debut" I would attend all of the latest movies. We would pay a dime to see a double-feature movie, a couple of short films, news and a cartoon. My hero at this time was an actor named George Brent. He was a good-looking, daring type who had the most amazing voice – very deep and powerful. Characters who had power and strength always impressed me. Tarzan was one of them and I would watch him in the chapter films. Each week he would find himself in some kind of high-pressure situation mere seconds before the segment's end. He would be about to go over a waterfall and we would all be on the edge of our seats waiting - then we would be informed that we could find out the ending next time. We would all be left wondering what would happen next, which, of course, had us coming back the following week for the next episode. During the next installment Cheetah the Chimp would throw Tarzan a vine and we were back into another gripping adventure. During these times my mind would often get caught up in fantastic adventure. I imagined myself as the hero, strong and powerful, ready to save the day. I suppose all young men have these kinds of fantasies, but mine were so vivid it was as if I was, in fact, living my life through them, a state of being that would, in future years, benefit me in many ways. These dreams, as they increasingly bordered on reality, would eventually lead me to heroic performance of a kind I had never seen, much less considered during those young years.

From an early age I developed a liking for physical strength. The feeling it gave me and the fact it helped me to win at sport was enough

The Dream Begins

to convince me to push my muscular limits in the hopes of gaining more of it. I particularly enjoyed, and became good at, gymnastics, Ping-Pong and badminton. After-school games included stickball and stoopball, the objective of the latter being to hit a rubber ball into the opposing team's goal - a point on a front door step - by whacking it with all your strength. We played this game curb-to-curb, rather than the length of the street as was done with stickball. To get a turn at bat, a fielder had to catch a ball on the fly. During these kinds of games my aim was to always hit harder, run faster and jump further. Later, at high school, I developed my athletic skills to such a degree that I became the only student ever at Tilden High School, possibly even in U.S. history, to graduate with a perfect score for physical education at that school. Along with this distinction I received the George F. Wingate medal for outstanding athlete.

The year was 1936 and I was well on my way to becoming a sports star. But what activity would I choose? That was the question I asked as I worked away at achieving perfection in tumbles, push-ups, running – whatever was on offer, really. I would say my school years were a time where my physical aspirations overtook all things scholastic. At this time my mind was focused on achieving sporting success rather than academic excellence, though I did become skilled at checkers, winning the New York State High School Checkers Championship's, and did win the Tilden High Spanish Medal thanks my sister Jean's help. In fact, so passionate did I become about checkers that this game of strategy would form a major part of my life. My Uncle Morris Rosenberg taught me how to play checkers and from the age of ten I would spend many hours with him, himself a master checkers player, and he would show me all of the traps and positions needed to win and how to make all the right moves - I would go on to beat him several times, which boosted my confidence tremendously. Adding to my high school checkers success, I won - at age 13 - the teenage division at the 1936 New York State Checkers Championship's and was eventually placed in the pro category for this game. If I had to, I would rate myself on a scale of one-to-ten, as an eight-to-nine pro player. To this day I credit the game for providing me with a good business mind – it has made strategic thinking much easier.

While certain areas of my early teens were shaping up nicely, others were less distinctive, by virtue of my still-developing confidence levels and smaller stature. At age 13 my character was further tested. At this time I must have weighed 100 pounds soaking wet and I would walk to PS 115 in Canarsie, Brooklyn, very underdeveloped and an easy target for bullies. Every so often I would see this boy, Raymond, across the street from where I was walking. Raymond, who would have outweighed me by at least 40 pounds and who stood a good five inches taller, would cross the street and follow me before attacking me with punch after punch. This went on for about one year. I would try to walk a different way to school each time, but again he would spot me. Running was of no use. He always caught me and the beatings took a more sinister tone each time, almost as if he was punishing me for trying to escape. I always tried to avoid him, but it did no good. I remember one time telling myself to stand up and fight, to hit him hard. But no matter what I did Raymond always got the better of me. Fortunately this all stopped when I entered Tilden High School, but the memories stuck with me for many years afterward. As I grew, so too did my strength. At age 14 I began boxing at P.S. 115 before, several years later, joining a pro boxing club called Ferkie's - where all the top fighters in my area trained. I too became a good fighter, gaining skills I would love to have had back when Raymond used to beat me. When I trained as a boxer, and later as a bodybuilder, I would picture Raymond in my mind and swear to some day get even with this "coward", this "poor excuse for a person". I would say to myself that one day I would catch Raymond and beat the hell out of him and the tables would be turned. Thirty years passed and I had grown to a bodyweight of 220 pounds of solid muscle. I was in my early-40s, at peak strength, and running several businesses at once. One day a man came into one of my fitness showrooms with his son and asked about buying a barbell set for his kid. He looked familiar. "Is your name Raymond and did you once live on East 98 Street," I asked sternly, physically overpowering the man standing before me. "Yes," he replied, his voice quivering slightly. I knew instantly it was the Raymond who used to beat me up. At that very moment, all of those years of accumulated anger overcame me. I could feel my heartbeat rise and my adrenaline soar. Placing my hands behind my back I clenched my fists. I was ready. Finally it was my turn to get even; the moment I had waited many years for had arrived and there was no holding back. But instead of sending him flying I looked him in the eyes, unclasped my hands, gave him a big hug and cried. Still holding this man who would routinely beat me to a pulp, I asked, "Why did you follow me and beat me Raymond?" He burst into tears, apologized and said he was just a stupid kid at the time. At that moment I felt a great release of pressure and the weight of 30 years of anger melt inside me.

Upon entering Tilden High School my life took a different direction. Whereas at Canarsie Elementary School my grades were very good overall – low-90s on average - at Tilden they became less of a concern. The subjects at high school were different and, by comparison, more difficult for me. This is not to say my time there was not productive. My sporting success shows it was. I even made friends with several of the teachers and got along fine with almost everyone I met. But my grades would drop to the point where I even flunked math and Spanish in my first year. Poor academic performance in my first year aside, though, my time at Tilden proved an important turning point in my life.

My first real exposure to a sport that required great strength came when I began training in gymnastics. I would work out with six other students on the parallel and high bars. My skills and strength quickly improved to the point where I would beat my fellow gymnasts on all disciplines and my overall athletic prowess progressed so much so that when I won the George F. Wingate medal for outstanding athlete I was told that I was the only non-football and basketball-playing student to ever achieve such an honor. Although my gymnastics performance was an important step toward getting this award, my overall academic record for physical education - 100 percent for each of the eight semesters I participated – sealed the deal. This also taught me a valuable lesson in that with strength of mind and determination, anything is possible.

Dan Lurie: Heart of Steel

Tilden High School's Top Athlete: a 17-year-old Dan Lurie (far left) out-muscling his class in 1940.

In my first year at Tilden, physical development became very important to me and I loved gym class, as it would give me the opportunity to improve my body and release my boundless energy. It was fun for me, recreation almost. In my very first gym class I overheard my gym teacher saying, "If everyone did push-ups like that fellow over there, they would get very strong. If he continues the way he is going I will give him 100 percent for the entire semester." When I realized he was talking about me I sprinted across to him and with much eagerness asked, "100 percent, what do I have to do to achieve 100 percent?" The teacher told me I would need to get 100 percent on all tests and not miss a class. For four years I did not miss a single class and with a disciplined mind that would enable the reaching of even greater heights in later years, came out on top in all that was asked of me.

The quest to become Tilden's top athlete, along with the many street games I played during my younger years occupied hours of

The Dream Begins

my time and helped to take my mind off the poverty I experienced. Though my childhood years were fun, and we kids had what we needed like food, a roof over our heads and our parents' love, a level of desperation on the part of both my parent's was a constant feature of family life for us. Although my father ran his furniture-removal business, money was extremely tight. When I was six my family, like all families on our street, experienced the 1929 stock-market crash. The after-effects were devastating. Large numbers of men found themselves out of work and those who were employed could hardly make ends meet, due to a lack of demand for their business.

One very sad moment of my life, a tragedy that stands still as a constant reminder of just how hard things were in those times, was to bring unimaginable grief to my family. My little sister Pearl, five at the time, was playing with one of our small cousins in the backyard of our home, but this harmless fun would soon become a living nightmare for us all. Pearl and her cousin played tag that day - a game we all enjoyed - and were running around the yard, laughing with excitement, and as carefree as only young children can be. Then it happened. As a joke, my cousin put a lit match into Pearl's pocket. Her clothing quickly caught fire and she was badly burned. From where I was standing inside our house, I saw everything, and was horrified to see the flames spreading fast as Pearl desperately tried to put them out herself. I ran into the kitchen for water and by the time I got to Pearl a neighbour had wrapped her in blankets. We quickly took her to the hospital on Linden Boulevard, but they would not treat her, as my parent's had no money. My parent's instead were forced to take her to King's Country hospital, where little Pearl died the following day. My family and I were devastated. One day Pearl was happily playing in the yard, the next she was dead. This poor girl's image haunted me years after she died. I still think of her today and imagine what might have been had she not been taken at such a young age. Her burns, and perhaps the delay in treating her, were too much. Such was the poverty that was so real for us, my parents had to ask several of our neighbours for money to bury Pearl. They all chipped in and Pearl was given a proper farewell. Losing a child is every parent's worst nightmare and with the little girl who brought so much joy into our lives gone, life would never be the same.

Though Pearl's death may not have happened had she received quick attention and if my parent's were able to pay the hospital, the poverty my mother and father experienced did not, on the whole, affect us kids in a bad way. We managed and got through. For example, we always had plenty to eat. My mother made sure of that. She could make something out of next to nothing and if 20 guests arrived at our home, my mother would disappear, only to return moments later with enough food to feed everyone. I loved my mother's cooking, and my favorite food was mashed potatoes. Often I would help her to make dinner and my job was to mash the potatoes, adding the milk and raw eggs. When she wasn't looking I would sneak mouthfuls of potatoes. My mother was smart and very resourceful, but not only in domestic jobs. She helped my father run his business with her bookkeeping and accounting skills. At one point, to make ends meet, my mother took in three orphaned children, a job that lasted for ten years. On New Year's Eve, 1952, my mother died of a heart attack resulting from water on her lungs. She was only 59. My mother was a dear, compassionate lady who will always remain close to my heart. My father died 21 years later at age 80. Diabetes took this very strong capable man. I was inspired by dad's strength. When he was in his prime he could, with one mighty blow, drive a 10-penny nail into a plank of wood with his bare hands. He could also carry an upright piano of around 800 pounds down a flight of stairs on his back, without any help. These are memories that had a massive impact on my life at the time and I believe they helped shape my future. Although he was never a professional strongman, my father, at five feet eight and 200 pounds of pure muscle, did train

The Dream Begins

at Coney Island with world-famous strongman, Warren Lincoln Travers. My father and mother were caring loving parents who provided for us as best they could. To them I owe a large part of the determination and drive that helped me achieve all I have today.

Loving Parents: Dan's father and mother, Abe and Ray Lurie.

As the years passed, my interest in physical performance grew. In 1939 at age 16, I decided to give boxing a decent go. Up until then I trained with my brother Morris at Ferkie's Gym in Brownsville. At 118 pounds my body was small but well developed through countless hours of gymnastics. At the time Morris was training hard for the local Daily News Golden Gloves Championship's, which offered the winner a chance to fight in the finals at Madison Square Garden. I helped him to improve his skills in preparation for this contest, where he eventually made it to the final bout, only to lose by a few points. Morris had built quite a solid boxing foundation and had also narrowly missed winning the New York Daily Sun Diamond Belt Boxing Championships, so he was no slouch.

Dan (left) spars with his brother Morris in the lead up to his first boxing fight that never was: the Daily News Golden Gloves Championship's.

Morris was the real fighter of the family and a lot better at boxing than I was. Before training with Morris at Ferkie's, I had boxed a bit at the Community Center in Canarsie and had a good, strong left-hook, as shown to great effect when weighing only 115 pounds I knocked out a 180-pounder in one of their bouts. With my developing skills, I made pretty good partner for Morris and he eventually talked me into entering the Golden Gloves with him. We both became extremely focused on making it all the way. For poor kids in those days, the Golden Gloves offered a way out. A win could provide recognition, which could lead to greater career opportunities. So there I was, all ready for my first big shot at glory. My first Golden Gloves fight had arrived. You can imagine my disappointment when, during the pre-fight medical examination, the white-haired doctor took his stethoscope away from his ears and shook his head. "What's the matter doc," I asked, bemused at

The Dream Begins

the look of dismissal on the old man's face. "You can't compete in the Golden Gloves son, you have a heart murmur," he said, again shaking his head, this time closing his eyes. Seems I had a leaky heart valve resulting from the hole in the heart I was born with, a problem I thought long gone. The murmur is the sound this type of valve makes through the stethoscope. "I can't let you fight," concluded the doctor. "Something serious could happen to you in the ring." All my life I had wanted to be just like my brother Morris. I looked up to him and he inspired me in so many ways. When I found I could not fight alongside him in the Golden Gloves, I felt crushed, like a piece of my identity had been taken away. The hole in my heart that was discovered at birth had come back to haunt me. And it would not be the last time either.

The Young Fighter: Dan practicing his right jab, while loading up with his left hook.

Later that evening, while trying to deal with my Golden Gloves rejection, I met a man who would transform my life. Terry Robinson had been a boxer before switching to bodybuilding where

Dan Lurie: Heart of Steel

he would place in the top six at the 1940 and 1941 Mr. America competitions. When I met him I was still dejected, but he told me to forget fighting. "There is always someone better than you out there and you will end up getting your brains knocked out," he said, raising up a couple of ham sized fists, scarring clearly visible on one of the prodigious mitts. "You have got a good build. Why don't you try bodybuilding competition? You could be a champion in no time." Terry, a tough looking, handsome man with a rugged physique which defied father time, had been training for a long time and would win the Mr. Brooklyn City title in 1940 in the lead up to his America appearances, so he spoke from experience. And he knew my potential. So this great man took me under his wing, and would provide me with advice whenever I needed it, and for this I will be forever thankful.

A Great Man: Dan's early mentor and role model, Terry Robinson.

The Dream Begins

The year was 1938 and I was a 116-pound muscular, though skinny, 15-year-old and I had just begun weight training earlier that year. Though Terry first inspired me to compete in bodybuilding, I had already begun to lift weights on my own. In fact, I became the strongest weightlifter on my block despite a lack of strength training knowledge and any kind of regular routine. I had the most basic of weight sets and would just play around with this in my garage, improving my technique as I went. But I built some pretty good size and strength over this time. In fact I could say that my father's furniture removal business was responsible for giving me my first start in bodybuilding, as it was through this that I got my first weight set. In those days, to ensure a customer paid for their services, it was typical for those in the moving business to take a couple of pieces of furniture as security. On one job my father left a barbell set on his van because it was to be delivered last. Sure enough, the owner of these weights, a lady, reneged on her bill, so we kept the iron. I immediately became attracted to the feel of cold iron in my hands and the weights become some of my closest friends during my teenage years. After a month of hard work with those weights - a bar and 100 pounds - I could perform some pretty impressive feats: like pressing the weight 50 times overhead. Impressed with my burgeoning strength, one local guy remarked, "I know a kid who lifts weights too. You will have to meet him." Eager to show my incredible power, I met this kid. Turns out what he could lift with one hand I could not match with both. That brought me down to earth in a hurry.

One day someone suggested I train in a regular gym with weights and machines. "What is that?" I asked, looking down at my streamlined physique, and wondering if there was some kind of secret to gaining muscle the others knew about. I was told these gyms were places where people lifted weights according to a routine, with an instructor to advise them. At the time I had my own routine going and was, through much effort, designing my own little set of training principles. I just figured all gyms were for fighters. I never knew they had places like that for bodybuilders and weightlifters. And so began my mission to build my body, just like the great champions Terry Robinson had told me about and like he himself had done. In 1939 I joined the Adonis Health Club on Sutter Avenue, Brooklyn, and this is where I met Hy Schaeffer, the founder of the club and AAU National Weightlifting132-pound-class champion. I initially competed in weightlifting competitions, because this was Hy's first love, but after several disappointments, I devoted my time to bodybuilding. I was 16 and ready to *really* focus on building my muscles. The bodybuilding bug had bit and after another year at the Adonis Health Club, this time training specifically for bodybuilding, I was eager to show off my results. I practically lived at the Adonis Health Club and spent every free minute building size and strength. At the end of the year I was ready, or so I thought. I had built my body to a respectable 150 pounds, I was 18 and it was the summer of '41. Bodybuilding had added 34 pounds to my physique, the Mr. New York City title beckoned and I was convinced I was the world's best-built teenager. I was ready to win. In the dressing room before the show I got the shock of my life. After seeing the other competitors I wondered to myself if I might, in fact, be the world's worst built teenager. I finished last in that show. Needless to say I had some improving to do.

Dan, The Ladies Man: at age 15 in 1938 - 116 pounds, ripped.

The Dream Begins

And… Press: Dan, hoisting the iron during his early weightlifting days.

Dan (left) at age 17 posing with his brother Morris in
1940: two years after lifting his first weight.

The Adonis Health Club gave me my first taste of bodybuilding as a sport, but I have to give full credit to my father for providing me with my first barbell set. I have him to thank for initially awakening my desire to develop one of America's best physiques. Dad began my love for the iron and Terry Robinson gave me the motivation to begin training seriously. Hy provided the structure. And even though my initial start in bodybuilding did not go quite as planned, highlighted by my rude awakening at the 1941 Mr. New York, I knew I was onto something. If I could add 34 pounds of muscle in one year, what could I do with further bodybuilding training? Like the screen legends of my youth, I too wanted to achieve greatness as a strong, heroic man of muscle. Slowly but surely I was beginning to see a change within myself that would lead to something big. My whole mindset shifted and I began to think like a champion. Those who have succeeded in any sport will tell you: there are mental boundaries you must first pass to develop the kind thinking needed to succeed in your chosen activity. With every new gram of muscle built and every additional pound of weight lifted, I could feel my attitude change to where I would visualize myself breaking through all limiting boundaries of self-doubt. My will to win became enormous. In my heart I knew great things were ahead. But exactly what I did not know.

Chapter Two:

America's Most Muscular Man

My first taste of bodybuilding competition did not go as planned, but I had made some pretty impressive gains, enough to keep me pushing harder to build more muscle size. My first experienced trainer, Hy Schaeffer, did give me quality weightlifting advice, but he was no bodybuilder. What I wanted was huge shapely muscles along with the power I was gaining by the day. To me a good physique must be symmetrically pleasing with good proportion and balance, not simply a mass of muscle with little shape. This shape *with* size is what I wanted.

At the time, the world's number one competitive bodybuilder was John C. Grimek, a man who had built his massive muscles through years of competitive weightlifting and bodybuilding training. Grimek was the current AAU (Amateur Athletic Union) Mr America, but to me he did not represent the ideal physique. Sure he was big, but I was more interested in perfect proportions to go with the size, and I had John in my competitive sights. But this was not to be. I would soon make my Mr. America debut, but I would not challenge Grimek on that particular stage. After winning his second Mr. America in 1941, the AAU decided to prevent previous titleholders from winning again, such was Grimek's dominance. No one could touch him at that time. Most consider him to be bodybuilding's first real legend.

At the time of Grimek's second America win I was 18 years old and had just been defeated at the Mr. New York City. Still, I figured with another year of solid training I would be on the same stage he once dominated, competing with the America's finest bodybuilders. In fact, I was determined to become Mr. America, but to get there I first needed expert guidance and a lot of hard work. The hard work part was easy for me, as I had developed an ability to out-train anyone. I had an almost endless supply of energy and would do whatever it took to improve my physique. After the Mr. New York City contest, rather than give up I became even more motivated to become a bodybuilding champion. At this time I worked with my father on his moving van, despite being offered a scholarship from Boston University in 1941 to study physical education. The work I did for my father was hard, just like my training at the Adonis Health Club. As well as sculpting my body, I was gaining a reputation for being very strong for my age. At 17, a year before my New York loss, I bent-pressed 190 pounds under the guidance of Hy. Hy taught all his lifters this movement, an extremely hard lift that involved hoisting a barbell with two hands to just below shoulder height before grasping it with one hand and powering it up above the head while bending the body to the side and outstretching the lifting arm; a complex move that required tremendous agility, speed, strength, flexibility and coordination.

Our training at the time was centered on power movements such as the bent-press, but I believe these built a solid foundation, which I was able to improve and refine for future bodybuilding contests. With gym training combined with all the work I did in my garage - where I would try different techniques and invent my own methods of attacking my muscles from all angles - I was beginning to resemble the bodybuilding champion I wished to be. I had the potential and I knew it. By age 19 my strength had skyrocketed: at a bodyweight of 162 pounds I managed a 210-pound right-hand bent press, a 190lb snatch, 260lb clean and jerk, 138lb pullover, 145lb barbell curl, 120lb reverse curl and a prone press of 260lbs. My endurance feats were better yet: 360 consecutive pullovers with 42 and a half pounds, 1225 parallel bar dips in one and a half hours, 1665 floor dips over the same period and 25 extended push-ups where, facing down, the arms are stretched overhead and the entire body is raised by the fingertips and toes. Incredibly demanding, as one extended push up alone was a major effort. As a bonus, my varied training program had made me extremely flexible and athletic, qualities that would help me in later years as a television strongman and performer. My performance had improved to where I could even do repeated full back bends, handstand walkovers, splits and half-moon hand stands, rare feats for someone carrying the kind of dense muscle I had at the time. Certainly, the specific strength feats I did - both power and endurance - were unmatched for many years after I performed them.

Mastering the One-Arm Bent Press: Dan, training at the Adonis Health club, weighing 150 pounds at age 17.

Dan Lurie: Heart of Steel

The Physique Takes Shape: Dan, age 18, contemplates his first Most Muscular title.

At age 18 I still had to face the realities of life, and pay my way, and this meant lots of hard work helping dad with his moving business. I did not complain. Rather I enjoyed the challenge of carrying large pieces of furniture around; my large muscles were more than just for show and I made the most of my time in the moving business. To further build my muscles I would carry a piece of furniture up two or three flights of stairs and then "exercise" on the way down. I had put together several routines that called for certain exercises to be done at certain times. For instance, one routine would require 25 push-ups to be done on the landing of the stairs before I returned to the truck for more furniture. Ten trips meant 250 push-ups. I had not heard about over-training in those days, and just kept pushing and pushing.

It was a foreign concept back then and bodybuilders would generally work until they dropped. Still, my physique grew and my strength skyrocketed. My father would tell me to stop exercising in between, as he feared I would wear myself out. "Danny what is taking you so long?" he would ask. "Are you stopping for ice cream between pieces?" "No Pop, honest. I am just getting a few push-ups in on the way down. I've got to build up my muscles." My father figured lifting heavy furniture would be enough for me. As far as I was concerned there was never enough. Others reacted the same way my father did. Many thought I was pushing too hard, but I knew if I wanted to challenge America's best bodybuilders, I would need to make some big physical changes. And they were coming. It seemed I was growing by the day. As 1942 approached I was training as hard as ever, both on the moving van and at the Adonis Health Club. At this time I had a training partner, Marty Rosenberg, who would push me even harder. While Marty would go onto become a New York City fireman, I was destined for the biggest bodybuilding stage there was.

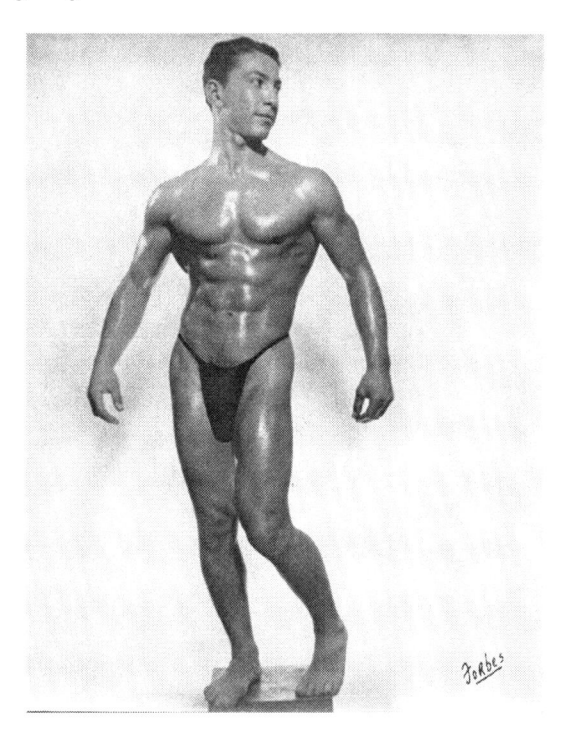

Dan at Age 18: one year out from his first AAU Mr. America contest.

Almost There: Dan (right) with old friend Ludwick Schusterich in 1941, moments after Lud won the 1941 America's Most Muscular Man title.

People have often asked me how I developed my strength levels with such backbreaking work. Looking back the amount of training I did do, the sheer volume of weightlifting, heavy manual work and long hours running my business, were excessive, but I never shirked from my responsibilities and never gave up. These days they would call what I did back then over-training, but it worked for me. And there were no steroids to improve recovery back then. All things considered, I would have to say that I was blessed with a better than average ability to recover. At my height I had a very large bone structure, which could take tremendous stress and bounce back stronger than ever. As a side note which might explain my strength and recovery abilities, it is thought that the larger ones wrist development in comparison to their height, the greater the potential they have to lift massive weights. I recently had my wrist taped at eight and a half inches, and according wrist size norms, mine is off the scale. While a man of six feet tall would be classed to have great potential to lift huge weights if his wrist measured seven to eight inches, my measurement was done at a height of five feet six inches.

When Marty and I trained together it was around the time of World War II and there would be frequent blackouts. The blackouts were done as practice for possible enemy air raids and would come without notice. I worked all day with my father so the only time I could train was at night and this brought with it many risks. If the lights suddenly went out, we would be in danger of hurting ourselves with the enormous weights we lifted. So we did around an hour of push-ups, sit-ups and chair dips on such nights, as it was the only safe training we *could* do. For this we worked on the honor system: both of us would do our exercises while counting at the same time. But neither of us could see what the other was doing so each of us had to fully trust that the other was doing their work. There were no shortcuts in any of our sessions. And as I was in training for the AAU Junior Mr. America, I would often do more reps: usually two to Marty's one. We would work up to 50 and down again and this unusual system combined with my additional training at home and work on my father's truck, really began to pay off.

Dan's developing physique as photographed by preeminent photographer "Edwin F. Townsend".

I entered the AAU Junior Mr. America, held in Bristol Connecticut in March 1942, and placed second, losing the overall by half a point. This, in my second ever physique show, was a big achievement for me as the contest was open to all ages and sizes. Back then, the word "Junior" meant it was a warm up for the larger Mr. America so it was a good way to test the competitive waters. At the junior show they also gave, in addition to the main title of Junior Mr. America, awards for the best body parts and overall muscularity as they did in all AAU shows back then. The body part awards were given for the Best Developed Arms, Best Developed Chest, Best Developed Back, Best Developed Abs and the Best Developed Legs. The muscularity award honored the winner as being "America's Most Muscular Man", an achievement that ranked only second to that of the main title, as it signified proportionate muscle size and impressive overall development. I won the Most Muscular Man title in Bristol that year.

After placing second at the Junior Mr. America, I had some great momentum, which placed me well for the AAU Mr America, which would be held in Cincinnati, Ohio, in July of that year. In the lead up to the Mr. America, pictures of me began to appear in muscle magazines and people began to learn who I was. As a result, I became known as a worthy bodybuilder, one of the favorites going into that show. In 1942 the Mr. America was the biggest bodybuilding show on earth. Competitive bodybuilding had yet to become professional and the main incentive bodybuilders had in those days was to capture glory and enjoy the title of world's best bodybuilder, which is essentially what the Mr. America crown represented. The Mr. America was really the only show in town when it came to competing against the best of the best, but it was an amateur show and this meant no financial rewards. We competed for the love of competing, nothing more. The Mr. America brought together the best bodybuilders around, but it came from very humble beginnings.

At the turn of the Twentieth Century, Eugen Sandow, a man known as the first real bodybuilder with a magnificent physique many years ahead of its time, organized a nationwide bodybuilding contest in Britain, but this was his only real attempt at this event. His promotional success on this front did not last that long, but bodybuilders kept training for the

America's Most Muscular Man

sake of building their muscles and improving their health. Early in the Twentieth Century, the father of physical culture Bernarr Macfadden held a series of "The World's Most Beautiful Man" contests, but these too did not last very long. With so many great bodybuilding physiques developing in America, there was a definite need for a well-organized bodybuilding show that would place one against the other. By the late 1930s, physique athletes were calling for such as show. Around this time a man named Johnny Hordines arranged two contests to decide "America's Finest Physique". His final show in 1939 - often referred to as the first Mr. America - but controversy still remains regarding his use of that title in this context - gave the overall to Bert Goodrich. The biggest development in bodybuilding, however, came in 1940 with the establishing by the AAU of the Mr. America, the first of which was won by John Grimek that same year.

Posing Experimentation: Dan practices new bodybuilding poses ahead of his first Mr. America competition.

Dan Lurie: Heart of Steel

Dan as photographed by famed photographer, Earl Forbes.

America's Most Muscular Man

The year I began training for the Mr. America, the event was still relatively new. The standard of competition was not all that high and only a few men stood out from the rest. I was one of them. For this show I traveled by car with my trainer Hy Schaeffer, not really believing how far my physique had progressed in such a short time. At age 19 I was thrilled to be accepted as one of America's best bodybuilders and vowed to do my very best to capture the 1942 Mr. America title. I guess I was a little naïve going into my first Mr. America contest. In fact, I was completely unprepared for what was about to happen to me. But at the time, big business drove bodybuilding. Though the competitors themselves received no direct financial rewards, in line with the amateur ethos that governed the sport, the title winners did bring business and money to the sponsors and equipment companies that supported them.

Show time had arrived and as I had expected, I stood apart from the others in the line-up due to my size, shape and conditioning. I ran up a desirable number of points in the competitive posing and the judges were impressed with my physique. When the prejudging concluded I had been awarded first place for Best Arms and Best Legs, second place for Best Abdominal development and Best Back and third place for Best Chest. I had also been crowned America's Most Muscular Man. The feeling was amazing. Back at my hotel I felt the overall title was mine for sure, given I had won two body parts and the most muscular. I could not wait for the following day to be crowned Mr. America. Naive. Local newspaper reporters were also convinced I had already won and in anticipation of the outcome, reported this as fact. The following day I arrived early at the exhibition hall. As I arrived there was a large crowd waiting for the doors to open. I made my way through, catching encouraging stares as I went. Once inside, my stomach began to tighten. I enjoyed the feeling of excitement before the great moment to come. But I was not aware that politics and business would combine to rob me of what many thought was mine and, moments later, was hit by news that almost floored me: I had been awarded second place behind Frank Leight. At the time I could not understand what had happened, but sometime later I discovered the truth. In spite of my being awarded two body parts, and America's Most Muscular Man, the judges were deadlocked on who would win the overall title: Frank

Leight or myself? In the end, one judge broke the tie. His name was Sigmund Klein who owned a gym on New York's seventh avenue. I still thought I was the clear winner but had to accept Klein's decision. That is until I discovered that Frank Leight worked for Sigmund as the manager of his gym. The honorable thing for Klein to do would have been to excuse himself as a judge, as having him on the panel presented a clear conflict of interest. It was he that ultimately cost me my first Mr. America title through the deciding vote he gave to Frank Leight.

Victory: America's Most Muscular man at last.

So what was Klein's reason for choosing Leight, who was less muscular and lacked the balance I had? He said even though I had won my body-parts and the most muscular, "a good big man would always beat a good little man." Given Frank was around six feet tall and I was five feet six inches, he towered over me. But he did not have the better physique. I figured that since I was only 19 years old I would give it another shot the following year. I returned home with the America's Most Muscular Man title, but not the overall. I felt disappointed that I had been conned by older more experienced men who had everything to gain by having their man win the title. Still, from this experience I gained some valuable insights, most notably that I had the tools to win the Mr America. I quickly got to work preparing for 1943.

As America's Most Muscular Man, I had become known as one of the front-runners for the 1943 Mr America. In the short space of one year I had gone from a relative unknown to one of the best bodybuilders in the country, and I had only just begun to hit my stride. People began to take notice of this new contender. But at the time of the 1943 America, America's Most Muscular Man was struggling to make a living by working three jobs. My jobs were as different as the physiques that entered the America contest in a given year. At night I sold candy-sodas and ice cream at the Jewish Theater on East 14 street and Third Avenue. During the day I worked with my father lifting heavy furniture. I was also running the Dan Lurie Barbell Company, a job that involved shipping exercise equipment across the country by railroad. These jobs allowed me to scrape up enough for the train ticket to Los Angeles, California, where the Mr. America would be held on June 27 and 28 of that year. While many of the other competitors had sponsors and other financial backers, I went it alone. My desire to become America's best-built man drove me to sacrifice money and time in return for such an honor.

As I made my way through the swarming crowd at Grand Central Station, en route to my second shot at glory, I felt some anxiety, but this was short lived: I had victory in my sights and the confidence of knowing that I had prepared as best I could. As I approached the information booth in the middle of the large waiting room, the afternoon sun streamed through the high windows on the north side of the huge waiting room in massive rays that seemed they would penetrate steel. I adjusted my suit, making it flat against my bulky chest as I approached the desk. I thrust my round-trip coast-to-coast ticket at the clerk, a ticket that to me meant hours of brutal training and endless sacrifice in pursuit of physical excellence. It was my personal ticket to the top of the bodybuilding world. Each railway station would claim its individual portion of the ticket as I passed from New York City to Los Angeles, but each step would bring me closer to my goal. The railroad man checked my ticket, before pushing it back with an authoritative "track 42."

On the train ride to Los Angeles, I became relaxed as a sense of calm came over me. After what I considered to be an unfair decision the previous year, I knew I had every chance of putting things right. The ride itself took nearly five days and to keep in shape I periodically did pushups between the aisles all the way to LA. The passengers must have thought I was crazy, but to me, an aspiring Mr. America, exercising at any opportunity came as naturally as eating and breathing. Once in Los Angeles, I took a bus to the YMCA. I entered the lobby with a single suitcase and wearing a rumpled suit. The first thing to hit me was the weather, which was warmer compared to New York. The weather was a nice surprise and so was the freedom I experienced away from the stuffy train car. Another thing that caught my attention were the palm trees. Up until then I had only seen them in the movies. In fact, everything looked different in California. However, the contest itself was really no different from the year before. It was a battle between myself and other principal contender, Jules Bacon, an outstanding, though smaller competitor, who placed second to John Grimek at the 1941 Mr. America. This contest was closer than the 1942 Cincinnati event though, as Jules was in very good condition with excellent size and shape. I too was in the best shape of my life so it made for a thrilling contest.

Jules, a very good-looking man, was a hard worker like myself. His body was built with hours in the gym in addition to long days of foundry work as foreman for the York Barbell Company. His boss was Mr. Bob Hoffman who owned the company along with *Strength and Health* Magazine. Unlike the year before, where I won two body part awards, this time we split them three apiece. Voting was especially close as the prejudging drew to a close. Finally, each judge awarded me 10 points for development - a perfect score. Then they took back one point for what they called "bad posture", which was strange since I was known for my overall presentation skills. That one point cost me the contest and Jules Bacon was named overall Mr. America. I later discovered the title was given to him, in a close decision, based on his good looks. Although we were equal on symmetry and definition, I was again awarded the America's Most Muscular Man title. These combined qualities strongly suggested I was the better bodybuilder, but it was not to be. I accepted what had happened as I sat on the green velvet of that old coach seat, as the train made its way back to New York and the click-clack of its wheels took me to dreamland. Jules died in 2006 and will be remembered as one of the great smaller bodybuilding champions - he became known as "little Mr. America" and I regard him as my toughest competitor.

"I was in the best shape of my life." Dan displays muscle size and definition many years ahead of its time during his preparation for the 1943 Mr. America.

My 1943 Mr. America appearance may not have happened. In 1942 my strength and development might have impressed more than just the AAU officials and fellow gym members, as this was the year I was called up for military duty, an opportunity I greeted with open arms. Back then, most young men felt great pride in the possibility of serving their country and I felt the same. When the medical examiners saw my physique they were amazed by my development and very nearly signed me up on the spot. But it was not to be as my heart condition, which I had thought completely cured through bodybuilding and healthy living, prevented me from passing the medical and the army had no choice but to reject me. In 1943, Time Magazine reported that, "before the army's physical examiners in Manhattan, Dan Lurie unveiled the flabbergasting body that had won him America's most muscular man. Despite the fact he could do 1625 push-ups, back to bodybuilding went Lurie with a slight heart murmur." At the age of 20 I felt I was in perfect physical shape to fight for my country, but despite routinely lifting weights that would break the average man's back, I was not fit for active service. So it was certainly back to bodybuilding for me.

The edition of Time magazine Dan appeared in - dated February 15 1943 - and the article on his army rejection.

America's Most Muscular Man

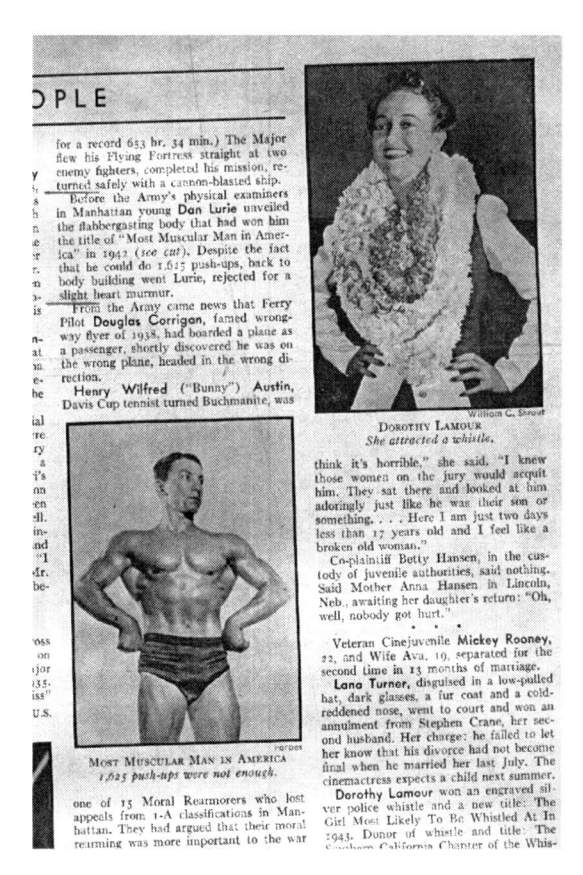

I mentioned earlier in this chapter that my teenage strength feats were unmatched in the New York area. In 1943, at age 20, I took it a step further and began to specialize in certain strongman lifts as a way to prepare my body for the 1944 Mr America. These lifts, or feats of strength, were not commonly done, but gave me some great results and brought me recognition as being one of America's strongest men. At one point I worked my way up to a 285-pound one-hand bent press. While an average super-heavyweight lifter might struggle with 350 pounds for a two-hand overhead lift, few could lift 200 with one hand in the bent press, as the technique was harder to master. But I was more concerned with developing my body, so these lifts were done in addition to my regular bodybuilding-style training, which featured many sets and reps. I was always a big believer in higher reps with the heaviest possible weight for definition and size development.

Dan Lurie: Heart of Steel

Beauty and the Beasts: Dan with fellow competitor Arthur Bianco and 1943 Ms. California beauty contest winner, Dannie O'Darl, shortly before placing second overall at the AAU 1943 Mr. America

So as 1944 approached I was again ready to take the America title. This time I had added some size and improved my definition. Again I was confident. Each year the AAU would hold the Mr. America in a different part of the country to make it fair for officials and competitors, as back then traveling was harder for all concerned. The 1944 Mr. America would be held in Chattanooga, Tennessee, on May 7 and this proved to be another great experience for me, as I had never before visited the Deep South. The train ride there was nice and relaxing and I used this time to think about the contest, to run through how I would perform when the time came. The contest would be held in a fight arena in downtown Chattanooga, which seemed a very small town for a boy from New York. My hotel, a second-class rundown affair, was a few blocks from the arena. The contest was the biggest event held in Chattanooga for some time, so on the night of the event it seemed the whole town had turned out to watch America's best musclemen compete and though most of those in attendance knew very little about bodybuilding, the show had an exciting, big city feel to it. Back at my hotel room before the show I sat in silence looking out into Chattanooga's main street. The traffic was scarce because of the wartime gas rationing that had kept most vehicles out of action. A light rain sprayed my window with a fine mist, which calmed my mind as it drifted to what might happen at the contest, now only moments away.

Since the AAU had ruled that no previous Mr. America could again compete, I wondered who my main opposition might be. The main question that played on my mind was, "who would the York Barbell Company sponsor this year?" Jules Bacon was out, as was Frank Leight. Before them there was John Grimek, another York employee. York was really the main player in the bodybuilding game at that point. They owned *Strength and Health* magazine, the bodybuilding and weightlifting industry's Bible and were headed by Bob Hoffman, a weightlifter who was the major player in the American strength training industry in the 1930s. I thought I might have had a legitimate shot that year because I figured York must have been running out of employees to sponsor. After all, their people had won every year from 1940 to 1943.

In 1944 I also decided to again challenge for the Junior Mr. America. Again I placed second overall and won the Most Muscular Man title. This did not bother me because my intention was to use this show as a warm-up to the main event, the Mr. America, and was not peaked to perfection like I would be at the bigger show. Finally the day arrived. The 1944 Mr. America was run differently to the others. For this show they had the contestants use a fight ring as a stage; when our names were called we would climb the steps and make our way into the squared circle much the same way a professional wrestler or boxer would. The only problem was, one contestant could not do this: the York sponsored ex-champion weightlifter, Steve Stanko. Steve was big, but he also had surgery scars on his legs due to the very bad inflammation of the veins he developed a few years earlier. This problem limited his movement and he had to be lifted into the fight ring to pose. He had trouble climbing the steps as with every footstep, he risked falling. The scars on his legs were unsightly and I thought they would not help his chances of winning, which gave me greater confidence in my own chances of success. After all the contestants had posed, Steve was called on. Given he was last, the people in the crowd naturally thought they were to witness some amazing force of nature, a competitor par-excellence. After all, they often save the best for last, don't they? Many leaned forward in their seats to see this bodybuilding gladiator make his way to the ring. Then all of a sudden all the arena's lights went out at once. Some panicked, many thought there may have been a power failure, a blackout. This widespread panic was short lived as an intense blast of light stunned the crowd. As the spectators' eyes adjusted to the light, a collective gasp was heard: in the middle of the ring stood Steve Stanko at just under six feet and 223 pounds of solid muscle. When he had finished posing, off again went the lights and Steve was carried from the stage. Stanko won that night, the first and only time in the history of bodybuilding that a championship-winning contestant had a noticeable disability requiring him to be assisted to and from the stage. The audience, who seemed to be moved by the dramatic appearance of Stanko, were not aware of his condition. I retained my Most Muscular Man title and, once again, finished second overall.

I truly felt this was to be my year as I was in my best shape yet, which made the train ride back to New York an extra lonely and downbeat one. Still I was not finished yet. In fact, I felt I had only just begun and was even more determined to fight for the title. However, something I considered at the time to be a small matter would return to harm me in the worst possible way and radically change the course of my competitive career. After my first America showing, I became widely known as one of the main contenders for the overall Mr. America title. My photos appeared in the top magazines of the day: *Your Physique* being the major one. Towards the end of 1944, my picture appeared in an advertisement in *Your Physique*, a move that would seriously damage my bodybuilding hopes. "From a Weakling to a Superman", it said. The advertisement, which featured two photos of me side by side, showed the improvements I had made to become America's Most Muscular Man. It highlighted the fact that I had been born with a weak heart and had used bodybuilding to overcome this setback. It was to prove my undoing.

America's Most Muscular Man

Dan at his Mr. America best

Dan Lurie: Heart of Steel

To begin my 1945 Mr America campaign I chose to compete in the junior version a few months before, as I had done on two occasions. The Junior Mr. America was held in Pittsburgh that year and promised to be one of the biggest ever. When I arrived, I received the shocking news. The man who controlled the AAU, Bob Hoffman, protested that since I had appeared in the *Your Physique* advertisement, I was a professional athlete and therefore ineligible to compete in their amateur show. I guess he forgot the fact that all his athletes, many having won the America title over previous years, were regularly featured in his magazine's advertisements and articles making them all professional by his definition of the word. My amateur status had been lost through the publication of a single picture. I was devastated. At the time, the AAU said that any athlete who earned a living through bodybuilding was a professional, but most of Hoffman's athletes were paid for helping him in his businesses. I never received a penny in exchange for my picture. I argued my case. It fell on deaf ears. The AAU would not budge and they ruled me ineligible to compete in Pittsburgh and in any other contests run by them. My life as a competitor was over, but my bodybuilding career was only just beginning.

The Offending Photograph (the "after" shot): the *Your Physique* advertisement that forced Dan out of bodybuilding's amateur ranks.

America's Most Muscular Man

All things considered, I feel my run for the AAU Mr. America title was a successful one. First of all I had distinguished myself as America's Most Muscular Man three years in a row, a record that stands today. I had also gained valuable insights into how the sport was run. I saw problems that needed fixing, one of the larger ones being the unfairness shown toward certain athletes. As I had found out the hard way, the main title of Mr. America would often go to whoever was popular at the time, sometimes to whoever was thought to be superior in looks and height and almost always to those who had some kind of business or political affiliation to the show - namely, whoever Bob Hoffman wanted to win. Sometimes the better guy lost out. By today's judging standards I may have won several Mr. America titles given my size and shape. Looking back on old photos comparing the overall winners of these shows with myself, the outcomes still amaze me. I walked away from the amateur scene feeling that bodybuilding promotion needed a fresh approach, someone to take it in a different direction. For the time being though, I had more pressing concerns, one of them being how to raise enough money to eat.

After my first Mr America competition, I received what I thought was the opportunity of a lifetime. At this time I needed to build my business, as training and eating to be a top bodybuilder cost a lot. When an opportunity to become more involved in bodybuilding was presented, I figured it would be a smart move and jumped at the chance. I teamed up with a man named Joe Weider, a magazine publisher from Montreal, Canada. This owner of the *Your Physique* magazine joined me as a partner in the barbell distribution business. At the time I was 19 years old, a very fast capable worker who was known throughout the bodybuilding world as an up-and-coming Mr. America. The partnership with Joe seemed promising to me and being a smart man, he surely knew that having me, as a partner, would aid his chances of reaching more people with his products. I was a name. He was a well-known publisher who had a knack for reaching the wider bodybuilding public through the passionate, call-to-arms messages he featured in his magazines. He told me he would help to finance and expand the Dan Lurie Barbell Company, the name I gave to my side of the then-small barbell business we were to operate together. His magazines, he told me, would provide me with much needed publicity to boost my bodybuilding career and my side of the business.

Our business partnership lasted just over three years and, early on, seemed to be working well. Then one day Joe decided he no longer needed me. The ads he featured in his magazines to promote our business directed traffic to my address, as I was his sole distributor for the United States of America. All of a sudden these ads were removed and replaced with the contact address of a new distributor – a barbell company I was not involved in. The case went to court and I was left hurting. Joe's lawyers got most of the money and I was personally forced to pay a 10 percent War Excise Tax on barbell profits that I had never collected. Joe walked away free, having benefited from me financially, while expanding his own market in America. He took the profits made in our business and put them into new ventures for himself. I was left to pay $18,000 in taxes, which left me completely broke.

Chapter Three:
Barbells, Contests, and Controversy

As I became better known in the bodybuilding world, business opportunities came my way. My first big venture, the partnership with Joe Weider, cost me a fortune but fortunately I was able to climb back and build on the competitive success I had achieved during my early bodybuilding years, though it seemed it would be many years before things would return to normal after Joe had left me with financial problems in 1948. It might seem that I am out to attack Joe but this is not the case. I discuss my dealings with him here as they formed a major part of my early bodybuilding days and it would be wrong to simply gloss over them. Actually, my initial relations with Joe were good.

In 1942, after I had just won the America's Most Muscular Man title for the first time and was getting fan mail from all around America, I received a letter from a Joseph E. Weider from Montreal, Canada, a magazine publisher who was just starting out in the bodybuilding business. In this letter he praised me on my development, congratulated me on winning my AAU titles and requested pictures of me for his magazine, *Your Physique*. He told me in his letter how he had started his magazine with very little money and that he worked as a dishwasher in a restaurant to make ends meet. I wrote back and thanked him for his kind comments and put him into contact with Earle Forbes, the New York City physique photographer who took all my photos at the time. One thing led to another and we became good friends. During my time as a physique model for Joe's magazine, he featured me on four *Your Physique* covers and gave me some good publicity. He also used photos of me to publicize his training courses. It was in the December 1943 issue of *Your Physique* that he told in a full one-page ad, compete with before and after pictures of myself, the story of how 'America's Most Muscular Man overcame his heart problem through the use of Joe Weider's "training methods"'. The irony was that I had been training using my own methods for many years before this article was published. I had developed my own system of training and had made very good progress with it. But putting respective training approaches aside (for now), this was the article that would get me banned from all AAU events as, according to AAU officials, it meant I had become a professional bodybuilder, as they thought I was paid for the use of my photos. The truth is, and as mentioned earlier, I was never paid a penny for appearing in any of Joe's advertisements, but I did enjoy the publicity they gave me.

"My initial relations with Joe were good." Dan (right): with Joe Weider (center), Mr. America competitor Joe Thaler (left) and Fitness authority Dr. Fredrick Tilney (seated).

Barbells, Contests, and Controversy

Cover Man: Dan on the March 1942, September 1943, June 1944 and January 1947 covers of *Your Physique*

Dan Lurie: Heart of Steel

Barbells, Contests, and Controversy

Soon after our initial contact, and before I was featured in his magazines, Joe and I met in person. He came to Brooklyn and we hit it off right away. We were kids at the time – I was 19, Joe five months older. My parents' home became his hotel, my mother's kitchen his restaurant. Our living conditions in my parents' home at the time were so cramped that Joe and I often shared the same bed. We would stay awake talking and planning our future. I recall Joe kept a copy of Hitler's Mein Kampf and would read this book every night. I would always ask him, "Joe, why do you read this book? We are both Jewish and you know how many Jews Hitler killed." Joe's answer was always the same: "think of all the power Hitler had." He told me that he was inspired by the dictator's words. "If you tell a lie often enough and put it in print, eventually it will become the truth," Joe would shout, punching his first in the air to drive his point home. To this I would always reply: "Joe, you are crazy."

Four years later, on a plane trip to Miami Beach in 1946, I introduced the 23-year-old Joe to his first wife, Dianna Ross, whom he married in 1947. I initially dated Dianna but arranged a date between the two of them after Joe took a liking to her; he found out she came from a wealthy family and because of this he was immediately interested in getting to know her better. He would always tell me that it was better to marry a woman from a rich family than one who came from poor stock. At the time he was engaged to a nice girl called Sally Berkowitz who lived directly above my first gym on Clarkson Avenue, Brooklyn. He broke her heart when he left her, but he felt Dianna would be a better catch. This was a tragic move for Joe because Dianna would cause him a lot of misery. Joe himself said recently in his book *Brothers of Iron* that his marriage to Dianna was the stupidest move of his life.

But before Joe's marriage to Dianna, and our relationship as business partners, we dreamt big together. As our friendship grew, Joe and I came to trust one another, which eventually led to us becoming business partners in 1943. Though he did not set up a manufacturing plant for Weider exercise equipment in the basement of my parents' home as he has said. Rather, we became 50:50 partners in a profit splitting operation distributing Weider barbells. I became his sole distributor for the United States of America. My business was registered with the City of New York, Kings Country, and I traded under the name Dan Lurie Barbell Company. My postal address was 1729 Rockaway Parkway, Brooklyn, my parents' home, and orders to be packed and shipped by myself were manufactured elsewhere and stored in its basement. In 1943 Joe began running ads for barbell sales in his magazine, *Your Physique*. 1944 was the year I was featured as his "*Your Physique* Equipment Manager" and these advertisements would direct customers to my address. A year later - 1945 - my end of the operation became Dan Lurie Barbell Company.

Happier Times: Dan (right) with Joe Weider and Joe's date, Dianna Ross (left), at the CopaCabana Night Club Miami Beach, Florida, 1946. Dianna was originally to be Dan's date that evening, but Joe asked to switch after learning that Dianna's family were wealthy.

At the beginning of our business partnership I would manufacture Weider barbell plates at a local foundry from wooden patterns Joe sent me. These patterns would be used for molds and the foundry would provide me with the finished cast iron plates and dumbbells. Before deciding on the right foundry, I looked high and low to get the best price and quality for our product. The best price was eight cents per pound for steel, and for the barbells and dumbbells I was able to get solid steel bars from a local mill, cut to the size of five foot, six foot, and 15 inches. The great thing about this business, from my side, was that there were few, if any major overheads. For one thing, it was a one-man business: just me. The business as a whole was never charged any expenses from my end other than manufacturing costs, and neither of us received a salary. For the first two years, all the orders would come from Joe Weider to be shipped out to people all over the U.S. But Joe received, and kept, all of the money at his business base at 4466 Colonial Avenue in Montreal, Quebec. And the orders kept coming for me to fill. During our partnership, I kept good records of all our sales and these show that Joe was sending out all of the training courses that went with each barbell set from his home base. In later years he would say that the numbers for finances received did not add up and that I was dishonest. This was not the case as Joe received all of the money while I filled the orders, after first notifying Joe of each order received. I only sent him bills that came with the cost of manufacturing the barbells. We had an arrangement where we would settle everything up after six months, but printing bills Joe ran up through his magazine ate up my 50 percent of the profits and he would give me equipment rather than pay me in money. I could hardly make enough money to continue.

In the first few years our sales were quite low as we took in around five thousand dollars for the first year, ten thousand for the second year and so on. By 1947 we were making some good profits. At this time we were doing over $100,000 annually in barbell sales and Joe showed increasing resentment every time he had to pay me my share, which he had finally begun doing. He then did something I have never been able to reconcile. Since everything was done through his magazine, Joe, in late 1947, simply cut me out of the business by changing the address in *Your Physique* from the Dan Lurie Barbell Company to Joe Weider Barbell with a 5th Avenue,

New York location. This instantly lost me hundreds in profits, as Joe was still collecting the money while I continued shipping out the barbells. When I asked him about this, he told me that his printer had mistakenly changed the address. After three issues with this "error" I knew what Joe's true intentions were. To me this double-crossing came as a major blow. After all our years as friends, all the good times we had together, he simply saw me as someone who stood in his way, a liability who would cost him profits. I took Joe to court for breach of contract, only to have him counter-sue. Neither of us got any money, but lawyers on both sides made a substantial profit.

One thing I learned about Joe is that he likes to counter-sue. If you were to sue him, he would sue you for four times as much. This was good practice for him as it ends with the jury finding it hard to believe who is telling the truth. It makes it a little better for the guy who is counter-suing because it puts the other person into a more expensive legal situation. You now have two cases: the one where you are being sued and the one where you are suing. The lawyer has twice as much work to do so his fees are going too be much higher. And Joe usually counter-sued regardless. He would counter-sue and his opponent would settle for a fraction of the cost because they had so much more to lose than Joe. That is how Joe operated.

The same year Joe cut me from the barbell business I married my sweetheart Thelma Rothman - on February the 1st, 1947 - and was blessed with my first child, Mark. So as 1948 approached, I needed a decent income to support my family. Given Joe had paid me little of the profits we had made together, giving me equipment instead, I was broke. In 1945, midway through my partnership with Joe, I opened my first gym, a small affair on Clarkson Avenue, Brooklyn. At 22 I was a gym owner, but was by no means making any money from this. In 1947 I moved my gym to 1701 Pitkin Ave, Brooklyn, and named it the Dan Lurie Physical Culture Studio. This new gym was larger with two floors covering 4000 square feet; with pool and ping-pong tables and a health drinks bar so members could hang

Barbells, Contests, and Controversy

out and enjoy the free facilities. I would go on to run eight separate gyms in the New York area and one in Miami, Florida.

But for the time being, after Joe cut me out of the barbell business I had to focus on my emerging gym interests along with other areas that could bring in some money to support my family. I called upon my business skills and in 1948 published a barbell catalog, placing advertisements in various magazines to sell barbells and dumbbells: I placed one-inch ads in dozens of national magazines, including *Popular Mechanics*, *Popular Science*, and various sports and comic magazines. I offered the catalog for free. As the orders came in, I began running close to 100 small ads each month. With my gym business growing and my reputation as a bodybuilding competitor and businessman my earnings began to grow. People trusted my name. Things were looking good and I was even making a few dollars when it hit me. Just when I thought my problems with Joe Weider were over, I was about to be hammered again. And this time it would almost knock me out for good.

In 1949 I received a letter from the IRS, which said that because my business had operated from 1944 to 1948, the Dan Lurie Barbell Company owed the Government excise duty and war taxes on barbell castings to the tune of $18,000.00. During World War II the American government had imposed an excise tax on all sports equipment, and all throughout my business dealings with Joe I was unaware of this law and never deducted the required amount from our business. I immediately contacted Joe Weider and told him he would have to pay half: $9,000.00. I could not believe his response. He simply laughed and said, "You idiot, why do you think I put the business in your name. I knew there was a war tax and excise duties back in 1942." He did not want to know anything about any back taxes. I felt betrayed. Here was a man I had trusted for years, a man who had attended my wedding and was Godfather to my son, and it seemed he fooled me all along. It later dawned on me that as I was asking him to be Godfather to my son, Joe was scheming to put me out of business - extremely callous. I ended up having to pay the U.S. government every cent of the $18,000.00, which nearly ruined the Dan Lurie Barbell Company along with my health, as hospital bills were also paid for the severe stomach pains caused by the stress brought about by having to pay all those back taxes.

Throughout my bodybuilding career Joe would continue to be my nemesis. You see, back in the early days there were only three main men in bodybuilding: Joe, Bob Hoffman and myself. Because of this you had to fight hard to get to the top and getting there often required a person to be as ruthless as possible. And believe me, Joe would try anything to push me under to monopolize the health and fitness industry. For the time being though – at the beginning of 1948 - Joe and I were, at least as far as I could tell, still good friends. In fact, January 15 of this year was the date of the first ever bodybuilding show to carry the International Federation of Body Builders name, the Mr New York State, which I ran. Joe was there and we enjoyed each other's company. It was only one month before that he had pulled my ads from his magazine, but at that point I hadn't discovered this. Months after the New York State we would be facing one another in court, and the relationship we had as friends and business partners would be irrevocably broken.

What is Joe Thinking? Dan and Joe Weider in the early days.

Barbells, Contests, and Controversy

In late 1944, one year after I began working with Joe in the barbell business, I decided to promote my own bodybuilding show. At this time the AAU had told me that I could no longer compete, as I was, in their eyes, a professional, and I was concerned with the way bodybuilding contests were being run and felt I could make bodybuilding more popular and reach more people through promoting shows of my own. At the time, as bodybuilding was not yet a professional sport, most bodybuilding events were run under AAU sanction. My first contest in 1944, the Mr Brooklyn, was AAU sanctioned, was well attended and attracted many contestants. It was given a big write-up in *Your Physique* and Joe Weider was right in behind my efforts to become a bodybuilding contest promoter.

Back in 1944, bodybuilding wasn't very popular, like it is today. York wasn't interested in running bodybuilding events back then and the ones that were run were done more as an afterthought. I wanted to change all of that. One thing that struck me was that shows then didn't even have the right staging and lighting. It was so crude. In 1944 your average bodybuilding contest, and there weren't many, would be held in a boxing arena where you would install a tiny platform and hang a single light from a basketball hoop. They would get whatever lights they could and then that was it. The same guy who posed in a show today would look 100 percent better than he would posing in those days, purely due to an improvement in lighting. One secret I found for presenting the physique to its best advantage was to have the best lighting possible – you need it to cast those shadows and separate the individual muscle groups. I remember when I was considering running my first show people had no idea what was needed to run a bodybuilding contest. One guy would say, "We are running a contest." The other guy would say, "Did you bring anything?" "No," was the usual reply. There were no lights, nothing. They set up whatever they had and it was a joke. Starting with the Mr. Brooklyn in 1944, my goal was to improve how bodybuilding contests were being run.

My second show, the Mr. New York City, non-AAU sanctioned, was held at Brooklyn's Ridgewood Masonic Temple on the evening of May 13, 1945, and again had an amazing turnout of athletes and spectators. Head of the judging panel was none other than Charles

Atlas, a man famous for designing and marketing the Dynamic Tension training courses and winner of the 1922 World's Most Perfectly Developed Man contest. I considered Charles one of my closest friends and admired his dedication to healthy living and bodybuilding promotion. Bernarr Macfadden, the man who awarded Charles Atlas the World's Most Perfectly Developed Man title, and who, in 1899, published the first ever bodybuilding magazine, *Physical Culture,* was another of my judges. Bernarr, himself a good example of healthy living and the bodybuilding lifestyle, was very influential in my early years as a contest promoter and bodybuilder, as will be elaborated on in later chapters. Also on the judging panel was Barton Hovarth, a New York bodybuilding champion who appeared on the cover of the first ever *Your Physique* magazine in 1940, famed physique photographers Earle Forbes, Gebbe and Lon Hanagan, world famous strongman Otto Arco, health authority Ray Van Cleef, actor and health and fitness educator Joe Bonomo, *Your Physique* writer George Weaver and Joe Weider himself. The master of ceremonies was Sam Taub, a famous boxing announcer and conductor of the popular Hour of Champions radio show.

A year later I ran my third event, the 1946 AAU Mr Eastern Coast contest, held at the 91 Auditorium 100 East Street, New York City on September 14. This show, a larger, more polished contest, had over 50 competitors in three height classes from gyms across the New York area: among those represented were the Holyoke boys Club, Dan Lurie's gym, Fritshe's Gym, Brooklyn Central YMCA, and the Bronx Union Weightlifting Club. One of bodybuilding's greatest ever stars, George Eiferman, made his contest début at this show. The Philadelphian had just come out of the U.S. Navy and did not know how to pose. He wore his trunks high above his waist, which caused many in the audience to laugh. Despite his lack of experience, he had a great build, but initially failed to make the cut and was not even placed at pre-judging. After re-consideration by all the judges, he was awarded third overall.

To take bodybuilding to another level as a contest promoter, and to give the crowd a total entertainment experience, I gathered talent from all over the U.S. Our featured guest posers were Boston's 1946 Junior Mr. America, Everett Sinderoff and the newly crowned 1946

Mr. America, Alan Stephan from Chicago. During intermission, Frank Giardine sang popular songs and at the piano was Lon Hanagan. A full "starsapoppin" entertainment package including parallel bars and side-horse exhibitions, magician, Frank Seims, and gymnastics displays given by the best gymnasts in America was also enjoyed. Weider Barbells were on offer as door prizes. All of my early shows were run this way; they were designed to promote bodybuilding, but also to entertain all who came to watch – they truly had something for everyone. For this contest I also decided to formalize a committee to lend a professional touch to this and all future contests. My committee included, as chairman, George Quintance, the art director for *Your Physique* magazine, Dietrich Wortman, head of the National AAU, Dr. Frederic Tilney, a famous fitness authority, and my wife to-be Thelma Rothman.

Meeting Again: Dan meets with George Eiferman in 1977, many years after George made his contest debut at Dan's 1946 Mr. Eastern Coast bodybuilding contest. With them is Maxine Reynolds, mother of American actress, singer and dancer, Debbie Reynolds. Photo taken backstage at the Debbie Reynolds Show.

Dan Lurie: Heart of Steel

Weider Star Athlete: Dan featured in *Your Physique* magazine.

By 1948 I felt it was time to promote contests on my own, once and for all, since the AAU had denied me sanction for a show I wanted to run in 1947. I had a good following of supporters and bodybuilding athletes from all across America were keen to compete in my events. My very own federation would also be a good way for me to reach more people and put into place changes I felt were needed for bodybuilding to grow further. This contest, the Mr. New York State Physique Contest and Professional Show, attracted a lot of attention. For it, I established the title International Federation of Body Builders - the IFBB for short - a name I had registered in 1947 to add some weight to my promotion efforts and to bring together bodybuilding worldwide. At the time I had seen many problems within the AAU, the most obvious being its exclusion of athletes who wanted to make money through bodybuilding, and the lack of financial incentive for the athletes to continue. No longer could athletes compete for the fun of it. While big business decided the outcome of many events, with certain athletes benefiting financially from exercise equipment manufacturing companies, other athletes struggled to survive. As an ex-bodybuilder who had to pay my own way to the Mr America three years' running, I had been there and knew what these men were going through. For me, the IFBB was a move toward making bodybuilding a legitimate, professional sport, to bring greater recognition to and moneymaking opportunities for bodybuilders. At the time, the AAU was heavily promoting weightlifting and in doing this they was holding back bodybuilding - bodybuilding was almost viewed as an afterthought. I wanted to put bodybuilding and bodybuilders center-stage. A great deal of thought actually went into choosing the IFBB name. When I published my first bodybuilding magazine, *Muscle Training Illustrated* in 1965 - which I will talk at length about in chapter six - I hired a fellow by the name of Emmanuel Orlick as editor. Having worked for Joe as a writer for his magazines, Emmanuel was someone I had known from a distance for many years. I admired his writing style and read all his articles. In many of his articles, Emmanuel spoke of an International Federation of Gymnastics that his son belonged to. In 1947 I simply borrowed the "International Federation of" bit and added Body Builders. This is how I originally came up with the name.

Joe Weider and I were still friends in early 1948 and he was at the Mr. New York State contest when I used the IFBB name for the very first time. In fact, the official program for this event advertised his magazines *Your Physique* and *Muscle Power* and the IFBB name was clearly featured on the front page above a photo of the magnificent 1945 Mr. America, Clancy Ross, who was the evening's guest poser. Joe's brother, Ben Weider, whom he became partners with, claims he established the IFBB name in October 1946 at their Mr. Montreal show, but I discovered that he never even registered it at the time, if, in fact, he had even thought of it then. In October 1947, Joe and Ben ran a Mr. Canada show and nowhere on the program does it mention the IFBB name. This was the year I registered the name. In 1948 I put the IFBB name on the Mr. New York State program and with Joe in attendance at the contest, and with his magazines advertised on the program, there was no questioning my use of this title. For Ben and Joe to say they registered the IFBB name in 1946 is nothing short of a lie. In 2005 I hired a Canadian law firm to check when the IFBB name was first registered as a non-profit organisation in Canada. After many weeks of searching they found no records to say the name had been registered in 1946. After seeing all the available evidence it is pretty clear for all who are willing to look hard enough that it was myself who first established the IFBB name.

It's Official! The Official Mr. New York State program with the International Federation of Body Builders (IFBB) title emblazoned on the cover.

As for the Mr. New York State itself, the show was rather successful, although it did not attract the number of competitors I would have liked. At the time the AAU had made it clear that anyone competing in a rival organization would be automatically banned from entering any of their shows, so fearing they would face bodybuilding extinction, many athletes chose to play it safe, a move that resulted in fewer competitors at my New York State contest. Though low on numbers, this show more than made up for it through its quality and the special guest appearance of Oakland California's 1945 Mr. America, Clancy Ross, who had a physique displaying previously unseen definition and shape. This was the first time Ross had been seen onstage on the East Coast and the crowd just went wild for him. He was truly great! We also featured Canada's most muscular man, Ed Theriault, along with the usual entertainment acts audiences had come to expect at my shows. Held at the Brooklyn Academy of Music, the best line up of contestants any of my shows had seen up until that point was on hand to pose for the many fans in attendance. We had Al Berman, Frank Leight and Fred Massaro among many others – all quality contestants. But with other business opportunities calling, this was my final big contest for the time being.

Between 1948 and 1965 I regularly ran a number of smaller shows including Mr. Brooklyn, Mr. Queens, various Country and Mr. Theater shows, which included the Mr. Pitkin Theater and Mr. Concord Hotel, Mr. Florida at the Fontainebleau Hotel in Miami Beach and the 1965 Mr. World's Fair. The theater shows were a good idea at the time, as bodybuilding was starting to catch on and moviegoers were thrilled by the muscular physique. Whenever there was a movie that featured an athletic, muscular actor such as Johnny Weismuller, I would stage a small bodybuilding contest at the same venue either before or after the movie. These kinds of movies provided the perfect tie-in for me to run my shows and a way to encourage interest among the general public towards bodybuilding. Most of these smaller shows were run in the local Brooklyn Queens area. In 1965 I would take my promotional efforts all the way to the top.

After moving my gym business to Pitkin Avenue, Brooklyn, in 1947, and after untying myself from the mess Weider had left for me, I decided to run the Dan Lurie Barbell Company from a little store on Bristol Street, near where my wife Thelma's parent's lived. My basement could no longer hold my growing inventory and the orders were coming in thick and fast. As the barbell business grew so too did the number of little stores, lofts and basements that held the equipment. This prompted a search for a new, more expansive, location and the Dan Lurie Barbell Company finally found its home in 1955: two large brick buildings of around eight thousand square feet in total, alongside one another on Utica Avenue in Brooklyn, just around the corner from our house on East 51 Street. The front building was the retail showroom where I sold my products and the rear was used for the manufacturing of goods. One of the great things about this new site was the room it provided for all of my equipment. It was next to impossible to fill large orders before, as the equipment was stored in dozens of locations. The new buildings made it possible to centralize my operations to reach a greater number of customers. But with all of the good we must accept some bad and whereas before I had paid next to nothing to store my equipment in a larger number of smaller locations, my rent for the new building amounted to $800 each month! At times I wondered if I had been too ambitious taking on such a large and expensive building. One thing I did have on my side, though, was a will to succeed and I worked all the hours I could to make enough of a profit to stay afloat. My intensive work schedule paid off and 25 years later I still had that building on Utica Avenue. The one thing I do regret slightly, however, was not buying this building, but I guess it is easy to look back today and say this was a mistake. I knew I would do well but did not really know exactly how big the operation would become. Back in the mid-'50s the Dan Lurie Barbell Company was less well known and I would have risked a lot buying it. It would be 25 years before - in 1980 - I bought my first major retail premises, a massive building on Conduit Avenue, Springfield Boulevard, Queens, overlooking the Belt Parkway near John F. Kennedy Airport on Long Island. This building had two floors and a total of 50,000 square feet, complete with a conveyer belt system that ran through the basement, which made it easier to move thousands of tons of equipment. It was the perfect location for my barbell business, and sales increased almost from the moment I moved in. For one thing, its location was ideal because it was highly visible from Belt Parkway, where over half a million cars passed each day. In a past life it was a supermarket so it was about the size of a city block, complete with space to park 50 cars. On the roof I had a trademark giant picture of myself hitting a front double biceps pose along with a sign advertising it as the largest bodybuilding equipment outlet in the world. On approach, this building really stood out: the display signs were five foot by five foot block letters with florescent lights inside. The size of the location, the amount of equipment sold there and its sheer presence made it the biggest of its day.

Along with this superstore, we also had other Dan Lurie sales locations and showrooms: one at 732 Seventh Avenue near Times Square, run by my then son-in-law Scott Epstein and another at 3475 Old Conejo Road in Newbury Park, California, overseen by 1941 America's Most Muscular Man winner Lud Shusterich, a man who I grew up and was very close friends with. We also had several manufacturing plants in Brooklyn. But the Queens store was our biggest. It was filled with fitness equipment made by several manufacturers along with my own brand of workout gear. Of course we stocked tons of Dan Lurie barbell and dumbbell sets, the equipment that gave me my start in this business. As well we had a large nutritional supplementation line, which included my own products, and a sports store and boxing and karate department. I employed many staff to help with the manufacturing and selling exercise equipment.

One employee, Tony Badal, came to me as a 17 year old and began by assisting my top salesman, John Jackson, before eventually becoming one of my best foundry workers. Along with the steel variety, we would make cement filled plates. One time I remember Tony worked so hard that he himself almost became a one-man conveyer system. As Tony recalled it, he was working on the assembly line up to his ears in cement, working on one of the five stations needed for making the barbell plates. I will let Tony explain: "One station put up the empty plates and then they slid them over and another guy would fill them with cement and then they would be slid over again and another guy would cap them with these caps, with a hammer, a rubber mallet. Then they would slide it over and another guy would hose them down and clean them then move them along and another fellow would take them off and stack them and put the empties back on. So it went in a big circle. And me trying to be the best worker, I was always ahead of the others so whatever station Dan had me on I was always waiting for it. So Dan being Dan he doesn't want to waste any energy. After that he had me doing two jobs: I was moulding dumbbell bars and stacking plates at the same time." You see, Tony was one of my best workers and his colleagues certainly didn't mind his desire to do more. I recall those days working the store as ones of productivity and fun. People were always joking around and the atmosphere was positive at all times. I can think of no other way to work.

On a Roll: one of the trucks Dan used to deliver barbells to devoted American bodybuilders (photo taken in 1958).

From the late 1940s to '88, the Dan Lurie Barbell Company had expanded to where it was the most successful company of its kind. It became a major supplier of bodybuilding equipment to large sporting goods stores and all major department outlets in the New York Metropolitan area. But a good business does not just happen. It takes great deal of planning and attention to detail. Customer relations were most important to me. The way I looked at it, I was in business not just to sell equipment, but also to make friends, and extra attention was paid to knowing on a personal level everyone that bought a piece of equipment. To do this I would have a card system, which contained all the important customer information: their name, age, hobbies, bodybuilding and sporting goals and physical statistics would be kept on this card-file system for easy access. If someone came in I would go directly to his or her name and their card would have all the information I needed to deal with them on a personal and professional level. One quick look and I would have enough to talk in a meaningful way with them about their wants and needs. A customer might have had weight gaining as one of their goals. I would ask them how this goal was going and what their current weight was. If it had increased I would say, "Wow, five years ago you were in here and your weight was 126. Now it is 180. Congratulations." It was my own form of good salesmanship. If customers feel like they are your friends they will return. My whole selling philosophy was very simple: always make people feel good and show a genuine interest in them and they will be your friends, and customers, for life.

My exercise equipment business was of my proudest achievements. But all good things must eventually end and so it was with this aspect of my professional life. In 1988, at age 65, I decided it was time to retire from the business that had given me so much. I had just had a silent heart attack, which I was told was more dangerous than the other more common painful type. Thinking I was experiencing physical exhaustion I decided to go see a doctor, but what I thought was stress brought on by overworking, was in fact a lot worse. Because of very low oxygen levels pumped to my heart without any major warning signs - the main trait of a silent heart attack - I may have, had my hectic schedule continued, expired before my time; the doctors forced me to stay in hospital for observation for two weeks before they could figure out how bad my problem was. When they let me out they told me I would be fine, but to take it easy. I considered it a sign from God to slow down. So before they put me a box for good, I turned the business over to my son Mark. 19 years later I am in perfect health and my life could not be better. In 1995 I sold the Conduit Avenue building for one million dollars.

My early days in business were good ones. I certainly learned who you could and could not trust. By 1948, at the young age of 25, I had achieved a lot in the bodybuilding business, and had done well competitively. As a manufacturer and distributor of barbells and promoter of bodybuilding contests in the New York area, owner of several popular gyms, and originator of the International Federation of Body Builders title, my name had become synonymous with bodybuilding, physical culture and healthy living. Throughout the '50s I would continue to promote bodybuilding through over 100 contests, in the running of my gyms and through my exercise booklets. The barbell business continued to grow, and so did my reputation as a businessman. But I had only just started. The 1960s would see bodybuilding become even more popular and I would be firmly at the forefront of this.

Dan, as captured in his early years, was a favorite muse of many of the times foremost photographers

Chapter Four:

The Grimek Challenge

By 1945 I felt good about my bodybuilding future. My competition career might have been over but I was still America's Most Muscular Man three years' running and there was no direct challenge to that title. Still, there were contenders knocking on the door. At the time, the AAU had just excluded me from all amateur events, and rumour had it that there was, within the amateur ranks, a challenger to my most muscular status. Even though I had won my titles fairly at the Mr. America, and this placed me as the man to beat, it did not stop people from speculating on who was the greatest muscular bodybuilder of all time. Despite my success, I had not won the overall Mr. America, and many found it hard to separate the two, that one - the Mr. America – (often) represented height, looks, affiliation and physique and the other - the most muscular - pure muscle, shape and definition. I felt I should have won at least two overall Mr America titles, but at that point there was nothing I could do to reverse what was to my mind political interference that allowed the wrong men to win. I accepted it and moved on, though I knew I deserved to be called America's Most Muscular man, as I had won the titles fairly and justly in 1942, 1943 and 1944. I had earned the right.

Dan Lurie: Heart of Steel

Best of Both Worlds: Dan showing the ultimate in size and shape in 1943, at his peak as America's Most Muscular Man.

I had won the titles, but many assumed, based on false media reports, that one man was superior to me. Winner of the 1940 and 1941 Mr. America titles, John Grimek was thought by many at the time to be more muscular than I. In fact, he was widely considered to be the world's most muscular man. Of course he did have a magnificent physique, and was larger than I was with more muscle mass overall, and he rightly deserved his America wins, but I *was* America's Most Muscular Man. I was definitely more defined and had better detail to my physique. Though this did not stop his sponsor, the Bob Hoffman-headed York Barbell Company, from printing in their magazine, *Strength and Health*, that Grimek was "the most muscular man in the world". After I won my last most muscular title, there was no mention anywhere in *Strength and Health* that I was America's most muscular champ. Hoffman's refusal to run any pictures of me or put me on the cover of *Strength and Health* seemed to suggest that I was not a worthy

The Grimek Challenge

champion. But they did put the title "world's most muscular man" under almost every photo of Grimek, which then, by implication, put him in the minds of many as America's Most Muscular Man. I worked extremely hard for my titles and it upset me that Grimek was falsely considered the more muscular of the two of us. Sure, he had more bulk but when I compare our muscularity I speak of defined muscle. My opinion was that since almost every sport had its own World Title champion, bodybuilding should have the same. But in 1945 the reality was that there weren't enough contestants to have a separate "Most Muscular" competition. Since I was opposed to the free use of titles, and people who gave themselves honors they did not win, or deserve, I decided to challenge John Grimek for the title of America's Most Muscular Man.

First I planned to stage a massive nationwide event to decide America's Most Muscular Man. I spoke with dozens of prominent bodybuilders from all over the United States and Canada to see if such a plan was workable. The whole show, which would be open to all comers, would be run at my expense, and I would advertise it as widely as possible. On the face of it, this plan seemed solid and people from all over liked what they heard, but one major problem stopped me: according to AAU rules, I was classed as a professional bodybuilder, which meant that any amateur who competed against me would automatically lose their amateur status. Since Grimek was an amateur, America's Most Muscular Man could not be decided between the two of us, which, to my mind, defeated the purpose of staging this event, as we were the best of the best. Many people considered him the most muscular, but I had proven I was on three occasions, and only a pose-down between the two of us would confirm the matter once and for all. The thought that Grimek was more muscular than I disappointed me because on paper I knew I could win: from top to bottom I felt I had more detail and better balance along with deeper cuts which better-delineated my muscle groups, and superior vascularity which gave my physique a refined, championship-winning look. By comparison, Grimek had a bulkier, rounder look with little abdominal development and small pectoral muscles. His chest was big, but flat. He was very large with good arm, shoulder and leg development, but I had a more pleasing complete look, I thought.

"From top to bottom I felt I had more detail and better balance, along with deeper cuts." Dan's legendary physique at its best: in 1943.

I wanted more than anything to set the record straight, but with no official contest to decide America's Most Muscular Man, I did the only thing I could at the time: I openly and personally challenged Grimek to a showdown at a time and place we would both agree on, in front of judges we both trusted. In a letter sent directly to Grimek, I suggested the challenge take place before the end of 1945, and offered to pay all of his expenses. In my letter I said: "I am confident that if we were both subject to close scrutiny, we would dispel any doubts as to who undeniably possesses the most muscular body." I had made it clear that if he wanted to maintain the reputation his magazine had created for him, he would have to step onstage with me and fight it out, one on one. I ended my letter by saying: "If you do not respond, it will be evident that you have rejected this challenge and that you have assumed an attitude of defeat."

I later ran my challenge in *Your Physique* and *Muscle Power* magazines. At the time, Joe Weider and I felt this challenge would be a good way to promote some interest in bodybuilding – his boy going up against the mighty John Grimek was sure to get people talking. Grimek's response was, to put it mildly, unnecessary and extremely hurtful. His 2000-word reply told me in no uncertain terms what I could do with my contest. His reply amounted to a barrage of insults and mud slinging, with no straightforward answer given. He just showered abuse and left it at that. The great John Grimek sure gave me a good going over, but I was not worried. As far as I was concerned, his response could have been viewed in two ways: either he felt such a contest was beneath someone of his stature or he was afraid Dan Lurie would prove him and Bob Hoffman to be liars for what they had published about him. I figured the latter was closer to the truth; that he was afraid. And so, it appeared, did Hoffman. Grimek did not directly accept my challenge, but it appeared Hoffman had thoroughly considered what the public might have thought had this showdown been avoided. And nine months later, *Strength and Health* published an article stating the challenge between John Grimek and me would take place at Turners Hall, Philadelphia, on the 4th of May 1946.

So it seemed the stage had been set. On one side was Joe Weider and Dan Lurie, and on the other, Bob Hoffman and John Grimek. In 1946 there was no bigger story in all of bodybuilding. Who would become America's Most Muscular Man, to put the question beyond doubt? I was confident it would be me, but would politics play a part in determining the outcome? This is the question I continually asked myself. But as the contest approached I became anxious to prove my point. The months seemed to drag, but I trained harder than ever. When the contest arrived, my muscles were the biggest they had ever been, with the same deep cuts and sharp definition that had won me my titles, and I was ready for Grimek. I should have known, however, that Hoffman's arrangement would not be a fair one. The moment I arrived at the Turners Hall, rumour had it that Hoffman had denied all involvement in the staging of this contest. I was supposed to attend with Joe Weider, but he refused to come as he had heard rumours Hoffman would beat him up, as there was a lot of anger between those two at that point. I was on my own. That night, Hoffman was hosting one of his York contests, which he had called "America's Most Muscular Physique Contest", where a number of amateur bodybuilders competed, but he said he was just there as a spectator, and that he had been persuaded to be the Master of Ceremonies against his will. Things just didn't add up. First, I had to buy a ticket and sit in the back row of the audience, despite supposedly being the main attraction along with Grimek. Hoffman was then heard saying that I was in the audience and afraid to compete. I was as confused as probably most of audience were. Was there not supposed to be a special challenge between John Grimek and Dan Lurie? Hoffman pretended there was no such thing.

Hoffman claimed to have been in attendance as a spectator, but it was clear he controlled the show. For one thing, his name appeared on the program as an official. And when one competitor applied late, he was told he would have to ask Bob Hoffman and John Grimek for special entry.

My patience wore thin as I sat in the audience waiting for the challenge. Finally the crowd, realizing that no direct challenge between Grimek and myself was to take place, started protesting loudly. Cries of "Lurie, Lurie, Lurie" swept through the building. It was becoming chaotic. Something had to be done to restore peace, before things got totally out of control. Finally they said over the loud speaker that Dan Lurie was a professional and John Grimek was an amateur and because of this no contest would take place. But this was exactly why a separate event was to be staged: to give us the opportunity to compete as equals, with no political interference. Hoffman then announced that they would have a professional most muscular contest, but it would be open to all non-amateur bodybuilders. Grimek, with his amateur status, remained in the amateur category. It was after this announcement that the crowd really went crazy.

Throughout his speech, Hoffman taunted me to come backstage. The crowd chanted, "we want Lurie, we want Lurie." But, instead of going backstage, I went onstage to ask Hoffman what was going on. Thinking about it now, I should have gone backstage to wait for my turn to compete. It was clear the Grimek challenge was off, but I still wanted to show that I was superior to John Grimek by audience approval, and to address them personally. I approached Hoffman face to face. I wanted to speak to the crowd. Hoffman, a rather large man at around six feet four and well over 200 pounds, told me to "get the hell off the stage." I considered what to do next. Rather than walk off, I stood my ground, took the microphone and again asked to speak. The audience began to chant "let Lurie speak, let Lurie speak." I took the microphone and told the crowd that I was there to compete against John Grimek, but it appeared I could not because of Hoffman's involvement and the fact I was considered a professional. I explained that I had checked with the Metropolitan AAU in New York and was told by the man in charge, Rudy Sablo, that the contest being held that night was not sanctioned by the National AAU, which meant that Hoffman had the final say, making it clear to all that things were definitely not right, that Hoffman's involvement prevented a showdown between Grimek and myself. Then Hoffman lunged at me. I moved to the side, clenched both fists and told him to move away. We were both enraged and fists were about to fly. The crowd were as worked up as Hoffman and I were to the point where there could have been a major riot. When Hoffman moved back I was completely shaken and lost all focus. I was upset that I would not be competing against Grimek, as promised, and felt sorry the crowd had been deceived. But when I spoke again, I made the mistake of saying that although I felt the judges might have been honest, Bob Hoffman picked them and since he had already tricked me that night I could not be so sure about the judges. After I said this I immediately regretted it and knew the outcome for me would be bad. Hoffman again grabbed the microphone and said the contest would begin soon. So they put me up against two other men Bob considered professional: Sigmund Klein, a well-built smaller man whose only real strength was his abdominal development, though he was never a competitor, and Walter Podolak, an out-of-shape wrestler who went by the name, "The Golden Superman". I figured I would be the clear winner. After all, Klein had never competed and was not at his best physically, and Podolak was no bodybuilder.

I told Hoffman the contest would not be a fair one because he picked the judges. He simply ignored me. I went on to say that there was only one way I could compete and get fair assessment: let the audience judge with their applause. The crowd agreed to this, but Hoffman went ahead as he had originally planned. Still, I figured I would easily win. Klein was 44 and had seen better days. Pololak, who later told me he had been paid $100 by Hoffman to compete against me, though a big man with a massive frame, did in no way resemble a bodybuilder. Funnily enough, *Strength and Health* reported a short while after this contest that Podolak had volunteered to compete in this show.

So with my "competition" decided I readied myself for an easy victory. The auditorium went quiet as we three professionals readied ourselves for battle. As I was putting on my trunks, I noticed Hoffman pushing Klein onto the stage. With Hoffman at the microphone, Klein went through his routine. Throughout his display, Hoffman spoke to the audience, and the judges, as he praised Klein's physique. "Look at Sig Klein," Hoffman said. "Look at his abdominal development, look at his obliques, have you ever seen such a great physical specimen." He went through all of Klein's good points before I made my appearance. As I posed, Hoffman went quiet, though the audience, much to Hoffman's obvious anger, responded well to my routine and physique. Then Podolak posed. He did the best he could, but could not match muscles with myself, or even Klein for that matter. I felt a degree of vindication as we stood there at our routines' conclusion. I did not get to pose down with Grimek, as promised, but the audience still saw both of our physiques on the same stage and they were able to make up their own minds as to who was the most muscular.

Grimek did continue his winning streak that night, taking the overall title later that evening. To my mind, though, the crowd response throughout both our routines - after my category had been decided - left little doubt as to who was most muscular. So there I was waiting for the professional winner's announcement. I figured if I could not beat Grimek directly, a win against Klein and Podolak might, after Grimek was declared the winner in his division, force a comparison between us. Based on the crowd response and all that had been reported in the magazines up until then, I felt the fans would certainly demand this. I was satisfied that a win would get me my shot at Grimek. When Klein was announced the winner, the audience was outraged and a riot began at the back of the auditorium. People began throwing chairs and loud booing rang throughout the building. The thought was that I had clearly been cheated. While Klein, at five foot four inches and 150 pounds, had never competed in a bodybuilding event and had no leg development to speak of, I was a past three-time Mr. America runner up and at five feet six inches and 180 pounds had some of the most balanced muscular development in America.

Most Muscular: Dan's size and definition was ahead of its time.

It appeared Hoffman had set the whole thing up to humiliate me. In fact, I have spoken to many people since who said they felt the show was a joke. But I never held anything against Sig Klein for placing ahead of me. In fact, in 1968 I honored him at my first World Body Building Guild (WBBG) Hall of Fame banquet held at the Granada Hotel, Brooklyn. If you will recall, Sig was also the judge who broke the 1942 Mr. American tie between Frank Leight and myself in Cincinnati, Ohio. Known as one of the world's best-built men of the 1920s, Sig was truly one of bodybuilding's great pioneers. Despite our early encounters, we eventually became friends and he even wrote for my Magazine *Muscle Training Illustrated*. Walter Podolak and I became best of friends. His engaging, larger than life personality and warm heart were his biggest attributes.

A Pioneer Honored: Dan honors Sigmund Klein (left) at the first WBBG Hall of Fame Dinner held at the Granada Hotel in Brooklyn, New York, 1968.

One month after this debacle of a contest, Hoffman's magazine *Strength and Health* reported that Sigmund Klein won "America's Most Muscular Physique" professional challenge by a wide margin of 48 points to my 43, and Podolak came a "close" third with 41 points. This statement did much to highlight the unfairness of this contest, but it also made me laugh. What would I have to do to get a fair deal?

I never did get my comparison against Grimek. I always did admire Grimek for his bodybuilding achievements but I really did want to

The Grimek Challenge

have it decided officially at one contest just which of us was the more muscular. It was a shame things worked out the way they did. The best chance I had to gotten to know John was when his wife Angelina and I met at an old-timer's barbell banquet, years after his death. She told me about his bodybuilding life and shared insights into how he was as a man. It was nice to hear how Grimek as a family man, not as his York-constructed personality, viewed the world and life. As I was a Weider athlete in the 1940s, Grimek distanced me. Weider and York were old rivals and because of this Grimek considered me the enemy. On a few occasions I would approach him at AAU contests and attempt to shake his hand and get to know him. He would always ignore my gesture.

Example of the Bob Hoffman bodybuilding judging system? Walter Podolak placed a close second to Dan at the AAU 1946 America's Most Muscular Physique contest - with 41 points to Dan's 43.

Dan Lurie: Heart of Steel

With Wives' of Champions: Dan with (left to right) Mrs John Grimek (Angela) and Mrs Marvin Eder (Adelle) at the 2005 Oldetime Barbell and Strongman awards.

Hoffman's contest left me with a sour taste in my mouth. All I wanted was a fair shake, but it seemed corruption was a big part of bodybuilding back then. My first show as a promoter, two years earlier, was partly a response to bodybuilding's corrupt state. I vowed to promote this show, and all others after it, with integrity and in the interests of good sportsmanship. As you will read in later chapters, my philosophy as a contest promoter was to accept anyone of any nationality or creed, and from any federation. It would be a non-discriminatory federation. With Hoffman, everything was underhanded. He would promise certain things and not deliver. It was also revealed that he was racist and it could be seen in the way he ran his shows that he was strongly opposed to anyone he did not personally like. His influence on bodybuilding was widely felt at the time and many a great competitor suffered through his discrimination. Joe Weider himself said in his book *Brothers of Iron* that in his many dealings with Hoffman he discovered him to have had a staunch anti-Jew streak. Did Hoffman's stance impact my ability to win the Mr. America? I cannot really say, but it does raise some questions. One thing was for sure: the Grimek challenge was a trap from the beginning. The challenge generated a lot of publicity, which only helped Hoffman attract more spectators - 3,000 people attended

The Grimek Challenge

this show and he made $30,000 in profits, a lot of money in those days. It seemed Hoffman knew what he was doing right from the beginning. I learned my lesson and, once again, moved on.

But the debate still raged. Who was America's Most Muscular Man? Of course I thought I was. After all, it had been proven. But Grimek was still considered by Hoffman to be the best ever. Given Hoffman largely controlled bodybuilding in the 1940s, many took his word as gospel. You have to remember, John Grimek was a weightlifter *and* a bodybuilder. He was very strong and built a lot of size, but on closer inspection it is easy to see his weaknesses – a massive frame does not make a complete bodybuilder. Two muscle groups to which the eyes are focused when viewing a bodybuilder's physique are the chest and abdominal muscles. Grimek's were not all that impressive. Mine were well developed. Overall, Grimek may have beaten me in a few of muscle groups, and I will admit he was the much larger man, but from all angles I displayed total development. Not convinced? Look at photos of the two of us from the 1940s and these should dispel any doubt. So who would have won the most muscular event between us? Take a look at our physique photos and there is your answer.

Balance and Size: the rugged physique of Dan Lurie in 1943 - aged 20.

Chapter Five:

Television Strongman

As the 1940s drew to a close, I had become known in bodybuilding as one of its top competitors, a good contest promoter and a successful businessman, the owner of a thriving barbell company and popular chain of gyms. I felt satisfied with what I had achieved but had a firm eye on furthering bodybuilding's popularity through continuing to promote contests and growing my businesses. I did not know it at the time, but my life would take a completely different turn, one that would put me more in the public eye than anything I had done up until then. The year was 1950 and a major opportunity, one that would change my life forever, came my way.

At age 27 I lived and breathed bodybuilding. Despite my hectic lifestyle I still found time to train, and my physique remained sharp. With added muscle size I was now much larger at around 185 pounds. This presented a more powerful appearance and I remained as strong as ever. In fact, it was my size and strength along with an unknown ability to entertain that landed me the opportunity to become a household name across America.

Television Strongman

It all began when I was asked to play the role of a strongman on the nationally televised Sealtest Big Top Show, a program that would become the number one children's show of its time. Airing on CBS from July 1, 1950 through to September of 1957, the Sealtest Big Top brought together all the fun of the circus with a cast of actors chosen for their ability to play various circus characters: Jack Sterling was the ringmaster; Bob Russell the barker; Ed McMahon and Chris Keegan were clowns; and Barbera Cubberly played Majorette. Naturally I played the strongman and became Sealtest Dan The Muscle Man. Before my role as Sealtest Dan, I was known nationally, but only within the then-small bodybuilding community. After appearing on Sealtest Big Top for several years I became known to a much wider audience, which, as it happened, only served to better promote bodybuilding. Of over 2,100 acts performed over the Big Top show's seven years, I would do the strength feats in a role where I would become known as America's most popular muscle man of the 1950s and '60s. Let me tell you how it all began.

After spotting a story about my bodybuilding achievements in the *Daily News*, a producer for the Madison Avenue advertising agency, N.W. Ayer, called me to arrange an interview for the role of Seatest Dan. At the time the agency was in talks with Sealtest Dairies, a company that produced milk, ice cream and other such products, who wanted to attract a younger market to increase product sales. They wanted to design a series of commercials that featured their product in ways that would appeal to children of all ages and I was of interest, as my physique was considered marketable, and would attract attention. I went along with no big expectations, more out of curiosity than anything else. The agency, though, had big plans for me. "Mr. Lurie," the producer began. "We are about to launch a very exciting television show to be called the Sealtest Big Top Show. The central theme of the show will showcase a circus, with a range of actors playing circus characters. Everybody loves the circus," he said with a big smile. He told me that professionals would play all of the main characters. "We want real clowns and a barker. We also want a real strongman, you!" I considered the promoter's words before turning him down. "Wait a minute, Mr. Thompson, I'm not just some circus strongman currently out of work," I told him. "I have a business to run and really can't be taking days off to rehearse and to be going to Philadelphia every week to do the show. Sorry, but I am just not interested." " I'm sorry to hear that Mr. Lurie," replied the producer, "because your reputation as man of strength and the fact you are a former America's Most Muscular Man would have been an asset to the show. Perhaps you could recommend someone for the part." I thought for a while and suggested they contact a member of my gym, Stanley Elkins, a young man I considered very strong and because of this felt would fit the part well.

With the opportunity of a lifetime having slipt away, I made my way back to my own office. During my 20-minute interview with the producer we discussed a whole range of things relating to the role of Sealtest Dan, but not once did Mr. Thompson mention salary. And I didn't ask. Meanwhile, Stanley Elkins auditioned for the job, and got it. His contract was for 13 weekly shows. But before the first show screened, who should arrive at my office panicking, but Stanley, a look of concern spread across his face. I asked him what was wrong. "Dan, I've been drafted," he said between tears. This was at a time when the Korean War was at its peak and young men were being called up and put into uniform. "I'm not afraid of going in the army Dan. The problem is, I have already begun some of the Big Top rehearsals and I won't be around to complete the 13 weeks," he said, wiping tears from his eyes. "I can't just keep going, then leave them. It wouldn't be fair." It was disappointing for me to see Stanley like this as I really liked the young man and had hoped the strongman role would work out for him. Accepting his predicament, I told him that his country was to come first and wished him well. As he was leaving, I asked, "Just out of interest Stan, how much are they paying you to do the show?" "$300 a week, as well as my hotel expenses and train fare," he said, eyes downcast. Then it struck me. When I refused to do the show, I had not once considered the money. Now I figured if I played my cards right, I could make some cash from this role, which, combined with the profits from my current businesses, would be enough to provide my family with the kind of lifestyle I figured they deserved.

Two days later producer Thompson called me. I was ready for him. With Stan gone, they desperately needed a strongman and I knew it. "I might be interested," I told him confidently. "But not for $300 a week.

I am an AAU national titleholder and businessman. My time is valuable and I know what I am worth." This bluff seemed to work because Mr. Thompson then asked me very politely how much I wanted. "Twice what you are paying Elkins," I said without hesitation. Finally we settled on $500 a show. I also negotiated travel expenses both ways as the live show was filmed weekly in Philadelphia. The rest is history, and the original 13-week contract stretched out for seven years.

Strongman: Dan displays the physique the earned him the role of Sealtest Dan, The muscle Man, on CBS' Sealtest Big Top Show.

The work was perfect for me because I enjoyed performing and displaying my physique and physical strength in front of an audience. It was like bodybuilding all over again, except this time I was paid handsomely for my efforts. My main role was to perform strength feats after consuming Sealtest products, which included milk and ice cream. These feats, made possible through the "special properties" of the strength-inducing Sealtest products, included one-arm dumbbell bent presses, an exercise I did well in as a youth, various barbell presses, loads of bodyweight exercises such as push-ups and sit-ups, and stunts where I would lift one or more people overhead. One time I lifted, from a lying position, a 100-pound dumbbell 10 times with each hand while the audience counted along. This was extremely hard, as I had to balance one side of my body while the other side pumped the weight. Passing it from my left to right hand while remaining stable on the small bench was a feat in itself. After this display I was given some Sealtest, homogenised vitamin-D milk – "it's Dan's favorite drink," the announcer proclaimed.

As I popped and strained, my muscles would pump up and become almost twice their usual size, and this delighted the live audience of over 1000. I would also make my back muscles do their own kind of Mexican wave – they would contort and take on all kinds of shapes as I flexed them in unusual ways. I also had little faces painted on my chest and by moving my pectoral muscles up and down I could make the faces move, smile and frown, just the kind of gimmicky stuff the Sealtest people wanted. My muscles would also open and close the show. The Big Top's title and credits were drawn on my back and by flexing my muscles I could make them move; at this point in my career I must have had the most televised back in the world. Using my muscles in various ways was just the type of novel approach to attracting viewers and potential customers the agency wanted, and the viewers tuned in to watch each Saturday at noon on WCAU Philadelphia, the CBS owned-and-operated televison station that served the Philadelphia and Pennsylvania market.

As a side benefit, Sealtest gave me as much ice cream as I could carry home. It was normal for me to take over 20 gallons of ice cream home on weekends and my popularity as father and husband increased enormously at these times. Naturally my family and I could not eat this much in one week, so I would give it away: friends, neighbours, even toll collectors on the New Jersey turnpike would receive frequent gifts of ice cream. I was happy with the ice cream arrangement and, more importantly, with my weekly wage. But I noticed several others on the show would constantly approach the advertising agency for raises. They thought they were indispensable. Meanwhile I kept my mouth shut, and this paid off, as although these staff usually got their raises, a few weeks into their new contract a sudden replacement would be found for them and they would be out of a job. In fact, when asked if I wanted a raise I would always say, "I leave that entirely up to you. The money I make here is small compared to the profits I make from my own business. I do this because I like the people I work with and I do it mainly for fun." And this was the truth. I did love my job and considered it a fun experience. As Sealtest Dan I met and made friends with many talented people and learned a lot about business and life. For one thing, I learned how far good organization could take you. Getting ready for my Sealtest Dan slot, which meant many hours preparing my physique and reading my lines, eventually became second nature, but there was no room for error and I was to be highly organized at all times. The money I made as Sealtest Dan did also mean a lot to me. I played it cool, but the money I earned would allow me to buy a very nice home for my family. And, yes, I did receive a yearly raise.

Try Lifting This! Sealtest Dan, before being lifted skyward by the show's resident elephant.

**All Together Now: Dan (left, with cape) with
the Sealtest Big Top show cast.**

For the seven years the Sealtest Big Top Show screened, my routine more or less stayed the same. Every Thursday I would take the subway to the advertising agency, N.W. Ayer, at New York City's Rockefeller Plaza. From there I would get new scripts for my three commercials, which were to be screened the coming Saturday. I would then spend two hours rehearsing in the studio room before returning to my other businesses. Every Friday at 9.00pm I would catch a train from Grand Central Station and arrive in Philadelphia around 11.00 that evening. I would then relax at the luxurious Comac baths with several other Big Top actors, before retiring for the night. We needed the rest on Fridays, as a long day of screening would begin the following morning. On Saturday morning we were up by 6.00, ready for the 6.30am TV rehearsals, which lasted until 7.30. After rehearsals we memorized our scripts and were then free do whatever we wished. While others went out for entertainment, my "free time" was spent reading and answering business orders and mail I took with me from my Brooklyn office. In fact, I turned my actors area into a makeshift office using a four-by-eight piece of plywood on top of some props for a desk. At 11.15am sharp, the letters and orders were put to one side and I had my makeup applied.

It is hard to imagine a circus strongman needing make-up, but remember, this was television and without cosmetics the bright lights would promote a sickly appearance – not the kind of look the health-promoting Sealtest products should give you. After my makeup had been applied I would pump-up my muscles by doing five sets of 50 push-ups. With a coat of oil on my body and muscles properly pumped with blood, I was ready to make the first of my three, three-minute appearances at 12noon. Sealtest Dan would then perform whatever strength feats were expected of him for that week.

As well as the strength feats, I sang and spoke of the benefits Sealtest products provided, all in front on an audience of over 1000 boy and girl scouts. Performing in front of a live audience was rather scary at first, but I did learn the importance of timing, a lesson that would help me in later performing roles, mostly at fairs and schools where you had little time to prepare and had to be ready to perform at a moment's notice. Since I had only nine minutes to do three, three-minute commercials as Sealtest Dan, with about five minutes for the opening parade, I had to be perfectly on schedule or I would risk stalling the show. Makeup, pumping, oiling and costuming had to be arranged to allow for smooth running every time. The show also had only 30-seconds to stretch and cut in order to be off the air by 1.00pm, so the pressure was on! Fortunately everything went smoothly and the show ran on schedule every time.

Many times I drove to Philadelphia with fellow New York based actors, so after Saturday's show we were able to make a speedy return home, often arriving back at 3.30pm. Then it was back to business for me. Often I would spend a few hours at my gym on West 57 street and Eighth Avenue. This gym had been an old YMCA basement that had steam rooms and a large Olympic pool, and these facilities were kept, and made good use of by my customers. After spending the afternoon at my gym, I would be back home by 7.00 to spend the evening with my wife Thelma and children. I never did business on Sundays, as these were family days.

Dan Lurie: Heart of Steel

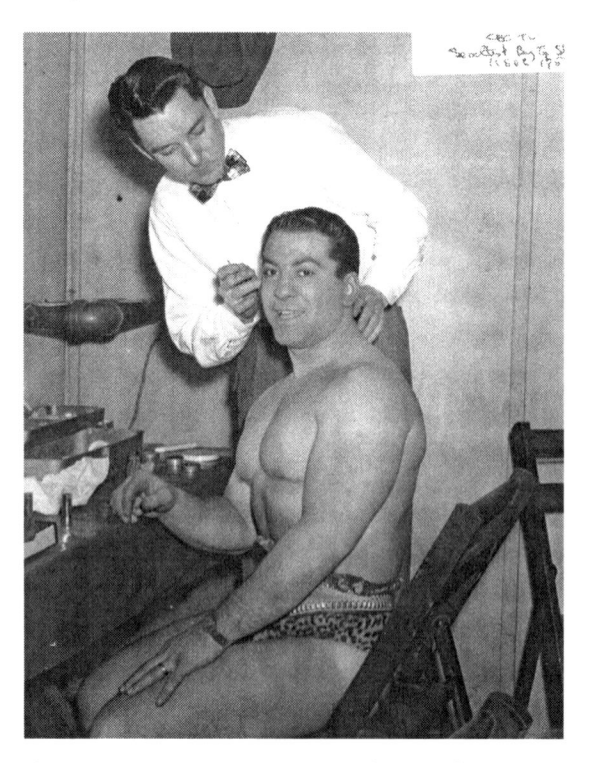

Makeup Time: Dan is prepared for the first of three three-minute commercials as Sealtest Dan.

What I enjoyed most about performing on the Big Top Show were the friends I made and many of them have had a lasting impact on my life. One man was Charlie Ryan, who was to be the original "Hymie" in my life. Charlie was a man of many theatrical talents, as could be seen in his production of the commercial music used on the Big Top Show, and as a former member, along with his younger brother, Little Ryan, of the original Smoothies singing group of radio and nightclub fame, who were also regulars on the Gracie Allen and George Burns show. He was the one who suggested that I join him and a group of his friends at the Comac Baths every Friday night before we filmed the show. Before then, Sealtest had been spending $50 every Friday night on a hotel room for me, and since the Turkish baths cost only five dollars a night I accepted this offer instead. At that moment Charlie Ryan saved Sealtest more than $4,000 on hotel fees - from the show's first episode to its final instalment – and this is not counting the towels we took from the baths.

Television Strongman

The baths provided a wonderful retreat during my hectic seven-year schedule as a Big Top Show performer. Along with the Baths themselves, there was a TV lounge, massage service, plenty of food and a small swimming pool. Our sleeping rooms were eight-by-eight in size, more than enough room to relax before the following day's filming.

Charlie Ryan was also a theatrical agent and was responsible for booking me on many of my earlier TV specialty show appearances. I would humour him over the fact he was Irish and had to work with so many Jewish show business people. "You should get yourself a Jewish partner Charlie," I would joke. "Ryan and Cohen would give you a better chance of booking more talent." The Jewish name "Hymie", an affectionate term used for a friend, was a name I gave him out of respect and I suggested he use this name to win over his Jewish clients. He often did. And to this day, it is still my name for him. Charlie is 94 years young and we have been close friends for over 57 years.

Another Charlie I worked with, but did not become as friendly with, was Charlie Vander, the show's producer. Mr. Vander was as serious as a heart attack and one hundred percent business most of the time. After the show he became more relaxed, but during the broadcast no one spoke to him.

My seven years on the Big Top Show also had me spending time on the road doing promotional work. The advertising agency had me appear at state fairs, on radio and television shows, and at everything from bridge openings to the arrival of a new elephant at the city zoo - it was not the first time I would be lifted skyward by one of these impressive creatures, as this would happen quite a bit on the Big Top Show itself. It was at the Michigan State Fair that I met Governor Gerhard Mennen (Soapy) Williams. It was planned that I would arrive at the fair with the Governor, have some pictures taken, then we would have lunch together. The agency people were already waiting for me in the lobby as I stepped out of the elevator of the five-star Detroit hotel we were staying in, dressed in a business suit and ready to impress with style and sophistication. "No, no, Dan, you can't wear a business suit," a disappointed looking agency P.R. man said. "What do you expect me to wear in the company of the Governor," I asked, "a white sheet?" "Dan, you have to *look* like Sealtest Dan when you meet Governor Williams." I argued that wearing my leotards and cape would not look good at such a formal time. I lost my argument and met the Governor wearing my Big Top Sealtest Dan outfit. I felt like a freak, but had no choice – I was meeting with this esteemed man cape and all. But this proved a good idea as the Governor loved my look and really got into the occasion. In keeping with my strongman persona, I lifted him overhead with one hand as part of the celebrations. The crowd loved it.

The Performer: Dan, acting on the Big Top Show.

The Big Top Show's master of ceremonies was Jack Sterling - whose real name was Jack Sexton - and he also became a good friend. I looked to him as an older brother as he had a few years on me and his kindness and advice was appreciated. Whenever Jack went on vacation, an announcer named Tony Marvin - the man with the very deep voice on the Arthur Godfrey show - would replace him. Tony lived on Long Island during his time on the Big Top Show - not far from were I was in Brooklyn - and we became close friends. He had one of the classiest singing voices I had ever heard, an operatic style that really shook the rafters. Sadly, few knew about his singing talents, but if they *were* widely known, he

Television Strongman

could have gone far in this industry. Tony also shared my passion for working out and keeping fit and strong and when we trained together he would inspire me with his great work rate. Tony retired in Boynton Beach, Florida, and died on October 10, 1998, at the age of 86. He was buried at the Pinelawn Jewish Cemetery on Long Island, only a short distance from my Family Plot in Mt. Ararat.

Who is That Clown? A Big Top performer displaying the show's title.

A most unlikely Big Top clown was Ed McMahon, who went on to achieve fame on Johnny Carson's, The Tonight Show. Ed, who lived in Philadelphia, graduated as an actor from the Drama Department of the Catholic University. His talents as an actor did not match his personality and I personally found him standoffish. While the rest of the crew, who were all from New York City, would gather at the Turkish baths on the Friday evening before the show, Ed would only join us at the Armoury where the Big Top was televised the following Saturday morning. 25 years ago I arranged and picked up the tab for a reunion of all the Big Top gang at the Waldorf Astoria in New York. Ed was the only one who never came. He sent his apologies from Hollywood and promised me he would call during the dinner. We hooked the phone up to a public address system so everyone could hear him speak. He never called.

A classy man: Dan (age 30) with Tony Marvin.

The Big Top Show's barker was Bob Russell. Bob was a consummate actor and a very professional entertainer who had a varied show business background, including a slot as master of ceremonies for the Miss America Pageant before Bert Parks got the job. In fact, Bob wrote the Miss America theme song, "Here she is, Miss America". Like many show business people, Bob had a superstition: it involved the number two. It seemed two's were connected to him in almost every way – his phone number, hotel number, his address all included the number two. For many years I called Bob and asked for extension

"222". He instantly knew who was calling. I kept in contact and maintained a strong friendship with Bob for 48 years, until his death in 1998; he died in Lido Beach in Sarasota, Florida, where he lived. Bob, who was 15-years older than me, was probably one of the smartest men I have ever known and had a great personality to match. He would have made a good diplomat because of his wonderfully charming nature and ability to make friends. In 1965 I had Bob MC at my WBBG Mr. New York State bodybuilding contest, held at the World's Fair. He was also Master of Ceremonies at most of my Hall of Fame dinners, beginning with the first one in 1968. In 1995, my wife Thelma and I drove to Sarasota, Florida, to visit with Bob. He was in fine spirits and looked well. He was a great guy. I learned a lot from him.

Mr. McMahon: Big Top clown Ed McMahon.

Dan Lurie: Heart of Steel

Helping Out: Bob Russell (center) assists Dan (Left) with the running of his 1968 WBBG Hall of Fame Dinner, where Sig Klein was honored. At the podium is famous American actor, Pat Hingle.

The 1950s were extremely busy and exciting for me. Along with working on the Big Top Show I managed my barbell and gym businesses and ran many small bodybuilding contests. This took a lot of juggling as orders were coming in left and right, and my gyms, one in Manhattan and two in Brooklyn, were taking in more people every day. My New York gym on West 57 Street and Eighth Avenue was home to many famous businessmen and celebrities. Among these men were Hollywood stuntman and bodybuilder, Joe Bonomo, actor of Rocky and Rambo fame, Sylvester Stallone and his brother Frank, and radio and television announcer for the New York Yankees baseball team, Mel Allen. Judges, lawyers and celebrities were this gym's main customers.

Though my gyms were very popular, when the Big Top show ended in 1957 I put most of my energies into my barbell business, packing sets and selling them to top department, sporting goods and toy stores. This is when this business really took off for me. My Sealtest Dan

Television Strongman

career actually helped me to sell more barbells. I would make many personal appearances as Sealtest Dan the Muscle Man and people would come to see me perform. As a business move, I would hold these displays outside stores that sold my equipment and big crowds would fill the parking lots. It was a good business practice for both the store and myself as they would attract more customers and I would sell more barbells. The barbell business was, at the time, run centrally from my showroom and factory on Utica Avenue, Brooklyn. At this time I rented the two buildings on the same site, and both served as distribution depots where we packed the barbells. All areas of manufacturing were handled from this warehouse base including the cutting, welding, and painting of all exercise equipment. 20 men were employed full-time and my son Mark oversaw the whole operation.

On Location: the Sealtest gang, including Dan (right), ready themselves for filming.

As well as taking care of the barbell and gym businesses, I continued doing television work. In fact, my regular appearances on the Big Top Show led to many offers to appear on television. I made regular appearances on the Steve Allen Show in 1954 and 1955; my muscles would impress his viewers and it was often requested that I return. At this time, actor Steve Lawrence, who was originally from the Brownsville area of Brooklyn and lived right across the road from Ferkie's Gym, where I used to train as a boxer, and his wife, Eydie Gorme, regularly appeared on the show. As was done on the Big Top Show, they would paint little faces and shapes with their fingers on my back and chest and flexing my muscles to change these faces' expressions would delight Steve Allen's crowd. I hit it off well with Steve, as he was the perfect gentleman and a clever entertainer. I love music and Steve was a great piano player. His shows were always full of the kind of quick-witted humor that keeps the audiences laughing. One of his approaches was to feature novel performers and, at the time, my strongman act was as offbeat as you could get. On one occasion I performed on Allen, who was 190 pounds at the time, the same one-handed lift I did with Governor Williams at the Michigan State Fair a few years earlier. But with Allen I put a different twist on what had become a signature move for me: I turned my body as I lifted him so that his behind, rather than his face, faced the camera at the end of the lift. The audience thought that was terrific.

I also appeared on other children's shows, during and after my time on Sealtest. I did commercials on the Captain Video Show for several years in the early 1950s. The show was based around the heroic adventures of great scientific genius, Captain Video, and his juvenile sidekick, The Video Ranger. While they battled various menaces from outer space and faced perilous situations on distant planets, I, upon eating the sponsor's product, became, you guessed it, very powerful and performed great strength feats. I was not Sealtest Dan this time, but the mighty Rewop ("power" spelled backwards). But the name "The Mighty Rewop" caused the sponsor to receive so many complaints from Italian-Americans that it was eventually pulled.

Meanwhile I continued to impress with my ability to do more than your average strongman. The Ayer agency executives, and particularly writer Maggie Kerns, learned I could do commercials with singing and speaking parts. So I did commercials quite different from the strongman-type work they first had me doing. There were also many times where I would dress up as an American Indian, cowboy, pirate, or even Santa Claus to entertain loads of children and their families at parades and openings around the country. During these appearances I would sing and act. I sang at many state fairs, where I would also perform 30-minute feats of strength in tent shows. And as the audiences had come to expect, I would always end these shows by lifting a 200-pound-plus man overhead with one arm. Performing in tent shows at state fairs, in parades and openings and on televised commercials was something that came naturally to me. I had never done any formal training to become an actor; I simply had a passion and capacity for making people happy through my muscle strength and an ability to engage with them personally, on their level. I never considered myself above anybody else and I think this was one of the secrets of attracting people to my shows. They enjoyed being entertained by someone who, though nationally known, was down to earth, friendly and in touch with them as people.

In addition to the additional acting work it provided, the Big Top Show gave me much more besides. There were the many life-long friends I made on the show and the business lessons learned. But the biggest thrill for me was getting paid for something I would have happily done for free. I encountered very few problems during my time on the Big Top Show. On one occasion, though, I managed to get badly sunburned on my back. This would not concern your average performer, but I had to display the show's title and credits on *my* back. It was a valuable commodity. I should have had it insured.

People often ask me, "What opportunities are there in bodybuilding?" My reply? Bodybuilding will lead to a life of riches. Health, vitality, strength of character, and a strong mind all come from the sustained efforts needed to build a great physique. But it can go even further than that. My slot on the Big Top Show and numerous other television appearances were made possible through my physique and strength, both developed through bodybuilding. These days, a well-developed, strong body is a commodity hired by movie and television producers who want actors with good marketability. Who knows where bodybuilding might lead you. It led me to the Big Top.

Chapter Six:

Muscles and Magazines

I decided to focus on my barbell company and gym businesses after Joe Weider and I split in 1948. I suppose I could have continued chasing the contest promoter's dream of massive audiences and competitions with top of the line physique stars, but without a magazine to promote my contests in, to get enough contestants, I felt it pointless to continue. So while Joe Weider went on to take the IFBB name, and to make a name for himself as a trainer of champions, my reputation as a contest promoter faded. These dreams would have to wait. Fortunately, opportunity came in early 1950 with the Sealtest Big Top television show, which put me back in the spotlight and gave me recognition that would set me up nicely for future contest promotion. The Big Top television show proved an enjoyable break from my real passion and my time as Sealtest Dan the Muscle Man was one of the highlights of my bodybuilder career, something I would never have traded for anything, but I still missed being part of the bodybuilding scene. I longed for the hustle and bustle, the camaraderie and excitement associated with running contests. I needed a way in. Magazines as official journals for bodybuilding promotion always served as valuable tools for the successful contest promoter, providing space to reach the masses, stir up interest and promote shows. This is exactly what I needed: my own magazine to attract audiences so I could once again begin promoting contests.

In early 1960, business was my main focus, and business was extremely good: my barbell company was distributing to major department stores and as the fitness and bodybuilding lifestyle caught on, my gyms were attracting many enthusiastic trainees. I had the capital and knew how I would use it to build what I hoped would be the biggest, most popular bodybuilding federation in the world. In 1965 the AAU was still going strong, and so too were English federation NABBA. Of course, Joe Weider was building his reputation as a professional contest promoter and at this time had just staged his first professional show, the Mr. Olympia, won by the great champion Larry Scott. After surveying the bodybuilding landscape, I could see where the sport was heading. A large number of young men were developing their muscles with a view to competing with like-minded fellows for bodybuilding glory. I had gotten a taste of how popular bodybuilding was as a sport - as a competitor and promoter - 20 years earlier and now it was time to supercharge my promotional efforts. I knew if I were to approach bodybuilding promotion in the spirit of fairness and in the best interests of the bodybuilders themselves, I would need a unique approach. For this I would need to separate myself from the other federations, so this is what I did.

My vision was to have a major bodybuilding magazine, the top federation, and a way to promote the achievements of physique stars that deserved the highest recognition. I always had an ability to think through major decisions to see the bigger picture and the best outcome for most situations I faced. My early days as a checkers champion and the fact that I always had to think for myself might have had something to do with this, and whenever I had a problem I would carefully consider all options and take the approach I thought best. The best way to bring major attention to bodybuilding and bodybuilders would be, I figured, to provide honest, clear advice and to profile all of the champions of the day in a way that would do them justice. This would be the first step in a three-step plan. So I established my first bodybuilding magazine in 1965.

From the beginning my aim was to publish a magazine that would provide the very best training instruction available. As a trainer I had many people coming to me seeking advice, the kind of information they said they could not find in the bookstore magazines. I wanted to help people but there was only so far I could reach, so I called my new magazine *Muscle Training Illustrated* (*MTI*) and placed a large emphasis on providing exercise routines and instruction from bodybuilding's biggest names. I even called each issue a course. Instead of 'issue 14' on the cover, I had 'course 14' and so on. Having a magazine where the readers could pick and choose which routines they wanted to try and read about the science behind what exercises did, and why a particular routine worked, rather than the usual gossip and filler people were used to reading, proved a major success and *MTI* flew off the shelves. Besides this, *Muscle Training Illustrated* was just a good, solid sounding name and the acronym *MTI* rolled nicely off the tongue.

My first editor was Emmanuel Orlick, a man who worked for Joe Weider during Joe's early publishing days. My business partner was Abe Glick. For the first issue, dated November 1965, we had the Herculean Reg Park on the cover, a massive star at the time and one of bodybuilding's biggest attractions. I would go on to work quite a lot with Reg, he would often feature in my magazines, and I was the first U.S. bodybuilding promoter to arrange for him to appear on nationwide television, on the Joe Franklin Show. Reg also guest posed at the 1972 WBBG Pro Mr. World and Mr. America contests, appearing in excellent shape for both. I felt fortunate to have worked with this great 1958 and 1965 NABBA Pro Mr. Universe winner, the man who strongly influenced Arnold Schwarzenegger to become a champion. It seems Reg's popularity has not lessened and he is still spoken of today as being one of the very first men to push bodybuilding to great heights. In fact, I recently discovered that that first issue of *MTI* with Reg of the cover achieves the most sales on E-Bay of any issue published over its 28 years.

Muscle Training Illustrated: Issue one.

Reg always struck me as being a humble and very down to earth man. When I invited him to appear at my 1972 contests, he chose to stay at a small hotel near Coney Island despite my insisting that he enjoy the luxurious accommodation afforded by the Waldof Astoria in New York City. The day after he arrived we planned to eat out and it was no fancy restaurant for Reg. He simply wanted to go eat the famous Nathan's Hotdogs so that is what we did. Over the years we kept in contact and I always regarded him with great affection and would call him "Mensch", which in Jewish means a truly good person. In August 2007 I heard Reg had skin cancer, so I called his son Jon Jon in Los Angeles and asked for his father's phone number in Johannesburg, South Africa. I spoke with Reg and his lovely wife Mareon and wished him a speedy recovery. I told him I would pray for him. He told me he was working out again and would beat this cancer.

On November 22, 2007, the great Reg Park died of skin cancer at age 79. His memory will remain in the hearts of many thousands of people worldwide. I feel blessed to have had Reg's support from the very beginning, and that very first issue of *MTI* will stand as testimony to this great man.

The moment *MTI* hit the shelves it was popular. I wanted to include as much information as possible to give the readers value for money, and that very first issue gave the readers this right away. The table of contents from this issue is printed here to show where we were heading with the magazine I planned would become the best in the business.

Welcome: Dan welcomes Reg Park to America ahead of Reg's 1972 WBBG guest posing appearances.

Editorial - Scientific Muscle Training	E M Orlick	5
Muscle Gossip		7
Feats Of Strength And Daring	Jack Holst	8
Spectacular World's Fair Physique Contest	A W Whalen	10
Eddie Silvestre Becomes Movie Star	Ronnie Orlick	13
How To Build "The Best Developed Arms In America"	Dan Lurie	16
Are You Getting Enough Muscle Building Protein?	Ronald James	18
How Many Sets And Reps For Best Results	Lou Lomazzo	20
The Truth About The Flushing Principle	E M Orlick	22
How To Build Terrific Thighs And Calves	Eddie Silvestre	26
Karate And Scientific Muscle Training	Sam Vasquez	28
Scientific Exercise Analysis	E M Orlick	31
For Bigger Muscles And More Strength Try Slow Motion Training	Dave Baillie	32
Scientific Muscle Training Hints		34
The Beginner's Corner - Selecting The Right Equipment	Dan Lurie	47
Your Fabulous Biceps	Terry Douglas	49
Mystery "Guess-Star"		50
Weight Trained Athlete Of The Month - Bruno Sammartino	Ronald James	57

As you can see here, I was a writer as well as the publisher and this was something I greatly enjoyed. I had gained a lot of training knowledge and was eager to put it in print. Look closer and you will see professional wrestling legend Bruno Sammartino as our featured athlete, a good friend and one of the many athletes I helped to train around this time.

Since I had built a solid rapport with many of the biggest stars of the day, by the time *MTI* went to press we had the input of many experienced professionals, men who led the way as bodybuilding champions. After 15 issues, though, my partner Abe wanted out. He felt the magazine was not making enough money. At first I knew almost nothing about the publishing business, but after two years I had learned a lot. Abe was right: we were not making nearly enough, but I persevered and continued to promote bodybuilding at the highest level through the pages of *MTI*. When I took over the magazine at issue number 16, after buying Abe out after two and a half years of loyal service, I instantly began making good money on sales. I gave Emmanuel one third of the profits instead of a raise, but since his focus was mostly on gymnastics, not pure bodybuilding, as I wanted, I had to ask him to leave. His heart simply was not in bodybuilding and I had to do what was right for my readers. I replaced him with a bodybuilding editor and Emmanuel and I remained good friends.

Magazine Publisher: Dan in his office with two of bodybuilding's rising stars, Pat Neve (left) and Tony Emmott (right), both *MTI* cover men.

Looking back I can see where we went wrong. Abe had an office in New York City with secretaries, and this took up valuable resources. Once all the expenses he attracted were out of the picture, *MTI* really took off. I didn't need anything fancy to put out a quality publication: I simply had one office, and with my wife and son helping out and my only real costs being for pictures and written content, both of which I paid for up front, an editor and the running of my office, I knew exactly how much each issue would cost me to produce. While most magazines would pay their photographers and writers after the publication hit newsstands, I paid for everything up front. Most physique photographers and writers had to keep a very good record of what the magazines owed them and to get paid they had to bill these magazines. My philosophy was different, and simple: writers would submit their photos and copy and I would pay them for the ones I wanted and return what I felt would not enhance the overall production of the magazine. This scheme ensured I always got the best content, as writers and photographers were getting paid at a good rate on acceptance.

Whenever I turned down an article or photograph, I would always give the sender a reason as to why their content did not make the cut. Usually I would say that there was simply not enough room in the magazine for their work, or that we were booked and had too many items to work with. And most of the time this was true. But sometimes when I didn't like an item I would still say the same thing, as I did not want to hurt the writer or photographer's feelings. I always believed in putting money into quality content rather than printing bills and other overheads. I even bought my own magazine paper and a printer, which would allow me to cut printing costs. If I didn't approach the running of *MTI* this way I would not have put out such a quality publication and may even have gone broke in the early stages.

Of course I could not have put out such a magazine without expert help. One of my early writers and photographers was Bob Kennedy of *Musclemag International* fame. He was tireless in his approach to covering events and putting out sound instructional articles, a real down to earth, nice guy. Anyone who knows Bob will know that as well as being one of the main players in the bodybuilding game today he is one of its most sincere. Bob had an amazing passion for bodybuilding and we would often just hang out together after contests and talk shop.

Another of my staff was John Balik, my West Coast editor, who went on to run Ironman Magazine. With a great physique, John was one guy who lived the health and fitness lifestyle to the fullest. John was like me in many ways: he had worked extremely hard to achieve what he did in bodybuilding and took chances. You don't get anywhere in life if you don't have the confidence and the ability to use it and underlying knowledge of the industry. John had both and today is a very successful magazine publisher and businessman.

Promoting Only the Best: The October 1968 edition of *MTI* with Freddy Ortiz (left), Harold Poole (center) and Warren Frederick (right) on the cover with Dan himself. Photo taken at the 1968 WBBG Pro Mr. America, won by Harold Poole.

One of my close friends at this time, who remains so today and who also became a regular correspondent for *MTI*, is Steve Michalik, a great bodybuilder who won the Mr. USA, Mr. America and Mr. Universe titles with one of the best physiques ever seen. Steve was a guy I could always rely on for quality article content and he would also double as a model for many pieces on training. In fact, Steve was with me right from the beginning and was featured in some of my earliest articles and advertisements.

Dan Lurie: Heart of Steel

In 1978: Dan with Steve Michalik (right) and, then NABBA head, Oscar Heidenstam (left).

At a time when *MTI* was in full swing, and contributions were coming in fast, I came into contact with a very powerful young man who impressed me with his enthusiasm for bodybuilding, especially the scientific side of the sport. Dr. Bob Goldman, a fellow New Yorker, was just starting out as a writer and I took a chance with him, giving him some of his first magazine exposure. This proved the right choice, as Bob was a tremendous contributor who also had an extremely sharp intellect. Needless to say, he maintained his high writing standard and over the years has written thousands of articles, and over 30 books on health, fitness and anti-aging. As an MD and PhD, he is a world authority on drug use in sports along with chairman of the board for the American Academy of Anti-Aging. As a medical expert, Bob was the medical researcher for *MTI*. His list of achievements and credentials is vast and so is his knowledge of bodybuilding training and nutrition. Along with a passion for bodybuilding, Bob and I also share a love of strongman competition and he too performed, and holds records for, many strength feats. We remain good friends.

Celebrating the Champions: Dan, 82, at the 2005 Oldetime Barbell and Strongman awards with Dr. Robert Goldman and a friend.

An *MTI* associate editor for three years was Tony Badal. Tony, who was 19 when he began working for *MTI* after two years' employment in my barbell foundry, also wrote articles and arranged for high profile athletes to attend *MTI* photo shoots. He was an efficient worker and we clicked right away. Recently Tony and I spoke, and his thoughts on our working relationship brought back some nice memories. Says Tony:

"I enjoyed working for Dan. Dan treated me like a son and I looked at him as a father. He was a nice man. I think he made a good contribution, a positive contribution because he promoted bodybuilding all over the place. His methods were a little unorthodox. He would have us parading down the street on the footpath to gather a lot of attention and we certainly did. But he did a good job in promoting bodybuilding in a very good light. I was glad to know him and work for him. I liked his sense of humour and I think I kind of modeled my business ethics when I ran a health food store and now as a doctor running my own business, on what he did, what he showed me in running his own business on Utica Avenue."

I use this quote to show another side to my business practices and key relationships. Treating my employees with respect and encouraging them do their best, to become better people, was always my aim and Tony was no exception to this rule.

As a magazine that provided solid training and nutrition advice, profiles on top bodybuilding stars and the latest contest coverage, *MTI* was a market leader. I would select the best photos and editorial content for each and every issue. As the publisher, I would deal with the day-to-day running of *MTI*, but I would also write editorials and help with other written content wherever possible. You could say I got my start in the magazine business around 24 years earlier when I appeared in *Your Physique* and *Muscle Power* magazines, where I would write articles and provide content based mostly on my bodybuilding experiences. One of my articles, *How Long will it Take,* appeared in the 1946 issue of *Muscle Power* and was very well liked. It had as its main message the idea that if a young bodybuilder wanted progress they would have to work at it and never give up, lessons I myself had learned nine years earlier when I was starting out as a bodybuilder. In this same issue I presented my challenge to John Grimek.

I knew a little about the publishing business from my start in Weider's magazines, but still had much to learn. One thing I knew right from the start was exactly how picky bodybuilding fans are. I was of one of them, after all. And I doubt *MTI* would have run successfully for 28 years had it not delivered the best content around. So this was always my main aim: to employ the best people to deliver the best content. Along with my U.S.-based correspondents, those from many other parts of the world would contribute to *MTI*.

Throughout much of the 1970s and early '80s I would regularly receive images from one of the most respected photographers in the business, Australia's Wayne Gallasch. Wayne would come to the U.S. several times a year to work with all the top athletes of the day. You name the athlete and Wayne worked with them. Franco Columbo, Arnold, Samir Bannout and Frank Zane were just a few to be captured at their best through Wayne's photography skills. In fact I have one of Wayne's Sergio shots sitting on my desk as I write this. This picture of Sergio posing outdoors after the 1972 Mr. Olympia in Essen Germany looking totally unreal with a wonderful rural landscape as a backdrop is breathtaking. Wayne, who today runs a successful bodybuilding movie distribution business, and I enjoyed a good working relationship and he valued my up front, easy to deal with manner and the fact his checks always arrived on time, practices that have kept me in the bodybuilding business for over 70 years. It touched me greatly when Wayne recently said that he valued my kind, thoughtful and honest manner to doing business and that he considered it a privilege to have worked with me. This was a common sentiment shared among most of the professionals I regularly dealt with. I did not believe in complicating the process, whether it was selecting photos for publication or staging a show. What you saw is what you got. There were never any hidden agendas.

From its first issue in 1965 to its last in 1993, *MTI* regularly featured bodybuilding's best in the 180 issues that went to print. From early pioneers such as Reg Park, Steve Reeves and Bill Pearl through to later champions Lee Haney, Rich Gaspari and Shawn Ray, *MTI* covered all of bodybuilding's top stars. Immortals Arnold Schwarzenegger, Lou Ferrigno and actor Sylvester Stallone also kept my quality-conscious readers happy. They wanted the best and I gave them the best. In fact, I was the first publisher to promote Arnold Schwarzenegger and Lou Ferrigno due in part to my ties to NABBA, where Arnold first competed, and through my early friendship with big Lou. Countless photos and profiles on these two could be found in *MTI* in all the years it went to press. You will be hearing more on these two later in this book.

Throughout its history, *MTI* reported on every major bodybuilding show or event from around the world. My reporters were asked to get interviews with all the major stars and we did not shy from featuring non-World Body Building Guild shows. In fact, Oscar Heidenstam, who from 1955 ran the National Amateur Bodybuilding Association (NABBA) in Europe, was featured on our official masthead as our NABBA representative. Oscar, who began bodybuilding around 70 years ago, winning the 1937 Mr. Britain, lived in London, England, and was a most respected official. I considered him the consummate professional and was happy to count him as one of my dear friends. When he passed away in 1991, he was widely known as one of bodybuilding's longest serving stalwarts. A great man whose contribution to bodybuilding worldwide remains untouched.

Featured Star: Dan in 1972 with *MTI* athlete, Lou Ferrigno, and *MTI* employee, Tony Schtinna, after Lou had appeared on television for the first time - on New York's Midday.

With my new magazine I could now begin contest promotion again, but this time on a larger scale. To test the waters, I ran a show the same year I started *MTI*, the 1965 Mr. New York State. Held at the World's Fair, Queens, this version of the New York State was more successful than the 1948 attempt, the show many athletes, fearing a loss of AAU eligibility, chose to avoid.

With bodybuilding taking a professional turn, after the birth of Joe Weider's Mr. Olympia show in 1965, it was now a more realistic option to compete as a professional. In 1966, one year after my Mr. New York State, I began my own federation, the World Body Building Guild (WBBG), and, in 1967, began promoting amateur and professional contests on a wider scale. In naming the WBBG, I wanted something that sounded both prestigious and welcoming to all athletes. A guild is, by definition, an association of people who have the same goals, that is formed to protect all these people's interests while maintaining certain standards. I figured this word best represented the way I wanted to run things, with the best interests of all my athletes in mind and with high professional standards in place at all times. By placing World at the beginning, I was opening my arms to athletes far and wide. Ask any of my former competitors today and they will tell you that my contests were always run fairly and that as a promoter I was a man of my word. And like *MTI,* and the IFBB before it, the name just sounded right. It had a nice ring to it.

The Winners Circle: Sergio Oliva winning the WBBG Mr. Olympus title, with Arthur Jones on the microphone and Dan looking on.

With *MTI* as the WBBG's official journal, my main aim was to bring all of the best bodybuilders in the world together to compete in the fairest contests run at that time. While other federations were excluding athletes for competing in rival federations, the WBBG took all comers. We did not discriminate. In fact, I did not disqualify anybody regardless of what federation he or she competed in or represented. We also set up amateur and professional divisions to cater to bodybuilders at all levels and to give those lower on the ladder something larger to aim for. The WBBG staff consisted mainly of just three people, including myself. My son Mark, as my right hand man, was instrumental in running my events. He would set up all the onstage lighting and ensure all the competitors were happy backstage. Come show time, he would line the athletes up in the right order. Some of the best physique photos were also taken at my contests courtesy of Mark. When it came to directing each show, we kept in contact at all times with walkie-talkies and I sat in the audience and managed the entire show from my seat with the help of headphones. There was nothing fancy when it came to running my shows but each event ran smoothly. That was my biggest concern. My shows had to have a certain professional flow to them. I felt I was the conductor of an orchestra: I directed with accuracy, balance and a certain style all of the action onstage and backstage, and ensured the bodybuilders played their respective parts to perfection. I had a list of every competitor and their number and memorized where their position was in the line-up. There was no room for error at any of my shows. I also took a hard line on the timing of my events; everything had to run like clockwork. One minute out from show time and you would hear my booming voice: "everyone get ready now, one minute to go." I had no time for contestants who were late, as I myself knew from experience that standing around forever backstage before competing was not the nicest feeling. I did not want any of my guys to wait.

I did mention there were three WBBG staff members. In addition to Mark and myself, there was my lifelong secretary, Eve Bessler, who handled all the contestants when they first arrived at the

Muscles and Magazines

competition venue. Eve helped to ensure the WBBG's principals of honesty and integrity were upheld, as she was also responsible for cashing the checks for the winners before they went home. Too many promoters were writing bad checks in those days and I am glad to say I was not one of them.

Muscleman Meets Superman: Dan - shortly before the January 21 1967 Pro Mr. America - with Budd Colyer, host of the popular To Tell You the Truth TV show and radio voice for superman. Bud is holding a copy of *MTI*.

From the very beginning, the WBBG grew at an amazing pace and at one point it had an international membership of over 25,000 competitors and members. As my intention was to promote world bodybuilding through *MTI* and look for international talent to increase and enhance its written content, I made sure the WBBG had directors all over the world. Our contacts covered Europe, Asia, Canada, the Middle East, Africa, Alaska, Hawaii, Mexico and the

Caribbean and would keep us updated on all the latest developments in the bodybuilding world. Our *MTI* editorial consultants, who also served time as top competitors themselves, were among the most knowledgeable bodybuilding insiders around: Steve Reeves, Sergio Oliva, Freddy Ortiz and Bill Pearl, along with many others of considerable talent worked tirelessly alongside myself to bring to life in my pages amateur and professional bodybuilding as it was.

Champions All: Dan onstage with three of his biggest champions, Freddy Ortiz, Harold Poole and Warren Frederick, at the 1966 Pro Mr. America. Harold Poole won this contest.

Shows run by the WBBG were very well contested and the winners were among the best bodybuilders competing at that time. 1963 IFBB Mr. Universe overall winner and 1965 and 1966 Mr. Olympia runner-up, Harold Poole won my first big WBBG show, the Pro Mr. America, in 1967. Through the WBBG I also ran Mr. Eastern America, Mr. Galaxy, Mr. International, Mr. North America, Mr. Olympus, Pro Mr. USA, and my other major show, the Pro Mr. World. Of all my champions I am fondest of Boyer Coe, who won my Pro Mr. World from 1971 through to 1975, Sergio Oliva, one of the greatest bodybuilders ever and winner of my Mr. Olympus in 1975, 1976 and 1978, and Chris Dickerson who won my Pro Mr. America in 1973 and went on to win Joe Weider's 1982 Mr. Olympia. Other top champions included Serge Nubret, Mr. Olympus in 1977 and Pro Mr. World in 1977, Bill Grant, Pro Mr. America in 1972, Warren Frederick, Mr. North America in 1972 and Pro Mr. America in 1974, Anibal Lopez, the 1980 Pro Mr. America and Pro Mr. World winner and Freddy Ortiz, second place finisher at the 1966 Pro Mr. America. One of the most famous bodybuilders ever, Lou Ferrigno, who went onto become known as television's The Incredible Hulk, competed in the WBBG before crossing over to Joe and Ben Weider's federation. Arnold Schwarzenegger also contemplated a move to the World Body Building Guild, but politics got in the way and it was not to be.

One of the Best: Dan awarding Johhny Maldonado the WBBG 1969 Pro Mr. America title.

In 1973 there was no bigger star in all of bodybuilding than Steve Reeves as far as commercial success and worldwide appeal was concerned. One of my main aims as a promoter was to feature at my big contests competitors the crowd would go wild for, those who would be considered

Gods by all in attendance. One such living legend was Reeves and I was determined to have him appear. So I began promoting this in my magazines. Many said I would never achieve such a feat. Since Reeves lived in Switzerland at the time and was often occupied making films and giving appearances, it must have seemed an impossible dream to get him to one of my shows in New York, but I set out to do my best and my persistence paid off. Upon contacting Reeves, he and I hit it off immediately and he said he would be delighted to guest appear at my September 18, 1973 annual Pro Mr. America show. This contest would be held at Hunter College, New York City, and Reeves would appear at 8.00pm.

When the big day arrived, Steve was ready and the audience could not wait. Partway through the show I had a massive screen where we featured him displaying his beautiful physique in his role as Hercules. And just as his Hercules screen persona broke down the columns with his massive arms, Reeves, his wife Aline and myself walked out onstage. I will never forget the crowd's response: they went completely wild, almost to the point of pandemonium. Many in attendance rushed the stage. Fortunately we had 100 people lining the sides of the stage in case such a thing happened. Steve Reeves' appearance went off without a hitch, although one small problem may have impacted our turnout. And this involved none other than my old business partner, Joe Weider. He, of course, knew when and at what time Steve Reeves would be appearing at my show and decided to run one of his events at exactly the same time, in the same city, at the Brooklyn Academy of Music. He had never run his events there before so I knew what he was up to. I figured he wanted to ruin my chances of running a successful event by diverting bodybuilding fans to his show. I have to say if this was his intention he failed miserably. While we had to turn hundreds of people away, reports suggest his contest had one of the poorest turnouts in the history of bodybuilding.

The day after the Steve Reeves appearance, I inducted the great man into the WBBG Hall of Fame. Meanwhile Joe Weider filed a lawsuit against me later that year for using the title *Muscle Training Illustrated* for my magazine. He considered it too close, in name, to *Muscle Builder*, the title of his own publication. He also failed in this attempt to bring me down.

Muscles and Magazines

The Legend Has Arrived: Steve Reeves addresses the audience.

Good Friends: wherever they went Steve Reeves
and Dan made the headlines.

Another standout moment for me, concerning one of my biggest stars, was also one of the saddest. Sergio Oliva, who always represented the WBBG as a gentleman and fine athlete of the highest standing, signed an exclusive contract with me in July of 1968 to endorse my Weight Gain 707 sports protein powder, but his full page ad would not appear in *MTI* until after he had competed in that year's Mr. Olympia. The advertisement first appeared on the back page of the December 1968 *MTI*, issue number 17, and ran for seven years, increasing sales for my protein product greatly, but part of this story is anything but pleasant. Having Sergio as a representative was a great moment for me. One of bodybuilding's largest, most muscular competitors, probably the biggest and best of all time, was advertising my weight gain product. What better endorsement could you get? Talk about an advertisers dream come true. Given the 1968 Olympia was in New York that year and my wife and I were invited by very dear friend and one time editor for *MTI,* Bud Parker, who was master of ceremonies for the event, we attended. The show ran very nicely. Though when Sergio was crowned Mr. Olympia, Joe Weider told him he would not get his $1000 unless he announced to the audience that the picture of him endorsing my product was a fake and that he had never signed an endorsement contract with me. As Sergio spoke I could not believe my ears. I was shocked. I had a copy of the magazine with me so got out of my seat, ran to the stage, and screamed "Sergio, you are a big liar. You know you signed an agreement with me so why are you doing this." I then went onstage and confronted Sergio with the full-page ad. Joe Weider reluctantly gave me the microphone and I spoke to the audience and gave them the facts as I am doing here. To me it was clear Sergio was under pressure from Weider to say what he said and that Weider put him up to it to make me look foolish. I had to say something. Weider was also behind Sergio's many controversial IFBB losses including the 1972 Mr. Olympia in Essen Germany, which, according to the opinion of many, he clearly should have won. The fact he robbed Sergio of his deserved contest victories time and time again shows how Joe operated.

A Partnership in Muscle: Dan and Sergio onstage at the WBBG 1972 Mr. Galaxy, which Sergio won.

Sergio remains one of the most professional people I have known, both as a person and a competitor. I harbour no resentment whatsoever over what happened, as Sergio did not know I was in the audience and Weider as far as I was concerned, forced him to talk. I discuss this here to set the record straight, as there have been various incorrect versions of this story reported over the years. Finally I can give the true account of what happened. As a bodybuilder, I always considered Sergio the very best and he was, no question about that. As a person he was always very outgoing, had a great personality and always took time to talk to his many fans. My family also loved Sergio. When he came to visit he would always bring my four daughters sweets and he used to call my wife, Thelma, "Momma". Today we are on good terms so much so that he accepted my offer for induction into the 2007 WBBG International Fitness and Sports Hall of Fame.

When I look back on my WBBG days, it seems I would often cross paths with Joe Weider despite the fact I was running a separate federation and had washed my hands of him many years earlier. While I built my federation on my reputation as a strongman and bodybuilding personality, Joe lied about his standing. This annoyed me, as through his lies he was able to secure a large chunk of the health and fitness market, which naturally impacted my earning potential. Here is a classic example. Throughout the 1960s Joe was, in addition to running his own shows, constantly calling himself a "trainer of champions". He even made bold statements in his magazines saying that through his training methods he had transformed himself into a man of steel. In his magazines Joe would state that within a short time he had, using his bodybuilding "principals", built a physique of solid muscle, which had allowed him to win the title of "perfect man", although no such title ever existed, and smash the strength records of the day, raising 600 pounds off the floor and lifting 230 pounds overhead with one arm. No proof was ever given to back up these amazing claims, but Joe continued to the point where he began pushing his muscle and fiction just a little too far for my liking. Look at any of the supposedly un-retouched pictures of Joe today and it is all too evident: he had many of his images airbrushed to present extreme muscle size he never had, and even had pictures drawn of himself sporting a greatly exaggerated physique.

Dan and Sergio backstage at the WBBG Mr. Olympus competition.

Muscles and Magazines

A Meeting of the Publishers: Dan (center), Joe Weider (left) and Ironman Magazine's Perry Radar at the 1980 AAU Mr. America.

The late great artist George Quaintance created Weider's famous arms crossed shot, a photo that was used for many years to promote his magazines. This shot appeared on the November 1947 cover of *Your Physique*, and I was in his studio the day George, who was the art director for *Your Physique,* created it using his extraordinary skills. George was a magnificent artist who was head judge at my 1946 Mr. Eastern Coast Contest and remained my dear friend for many years. He also painted the January 1947 *Your Physique* cover shot of myself and one time he gave me a magnificent portrait he had painted of Steve Reeves.

Joe also presented bodybuilder Robby Robinson's massive physique as his own in a statue he created of himself as a corporate logo for the Weider publishing and sales empire. Robby, in turn, filed a lawsuit against Joe. In 1977 Robbie posed for a sculpture he believed Joe was having done of him to be erected in Weider's corporate headquarters in Woodland Hills, California, as a monument to strength training. When the statue was unveiled, Robby was shocked to see Joe's head atop of Robinson's body - yet another example of Joe falsely boosting his credibility.

Joe's comments and bragging weren't just done in his magazines. In his Weider strength training system manual, he says his top muscular bodyweight was over 220lbs. Laughable when you consider he was, in person, a rather slight man. In his book *Brothers of Iron,* Joe has a picture of himself hitting a most muscular that would put many heavyweight competitors of today to shame. If you look at this picture closely you can see it is clearly a fake.

So because of Joe's ridiculous claims and since he had openly tried to embarrass me using Sergio, and on the day of Steve Reeves' appearance, not to mention double-crossing me out of business in 1949, I decided to openly challenge him to a physique contest, to be held at the 1967 WBBG Mr. America contest. This show was to be held at the Roosevelt Auditorium in New York on Saturday 21 at 8.30pm and a special pose-down between the two of us would be the main event. In an open letter published in the January 1967 addition of *MTI,* I commented on his claims and said: "how about it Joe? You have been tossing around some mighty fancy superlatives for many years. Here is your chance to back them up in person, in public." He never accepted. I felt it was time the public knew the deceptiveness behind his claims, feats that no one ever challenged at the time. While what I stated in my magazines about my physical accomplishments were 100 percent verifiably true, Joe simply made things up to promote his publications and boost his invented reputation as a trainer without peer. The facts speak for themselves: Joe was never the muscular strongman he made out he was.

In its first manifestation, the WBBG ran its last show in 1980, but those contests are still spoken of highly today. Running these contests was my passion and the biggest thrill for me was to see my competitors arrive in top shape. I also appreciated my champions as people. I closely studied the different attitudes and personalities they brought to the stage and the way they conducted their lives and acted in the public eye. To honor what I considered exemplary behavior I presented "The Man of the Year" award, which, since I began it in 1967, was given each September around the time of my Pro Mr. America and Pro Mr. World contests to the worthiest competitor or athlete from any federation, who projected greatness beyond their physical achievements. Bill Pearl won the very first of these awards – other winners included Sergio Oliva and Steve Reeves. Later I updated this award to include anyone who best represented the health and fitness lifestyle. Among these inductees were Peter Lupus, Burt Reynolds and Robert Redford.

The Challenge Cover: the January 1967 issue of MTI featuring Dan's challenge to Joe Weider.

In 1975 I presented a "Sexiest Woman of the Century" award to Mae West, a lady I introduced to weight training and who I would "go up and see sometimes", to train, of course. Around the time of my Man of the Year awards I began running Hall Of Fame dinners, which honored personalities from the bodybuilding, sports, film, business and political worlds that best represented the bodybuilding and fitness lifestyle. The first Hall of Fame banquet was held on February 18, 1968, at the Granada Hotel, Brooklyn New York; at this event 1920s trainer Sigmund Klein was honored. Inductees at other Hall of

Dan Lurie: Heart of Steel

Fame dinners included bodybuilder Chris Dickerson, movie stuntman and bodybuilder Joe Bonomo, strongman Joe "the Mighty Atom" Greenstein, Johnny (Tarzan) Weissmueller, Buster (Flash Gordon) Crabbe, Wrestler, Superstar Billy Graham, Sylvester "Rocky" Stallone and World Heavyweight Boxing Champion, Joe Louis. For my Hall of Fame award ceremonies I would book a venue and host a dinner. This would provide the opportunity for whoever was being honored to share this moment with those closest to them and for the fans to get close to their heroes.

One of my fondest Hall of Fame banquets was in 1977, where Steve Reeves was honored along with Superstar Billy Graham, Serge Nubret, Joe Louis and Sylvester Stallone, the greatest number of major stars I had seen under one roof up until then. Recently I came out of retirement at the age of 84 to stage another Hall of Fame event, which I will remember as my best yet. The 2007 WBBG International Fitness and Sports Hall of Fame awards, held in conjunction with my first WBBG bodybuilding show in 27 years, the North America Bodybuilding and Figure and Fitness Championships, honored 14 great bodybuilding and fitness champions and gave special awards in memory of Steve Reeves, John Grimek and Charles Atlas.

Awards Time: from left to right, Jim Morris, Bill Pearl, Sergio Oliva, Dan, television star Alan Burke and Jack LaLanne at the 1978 WBBG Hall of Fame awards.

Muscles and Magazines

The Great Bill Pearl

Along with running *MTI* for 28 years, I published several other muscle and sports magazines. As *MTI* was my number one magazine, I was happy to develop it further. But I also sought to broaden my publishing approach as I felt the need to appeal to the wider health and fitness market, and there are only so many people interested in exclusively building massive muscles. *Boxing Training Illustrated, Wrestling Training Illustrated and Karate Training Illustrated* kept those who used bodybuilding more to improve their sporting performance happy, while *Fitness and Nutrition* appealed to those not chasing extreme muscle size. For my bodybuilding faithful though, there were four *MTI* companion magazines: *MTI picture book and pen-pals*, where readers could keep in touch with one another - an important way to keep the sport growing I felt at the time - a *Who's Who of Bodybuilding* directory, where fans could better get to know their favorite stars; *MTI Exercise Courses*, for specific training instruction; and *AAU Mr. America*, to commemorate this prestigious contest.

My reason for publishing these companion magazines was to give my readers more of what they wanted. You can only fit so much inside one magazine and people wanted more. For *MTI* I would select the best of the best, so every issue would be perfect. With my sporting magazines the title of each was a pretty straightforward choice for me: the name of the discipline followed by *Training Illustrated,* as I continued my practice of providing the best quality instructional information. The *AAU Mr. America magazine* was intended to put the record straight about and publicize the AAU Mr. America show and all the competitors so the fans could get detailed information on this contest, while the *Picture and Pen Pal* magazine was designed for bodybuilding fans to reach out to one another and to become inspired by the highest quality pictures of their favorite bodybuilders. I felt that too many people never made competition shape for lack of motivation, but if they had quality pictures they would be inspired to try harder. And if they had addresses of fellow bodybuilders they could write to, they would have a greater chance to learn more about how other bodybuilders at their level made gains. In publishing these magazines I received many letters from happy readers who had made contact with bodybuilders like themselves and, at the same time, made friends and learned more about how to progress in this tough sport. The magazines didn't stop at sport and bodybuilding. I even ventured into the music industry with *Hot Rock Magazine*, which profiled many of the hottest music acts of the day.

Another reason for publishing a variety of magazines was the simple reason that I could sell more of my products through the space they provided. At this point my products were mostly mail order and I discovered a formula where with every issue sold I was making money from the distributor, and whatever came in from the mail order was extra money. So it didn't pay for me to take outside ads because half the time the publishers didn't end up paying. With my magazines I had my own mail order going. It wasn't only boxing athletes who bought the magazines. It was all fans of the sport and with wrestling and karate it was the same thing. And they all had the same thing in common: they wanted to build up their body. And to achieve this they would buy my vitamins and equipment. It all paid off for me and for them. Each one of my magazines was bringing in about ten thousand dollars per month in product sales.

Dan the Photographer: Dan with two of his WBBG athletes in 1975. Josh Rivera is on the right.

A women's bodybuilding magazine was something I had always wanted to produce, as I was a big fan of women's bodybuilding and could see it wasn't given the recognition it deserved. As far as I'm concerned there is nothing nicer to the eye than a well-shaped female bodybuilder. Not the overly massive ones you see competing on the pro circuit today, but those who have the kind of shape and accentuation of womanly curves that only an effective drug-free weight-training program can create. And though the first real bodybuilding contests for women weren't run until 1978 with the U.S. Women's National Physique Championship's, promoted by Henry McGhee and held in Canton, Ohio, I was always pushing for greater recognition for the female bodybuilder. The main problem was the public perception of muscular women. People, it seemed, were just not ready for the onstage display of women who lifted weights for the sole purpose of adding muscle. My view was that it was perfectly natural for women to increase their strength and improve their shape through bodybuilding and said as much in my magazines. In 1979 I could see that women's bodybuilding was becoming very popular, as I would receive many letters from women who were just as interested as my male readers in building up their muscles. A good friend, Doris Barrilleaux, one of the premier female bodybuilders at the time, and one I would regularly feature in *MTI*, suggested the time was right for me to launch my own women's bodybuilding magazine. Sitting across from Doris in an Atlanta restaurant during one meeting, we discussed all of the possibilities: what would we call such a magazine, what would its focus be and who would be its editor? Doris immediately offered her services as editor, which pleased me as there was no women with more passion for bodybuilding than she. She knew the sport inside and out and, like me, simply loved it, which made her an obvious choice for editor.

I later realized that it was always Doris' dream to have her own women's bodybuilding magazine, so I felt good giving her this opportunity. She did not have the money to get such a project off the ground, so I came up with the finances and we were away. At this first meeting, which lasted many hours, and where I coined the name "first lady of bodybuilding" for Doris, a name that she is known by today, we decided which direction we wanted the magazine to go in. It would be the women's equivilent of *MTI*, a knowldege-based publication with just the right amount of photographic content to inspire and enthuse the reader. Naming the magazine was actually the hardest part. Doris and I came up with about 20 names, all very good, but only one could be used. Faced with this dilemma, I asked the bodybuilding public from various gyms through to my magazine readers and those off the street what they thought. I would collect all responses and the name that was most often mentioned as being the best choice we would use. This name was *Body Talk*, and we were now ready to publish the first issue, which became the only issue that ever went to press. It was a flop. At the time the demand for such a magazine simply wasn't there, despite the increasing popularity of women's bodybuilding. I never did get around to fullfilling my dream of publishing a women's bodybuilding magazine, but I did promote women's bodybuilding in *MTI* whenever I had the chance and would regularly feature emerging female bodybuilders as a way to show my respect and appreciation for their efforts and to further promote their sport, a sport I continue to love.

Taking Bodybuilding to the Masses: Dan introducing Joe Spooner (left) and Mrs Spooner (right) on talk show television. Host, Pat Collins, is seated on Dan's immediate right.

Of all my magazines, *MTI* will always be my baby. Actually, without it the WBBG may never have been born and many bodybuilding champions may never have been honored in my Hall of Fame. In 1993, at age 70, I put *MTI* to bed and retired from publishing. 13 years earlier I stopped running shows to devote all of my time to providing the best magazine I could offer. I achieved what I wanted and felt the time was right to sit back and enjoy the fruits of my labors. And enjoy them I did. But old habits die hard, and 14 years later I am back at it again. Today, the WBBG is back with a new team, but the same approach: quality and fairness. Above all, what I hope to achieve with my new WBBG is to instigate a golden era bodybuilding revival. My aim is to return bodybuilding to its roots - a time where the spirit of competition was largely based on fair play, honesty and hard work - while keeping with the changing times.

Jim Morris winning the 1974 WBBG Mr. International held in Tijuana Mexico

Over the 28 years *MTI* was published and the 13 years the WBBG ran contests, my overall philosophy was pretty simple. My aim from the beginning was have fun and make friends while providing a quality service to the bodybuilding community. I always felt that if you keep a friend you would end up with a lot of good friends. In fact, one of my personal life slogans is: "in order to have a friend, you must be one". As a vehicle for bodybuilding promotion, *MTI* was fundamentally a success because it appealed to many bodybuilding fans, provided solid information and made me a lot of money in sales. But it would not have been half as successful if it weren't for the way I ran it and the values that influenced its production. My aim was to run *MTI* like a newspaper and to this end I would print bodybuilding stories and use athletes from all over the world regardless of their political affiliation, with the underlying purpose of getting to the truth. With the WBBG my main aim was to support bodybuilding's growth while building a federation that placed the athlete above all else. As a former competitor, I knew what they went through to get to the top and I wanted them to experience quality competition and fair play. As you have read, the WBBG and *MTI* have had their share of ups and downs, but I think it is safe to say their successes far exceed their failures. With any major project there will always be risk and things will not always go as planned. Looking back I am happy with what the WBBG and *MTI* achieved and feel the contribution both made to bodybuilding helped to develop the sport and lifestyle to its current level, where millions of people worldwide are enjoying its positive benefits.

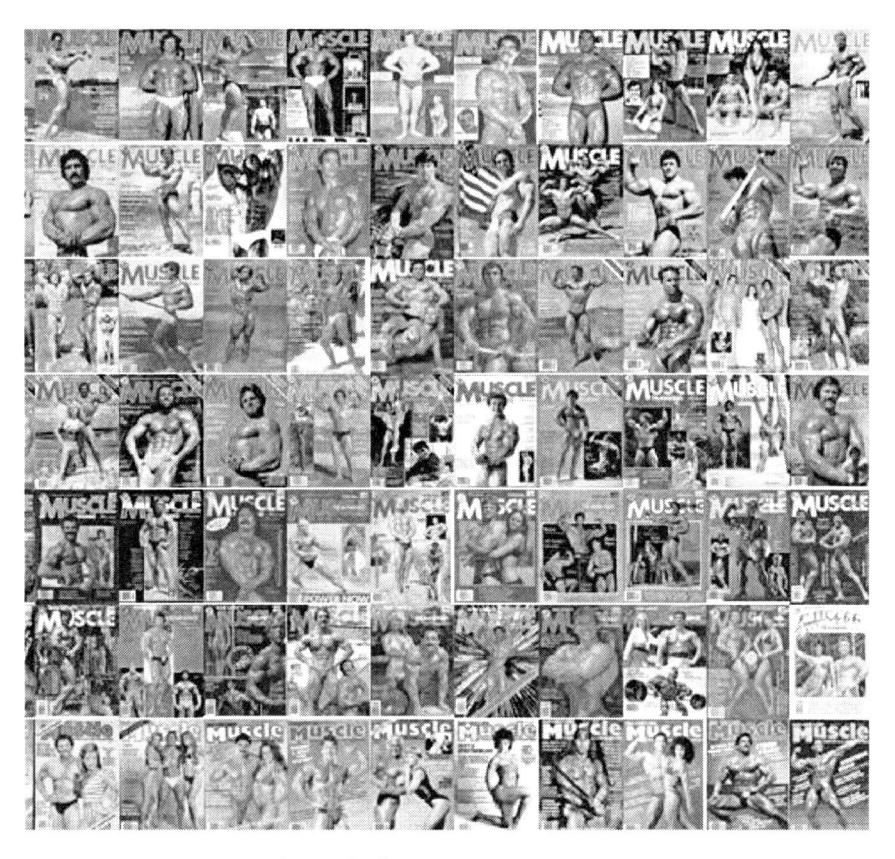

Through the years: MTI Covers.

Chapter Seven:

A Hulking Challenge

Of the many champions I have trained, one man stands head and shoulders above the rest. When I first met Lou Ferrigno in 1967, he was a rather shy and introverted young man of 16 whose single wish was to become the greatest bodybuilder the world had ever seen. His six foot five, 165-pound frame suggested to me at the time that he had a long way to go, but I could tell by the way he spoke about his love for bodybuilding that he had the determination to make it to the top. What he lacked was a mentor, someone to guide him to great heights. At the time, Lou lived with his parents, Victoria, a loving mother of the traditional Italian style, and his oppressive father, Matty. Matty would demean Lou and constantly criticize him for what he felt was excessive weight training. Lou, though, did not let his father's ways stop him from training with a single-minded focus on becoming the world's best-built man, but he did suffer from low self-esteem and a lack of confidence, a problem made worse by a hearing problem he had had since birth.

As I began working with Lou, he slowly began to show the traits of a champion that would eventually take him to the top of the bodybuilding world. Always motivated to train, Lou, despite hearing

A Hulking Challenge

difficulties that would often cause him to withdraw from the outside world, eventually became more confident. He developed a tunnel-visioned approach to bodybuilding and was determined that nothing would stand in his way. Bodybuilding became his life. But before he could achieve bodybuilding superstardom, we needed a plan. My first meeting with Lou was a big turning point in my life as a trainer and promoter. Brought to me by good friend, former employee and WBBG Pro Mr. America competitor Tony Badal (Badalamenti), Lou captured my interest from the very first. I intuitively knew there was something special about this tall, lanky kid, although physique-wise he showed no real signs of being anything more than just an average competitor. I asked him what he wanted to achieve in bodybuilding, suggesting that he might, under my guidance, win the Mr. American in five years. His reply? "I do not want to be no Mr. America, I want to be the best built bodybuilder that ever lived." From that moment on, I knew I had a champion in the making. And Lou proved me right. Six years later he won both the 1973 IFBB Mr. America and Universe titles. A year later he again won the Universe making him the only man ever to win this title twice in two years.

A Work in Progress: a young Lou Ferrigno with Dan (left) and the great Reg Park (right).

Lou's bodybuilding career peaked in 1975 as he competed alongside Arnold Schwarzenegger at the Mr. Olympia in Pretoria, South Africa. He placed third, one of his highest achievements as a professional bodybuilder. Standing tall and weighing around 275 pounds at this show, Lou had become the largest bodybuilder in the world. Seven years after we first met, Lou had proven that he was among the very best bodybuilders on the planet. Lou had definitely come a long way in those seven years, but before we could achieve this dream we had a lot of work to do. Tony Badalamenti had done some nice preparation work with Louie before he brought him to me, but he was lean with very little of the muscle he would develop. Lou had, though, built a nice base, developed through training with Tony in Tony's basement gym.

When Lou arrived in my office he was quiet, shy and reserved. In the years leading up to our first meeting, Tony would take Lou to clubs, try to get him involved in the social scene – Louie would be introduced as Mr. Universe and the girls would follow him all over the place. In fact, Tony and Lou were best of friends and would spend almost every day together. Tony flew airplanes and would take Lou out flying and, of course, they regularly trained together. Tony did a great job helping Lou to overcome his shyness, but Louie still needed to come out of his shell more.

I remember saying to Louie at our first meeting that I would love for him to one day compete against Arnold. He seemed to gain a lot of self-esteem just hearing these kinds of comments. After all, Arnold was, at the time, one of Lou's bodybuilding heroes. On the East coast we really had nobody of Arnold's status and I figured I could develop Lou into a worthy challenger. But I knew he had a lot of growth ahead of him. Initially Lou and I worked together much the same way a father and son would. I offered him sound advice and he followed my suggestions. I also provided him with protein supplements, clothing, money and many business opportunities, while advising him as a coach and mentor. I never asked for anything in return. There were no contracts and everything was based on trust and done in the spirit of friendship. Our relationship as trainer and athlete was very much based on friendship and Lou's willingness to train hard. And when it came to training, Lou was ferocious. Outside the gym he would stand out not so much for his massive size but for his gentle personality. He was like a big teddy bear, very emotional and sensitive. It was very hard to get Louie upset but if you did, watch out. But generally he saved his aggression for the gym where he really shined. The gym was like his home, a place where he felt most comfortable.

Father and Son Relationship: Dan assisting Lou with his posing, four years after their first meeting.

In 1971, after four years as Lou's trainer, a 19-year-old Lou got his first real taste of national-level victory at my WBBG Pro Teenage Mr. America, held at Ashbury Park, New Jersey. For this show, we increased Lou's bodyweight from a lean, though muscular 220 pounds, the size he had won the WBBG Teenage Eastern America weeks earlier at, to a massive 230 pounds. He smashed the opposition. This same year, Lou also competed in the AAU Teenage Mr. America, but had to settle for 4th in his class. These were proud moments for me. The numerous hours spent together perfecting Lou's posing and developing his muscles, the long conversations we had on bodybuilding and other areas of his life, did have a major positive impact on Lou. I could see a new, more engaging personality emerging. As our relationship grew stronger I had bigger and better things planned for him.

Muscles by the Sea
By the Editors

Hulking the Opposition: Lou (holding the American flag, to the right) dwarfs his fellow Mr. America competitors in Ashbury Park, New Jersey, 1971. Lou won the WBBG Teenage Mr. America at this event.

Before his win at the 1971 WBBG teenage show, I publicized Louie in my magazines, giving him maximum exposure as the next big bodybuilding champion. Around this time Arnold Schwarzenegger was the defending Mr. Olympia and no one really came close to beating him because of his shape and gigantic muscles, and the sheer confidence and charisma he possessed. However, Lou in my view was Arnold's match physically and I made this view known in my magazines. In fact, from the very first moment I began training him, I issued a statement in *MTI* saying that in four short years, this 16-year-old kid would be challenging Arnold for the Olympia title. Prophetic words since this is what happened in 1974 and '75. After Lou's teenage wins, he began to train even harder to capture bodybuilding glory at my WBBG Pro Mr. America contest in 1972. In training for the '72 Pro Mr. America, Lou made the biggest gains he had ever made in overall size. In fact he went from around 240 pounds to an incredible 315 by training with intensity rarely seen and eating everything that moved. He was then placed on a special "meat and water" diet to reduce his weight, to achieve a ripped to shreds, competition look. Bodybuilders wanting to preserve muscle while losing fat frequently used the meat and water diet back in those days, and it had worked wonders for champions like Vince Gironda, Rheo H. Blair and others dating back to the 1950s. It was a diet that featured meat of any kind, a few vegetables and water, which made it high protein, moderate fat with very little carbohydrate. And Lou made great progress on this plan. Around this time, Louie got so big that when Tony took him flying they had to use more of the runway because it took much longer for the plane to take off because of Louie's size. The planes they rented were usually rated for two people of average size. Louie was not average sized.

So with his amazing training efforts and diligent dieting, Louie arrived ready to do some damage at the Pro Mr. America. Sadly, for him it was not to be. The night before the show, Lou came to see me for a final assessment of his physique and a little last-minute posing advice. We spent two hours together and I have to say, Lou looked great at this time. He weighed 265 pounds, a massive increase of 35 pounds from the previous year. Everything was perfect and it seemed that he would easily win the following day, based on the size and conditioning he showed that evening.

The next day Lou looked dreadful. He had taken a water pill - a diuretic - on the advice of someone who told him this would further improve his conditioning. And instead of winning, which was predicted by most, he lost to Weider athlete, Bill Grant, who looked magnificent. Bill was overjoyed with his win and wept as he received his first place trophy. In my view, Bill's win was a fair one. Before this contest, people advised Bill Grant not to compete, as the "biased" Dan Lurie would overlook him. When he won it not only underscored my integrity, but also helped to silence people who thought I would support my boy Louie. After this show, Lou's father Matty came to me and demanded to know why I did not fix the show to allow Lou to win, as Lou was supposed to be my man. I told Matty that the winner of any of my shows would be the best man onstage, period. Sadly, this was Lou's last show with me and in 1973 we parted ways.

The Emerging Star: Lou and Warren Frederick onstage at the 1971 WBBG Pro Mr. America – That night Lou won the amateur Pro Mr. America division and Warren won the pro event.

At this time I was disappointed to learn that Lou was beginning to use steroids to help build his muscles. Frustrated, I approached his father to determine whether he knew of Lou's drug taking. I have always had a strong anti-drug stance and believed, and still believe, that anabolic drugs in their various forms are unnecessary for bodybuilding progress, and can only lead to ill health. Being very proud of Lou's achievements and treating him like a son for six years, I needed to know why Lou had turned to these drugs to succeed. "Do you know that Louie is taking steroids?" I asked Lou's father. "Do you know the dangers of these drugs, they could end up killing him." Lou's father simply said: "It is not important whether Lou lives or dies, it is important that he wins." Throwing my hands up in disgust, I said, "Matty, you are a sick father." I had to accept the fact Lou was taking steroids and that there was nothing I could do to stop it.

Soon after his disappointing result in 1972, Lou was to compete for redemption in my 1973 Pro Mr America, but he wanted all of the publicity for himself. For this show I had the great 1950 NABBA Mr. Universe Steve Reeves scheduled to appear and, of course, he would be the star attraction. But Lou felt that as he had been with me for many years, he deserved to be the main event and wanted to be promoted as such. At this time, Steve Reeves, star of the popular Hercules movies, was an international superstar and probably the world's best-built man. He had to be the main attraction, as he would fill the house, unlike Lou, who was, at the time, a relative newcomer. Lou reluctantly said he would compete in my show. I asked him a day before the show, "Are you sure Louie", as I had heard rumours that he was to enter an IFBB show the same day, in the same city and at the same time as my WBBG show. Lou looked me in the eyes and said that he would be at my show. "You can see for yourself if I am lying," he said shaking my hand and giving me his word. I wouldn't hear from him until months later. And the circumstances would be completely different.

In later years Lou would show anything but appreciation to me for all the sacrifices I had made for him. From my very first meeting with Lou I treated him like a son. I could see his potential and dearly wanted him to overcome his personal problems to become the champion I knew he could be. From 1967 on, I oversaw his posing, training and eating, guiding him with the knowledge I had accumulated over my 25-year involvement in bodybuilding.

The Hulk Meets the Park's: from right to left, Mareon Park, Dan, Reg Park, Thelma Lurie and Lou Ferrigno.

Based on my experiences with Lou and many other bodybuilders dating back to the mid-1940s, I became one of the first main bodybuilding trainers and Lou benefited greatly from my knowledge. I recall a 17-year-old Lou coming into my office at WBBG headquarters in Brooklyn for posing practice three times a week. This went on for over five years. We would spend hours and hours on his presentation, as this was to be a major part of his success. He had the physical gifts, which became even more noticeable as he grew to his full size. For posing, Lou would come to my office around 7.00 most nights. I eventually had to change this time to 4.00pm, as his practice would interfere with my family time. During our sessions I made a point of improving Lou's confidence and focus. I would have him focus on conveying a winning look; would encourage him to keep his head up and smile while hitting each of his poses with great impact and authority. On Sunday's he would train in my home gym on Long Island, where I would push him to his limits and introduce him to various training concepts, which would helped him to gain further size. I believe these early days together helped Lou move beyond his disability and disruptive home life to become a champion. When I sent him to compete in the '72 NABBA Mr. Universe in London, his mother thanked me warmly for taking Lou out of the shell he had been in for most of his life. My constant encouragement and support made him feel important, like he was someone for the first time in his life.

As Lou grew and became more marketable, I put him in my magazines to promote his achievements. I gave him his first major exposure on the cover of my May 1972 *MTI* - issue number 32. On the front cover, alongside Lou hitting his famous arm-behind-head, single biceps shot, I had the words: "Exclusive Pictures, New Giant Rivals Arnold Schwarzenegger". In this issue I introduced the 20-year-old Lou to the world, in the editorial where he openly challenged Arnold. "Enjoy the Mr. Olympia title while you are still holding it as your name will never be associated with that, or any other major physique title again," Lou said as he proclaimed himself as the next champion. In this article it was made clear that Lou would be the biggest thing bodybuilding had ever seen. It boosted his confidence like nothing else.

In sending Lou to London to compete in the '72 NABBA Mr. Universe, I paid all his expenses like I did for many years prior. For his first Junior Mr. America contest I remember buying him clothes so he could travel out of state. He had never traveled this far before and I wanted him to be presentable, to look like a professional. Lou's protein needs were also taken care of over these years courtesy of a generous supply of my Jet-707 sports protein supplement. Remembering these times gives me a special feeling. As one who helped transform Lou into the muscular champion that would go on to become an international superstar, I felt, and still feel, my efforts were worth every ounce of sweat.

With Lou's tremendous physique, I knew sooner or later he would become a star. No one in the world had Lou's look. He was imposing at six foot five and 275lbs. In 1972 I had Lou appear on Midday in New York City, his first television exposure. For this show I had Lou sit in the audience and show off his muscles at a pre-arranged time. He also spoke a little and people were amazed by his size. Soon after, I introduced him to Joseph E. Levine, the man who made the Hercules pictures starring Steve Reeves. I was hoping to get Lou into similar movies, but Levine told me that Lou's voice would not sell movies and they would need to dub another over the top. Too much expense he said. But I still felt all this initial publicity helped Lou to secure a firm spot in Hollywood history. In the early 1980s Lou did go on to star as Hercules, after having become a regular fixture in living rooms around the world as the Incredible Hulk, a role that would gain him a worldwide fan base and secure his place in entertainment history.

Lou Ferrigno featured in the pages of *MTI*.

A Hulking Challenge

His Arms Must Match His Age: a 21-year-old Lou with Dan in 1972, outside the Midday television studios.

Initial Showing: Lou showing his physique to Midday television audiences .

Taking Lou from a shy, socially backward kid to a man everybody wanted to know about, a star only years away from becoming a major Hollywood attraction, was a very special time for me. But despite all I had done for Lou, he chose to go with Weider, and his reasoning for this still escapes me. Lou's departure was like a knife to the heart. Instead of attending my Pro Mr. America as he had promised, Lou, as I later had learned, contracted himself to Weider. Lou's father set up the contract, which was fifty thousand dollars for five years and Lou, thinking this was a lot of money, jumped at the opportunity. But it was only ten thousand dollars a year. It broke my heart. If Lou's sudden choice to turn his back on me was not enough, he was to plunge the knife further still.

In 1974, Lou along with his father decided to sue me for using his image to promote my Jet-707 protein product. I had a release from Lou, but he said he was under the age of 21 when he signed the contract. Under normal circumstances at the time, this would have meant Lou was under a false contract. However, I proved that the contract was valid and its date showed quite clearly that Lou was, in fact, over the age of 21. I was justified in my choice to use Lou's image, and he had agreed for me to use it from the beginning, but he successfully sued me, as he managed to get a team of lawyers that were to achieve the impossible. I later discovered that one of them was in cahoots with the judge. In a case that dragged on for six years, ending on October 18, 1980, Lou, who was filming for the Hulk television series at the time, was awarded $65,000 dollars; I paid this amount in addition to all my legal expenses. The man who I had guided for many years, who I had helped transform into a bodybuilding superstar, got thousands of dollars out of me that day. It was one of the sadder days of my life. But what Lou did a year after he decided to sue, floored me completely.

Backstage at the 1975 AAU Mr. America in Los Angeles the unmistakable figure of Lou walked through a crowd that was forming near the stage entrance, and straight toward me. At this time he had already won the IFBB Mr. America, and the Mr. Universe twice, and was in peak physical condition. I guess I surprised him, as he said,

A Hulking Challenge

"Dan, how are you? How are your wife and son?" As he greeted me with open arms, it seemed he had forgotten he had double crossed me and gone with Weider two years earlier and began legal action against me the year prior. We spoke for a while, then he excused himself and we went our separate ways. About half an hour later we met again backstage and what he said to me left me speechless. He looked right at me and said: ""You dirty Jew, son of a bitch. The happiest day of my life and my father's life will be the day you get buried." We almost came to blows there and then. I gathered my thoughts and said, "Louie, God will take care of you. For how you have treated me after all I had done for you, God will take care of you." At five foot six I needed a crate to even get one good shot at the six foot five Lou, and thankfully we were broken up. I never heard from him again.

**Exhibit One: the photo that caused the controversy -
Lou advertising Jet Weight Gain Formula 707.**

Dan Lurie: Heart of Steel

During my years with Lou, I considered him a very smart guy, under-confident, sometimes, but stupid, never. Lou became a son to me. His home life was so depressing that I took it upon myself to become his number one mentor and father figure. In return Lou completely shut me out and insulted me with words that I could never forgive at the time. It has been many years since Lou and I worked together as close friends, but I still remember our good times with great affection. Today I forgive Lou and wish him well.

Dan's Champions: Lou posing for a *MTI* advertisement with fellow athlete Steve Michalik.

A Hulking Challenge

Bodybuilding East Coast Style: Dan with Tony Badal (second to left), Warren Frederick (immediate right) and Lou (immediate left).

Lou Ferigno on the cover of "Dan Luries's Muscle Training Illustrated Magazine"

Chapter Eight:

The Arnold Years

Another champion I would work with during early contest promotion and magazine publishing years was none other than the man many consider to be the greatest bodybuilder of all time: Arnold Schwarzenegger. Like Lou Ferrigno, Arnold was physically one of the most impressive men I had ever met, a man who had incredible power and the kind of will to win that turns the average into the unstoppable. But Arnold was never average. My very first impression of Arnold when I greeted him in September of 1969 at New York's John F. Kennedy International Airport, the day he and fellow bodybuilder, Franco Columbu, a major bodybuilding star in his own right, were leaving for London to compete in the NABBA professional Mr. Universe, was of his massive size and outgoing personality. My wife Thelma and I spent many enjoyable hours with Arnold that day. Several days later he would become a two-time NABBA professional Universe champion.

From what I could gather during the limited time I spent with Arnold just before his Universe win, it seemed the 21-year-old, who at that point had been competing as an amateur since 1965, was destined for greatness. He had a certain look in his eye and manner about him that said he was heading to the top and no one would stand in his way. And,

The Arnold Years

of course, this is exactly what happened. History shows that Arnold had developed the mindset of a champion well before he had even set foot in America. When we first met, Arnold had been in the U.S. since 1968 - after shifting from his home country in Austria - and his English language skills were not the best, but they were good enough for us to communicate freely and to discuss his bodybuilding plans.

Dan Meets the Austrian Oak: Arnold Schwarzenegger and Dan meet in 1969 and immediately begin business discussions. With them are Dan's wife Thelma (to Arnold's right) and Franco Columbu (left).

As Arnold boarded the plane I remember people staring at the massive young man with the funny haircut and white dress shirt. As he walked from the terminal carrying a TWA bag, which was tiny alongside his massive bulk of around 240 pounds and dwarfing Franco, who, at five feet four inches tall, looked almost half Arnold's size, Arnold resembled something else. There was no one like him at the time. I mentioned that Lou Ferrigno, who in 1969 was still a skinny teenager with dreams of bodybuilding greatness, was larger than Arnold when he challenged him in my magazines in the early 1970s, and he was. But the Austrian possessed the poise to go with his size; a quality that automatically added pounds to his already impressive look. To me, a bodybuilding promoter, he was a blessing from the Gods, a magazine publisher's dream. I had big plans for Arnold and before he boarded the plane I spoke with him about his future involvement with my magazine, *Muscle Training Illustrated*. In fact, that year, a short time before we first met, I featured him In *MTI* for the first time and in our October 1969 issue, a month after our first meeting at J.F.K. In our December 1968 issue we ran a four-page feature on Arnold written by Ricky Wayne, along with six photographs. I knew potential when I saw it and figured Arnold would be, as Lou became, one of my biggest stars. But unlike Lou, who in later years would impress with his great size, it was clear that Arnold had the charisma and charm to win readers over and make the biggest impact of any bodybuilder, ever. I wanted to feature him regularly in my magazines and he was more than happy with the initial publicity. In fact, I was the first publisher to promote Arnold in a big way, a fact very few people know.

During the pleasant few hours Arnold, Franco, my wife Thelma and I spent at J.F.K Airport, we discussed many topics. Today, Thelma and I recall the two bodybuilders being very nice and friendly. Of course we also discussed business. I wanted a good report of the NABBA Mr. Universe and Arnold had promised to bring me a detailed account. Arnold had only been in America for a few months, having arrived from Austria with only a duffle bag and $20 to his name, and he could barely speak English. But I do remember him listening closely to what I was saying and his English skills were good enough for the purposes of our first business arrangement: the contest report for *MTI*. Our conversation was additionally rewarding, as we also discussed the possibility that Arnold compete in an upcoming WBBG show. Before he and Franco boarded the plane, I gave him a $100 check to help him with his expenses and we all wished him well.

Arnold and I got along fine from the very first. My wife also liked him and thought he was pleasant and well mannered. And he was very charming and warm, but at the same time, as I would later learn, was ruthless and would do whatever it took to get to where he wanted. He knew when to turn it off and on and could charm you one moment and plot to defeat you the next. He could appeal to your emotions probably better than anyone I have ever met; with his intelligence, Arnold would have you fooled into believing anything, then tear you apart when you least expected it. And Arnold's ability to manipulate a given situation would strengthen with practice, and he would get plenty of opportunities to practice this skill. But for the time being things were good. I would learn of his deceptive side later.

One thing that did cross me as being strange during our first meeting was Arnold's fascination with women. This might not seem like a strange fascination until you realize that Arnold's interest went beyond a mere smile and glance. He would grope. Our waitress discovered this firsthand when Arnold reached out to fondle her breasts and backside. As he did this he said, "I vant sex." It made me uncomfortable and I told him, "You can't talk that way. You could get killed. She may have a husband or boyfriend. Besides, it is just not appropriate." He simply said what he did at the airport is what he did in his country if he wanted sex. "I don't have time to do all that other stuff," he told me. I could see tremendous potential in Arnold, but his social etiquette left a lot to be desired. In later years he also told various media that back in Austria this is how he would pick women up. So it is no secret how he operated on this front.

I choose to share the information in this chapter to give my personal insights into Arnold's character. In the early days I never had anything against Arnold. I liked the guy and considered him bodybuilding's biggest star. But like many others, I had my share of altercations with him, and would eventually discover his true nature. I mentioned earlier that Arnold would manipulate any situation he was in to his advantage and if this meant hurting others it was all part of the game. I too had been on the receiving end of his deception but let me make it clear: despite what he would do to me, I harbour no personal hatred toward Arnold. Like any publisher my aim has always been to get the facts on the table for the public good. Along with detailed look at another period of my life in bodybuilding, that is what this chapter is all about.

When I first met Arnold, we discussed many things including a possible appearance at my WBBG Pro Mr. America show. Arnold was very interested and told me he would seriously consider my request. Around this time, he had also made arrangements with Joe Weider to appear in his magazine, *Muscle Power,* and to promote Joe's bodybuilding supplements. This was fine with me and Arnold and I kept the lines of communication open. One thing most people don't know is that the man who discovered Arnold was not Joe Weider, but Mr. America competitor and 1960s Weider representative for Europe, Lud Shusterich. An architect who built the Weider headquarters in Woodland Hills, Lud, who originally came from Brooklyn and became partners with me in the gym equipment business in the 1970s, brought Arnold to Joe's attention and made the arrangements to bring the massive Austrian to America. He told Joe that he had found a European-based guy who had enormous potential and would look good in Joe's magazines. At the time, Arnold was very well known as a bodybuilder and strongman in Europe and had already won several NABBA Mr. Universe titles. As we know, Joe did show an interest in Arnold and that was the beginning of their bond. And right from the beginning Joe and Arnold plotted a course that would take Arnold to the top.

Once Arnold had sided with Joe he was asked to stir up controversy in *Muscle Power* as a way to increase sales and promote Arnold as the number one bodybuilder in the world. In rebuttal to this, I had one my biggest champions of that time, Lou Ferrigno, openly challenge Arnold in *MTI* in 1972. Arnold had, at this time, just beaten Sergio Oliva in Essen, Germany to win his third Mr. Olympia title and much of the gossip surrounding him made out that he couldn't be beat. He was labeled as a Teutonic warrior ready to take the head of any American who stood in his way. Two years earlier, in the October 1970 edition of *Muscle Power,* Arnold said in no uncertain terms that American bodybuilders were weak and would not stand a chance against him. "American bodybuilders are paper tigers," he stated. I still had much respect for Arnold as a bodybuilder, but as a patriotic American and a big believer in American bodybuilders I disagreed with him. Besides I was training a man who was larger than Arnold and felt this man would be the one to push Arnold off his pedestal. So when Lou Ferrigno made his challenge in *MTI,* it was partly in response to Arnold's arrogant statement that he was superior to all American bodybuilders. Eventually

Lou, too, would go on to sign with Weider but, unlike Arnold, would not reach his full potential as a bodybuilder.

The Greatest? Dan in 1969: with Arnold, Franco and Thelma Lurie at JFK International Airport shortly before Arnold and Franco's departure for the NABBA Professional Mr. Universe in London.

In the early 1970s *MTI* was at its peak and would profile many top competitors. And thanks in part to Joe Weider, and with a lot of help from myself, and my magazines, Arnold had made it to the top of the bodybuilding world. However, there was a lot of controversy regarding Arnold's 1972 Mr. Olympia victory over Sergio Oliva, a bodybuilder I profiled often in my magazines. Sergio, whose image advertised my bodybuilding supplements, had, in the eyes of many, received unfair treatment from Joe. The fact he was widely considered genetically superior to Arnold yet, in his best shape, lost to Arnold at the 1972 Olympia caused bodybuilding fans and insiders to wonder aloud how such a thing could have happened. In fact, at that time many thought that Sergio should have beaten Arnold and it was one of the most hotly debated judging outcomes in all of bodybuilding at that point. Since Joe Weider, who ran this contest, had a vested interest in having Arnold win this show, was it fixed? No one knows for sure, but many speculate that it was. In the midst of all the questioning and speculating surrounding the 1972 Mr. Olympia outcome, I decided to stage my own Arnold/Sergio challenge to set the record straight once and for all.

Arnold's involvement with the WBBG begins three years earlier, in 1969, the year Arnold and I first met. Before our first meeting and discussions, Arnold seriously considered my offer to take part in the WBBG May 24, 1969 Pro Mr. America and replied in a letter, "I would like to take part in your Mr. America contest this May. What do you think?" Well I was of course delighted that Arnold might enter my show. But there was a question mark over whether he would take part as a competitor or as a special guest poser. "Would it be more profitable for all concerned if I exhibited rather than enter the show?" Arnold asked in the same letter. He ended by asking me to give him my assurances that the show would not be fixed in any way. "Like so many of them are in America." I responded by assuring him that he would be treated fairly as a competitor. I also told him that since he was one of the world's best bodybuilders he would stand a good chance of winning the $550.00 first place prize, a large sum at the time. Since we had already hired our guest poser for that evening - Mr. America, Dennis Tinerino - I told Arnold his only option was to enter the contest. He eventually decided he would not compete and went with Weider.

During his time with Joe, Arnold kept his options open and in 1974 again decided to discuss the possibility of competing in the WBBG. This time he would have a strong challenger in the man he had beaten two years earlier, Sergio Oliva, who had at that point crossed over to the WBBG. In arranging this showdown, I made doubly sure that we covered all our bases, as I did not want to let such an opportunity slip. Sergio had already agreed and a nod from Arnold would seal the deal. To gain his acceptance we firstly set up a phone conversation between Arnold and Nat Haber, a sports writer and promoter who I knew and trusted well. When Nat called Arnold at Gold's Gym, Arnold agreed that he would compete against Sergio in my September 1974 Pro Mr. America. Nat, who recorded the entire conversation, was told by Arnold, "For $5000.00 dollars I will compete against Sergio Oliva, anytime, anywhere." Nat put Arnold's acceptance in writing and we were on our way. Arnold also said he thought the challenge would be a great success and gave me his word, through Nat, that he would compete for the cash prize of $5000.00 dollars.

The challenge would be a special event, a bodybuilding first, between the two greatest bodybuilders the world had ever seen. With both Arnold and Sergio agreeing, I began publicizing what I felt would be the greatest bodybuilding extravaganza ever. In promoting this event I featured pictures of Arnold and Sergio in *MTI,* placed alongside one another, to get the fans guessing as to who might win. Expectations were high and by all indications it was going to be a great event. On August 29, one week out from the show, Andy Bostino, who was a friend of both Arnold's, and mine, called Arnold's private telephone line in California from my office in Brooklyn to see how things were going and to determine what flight he was coming in on. Telephone records show that Andy and myself spoke with Arnold for exactly 21 minutes. Much to the surprise of all, Arnold said he would not compete against Sergio, stating that Joe Weider advised him against this. According to Arnold, Joe did not want the contest to take place because he felt that the show would be fixed to prevent Arnold from winning. Right from the beginning I made it quite clear that this would not be the case. It would be a fair contest. Arnold apologized that he could not compete and said he would send either Andy or myself a letter or telegram explaining in more detail the circumstances of his withdrawal. No letter or telegram ever came regarding this.

Several weeks before this conversation I contacted the Tom Snyder television show and suggested a verbal battle between Arnold and Sergio would attract a lot of interest. I then put the producers in touch with Arnold and Sergio and they both agreed to do the show. The producers also wanted Joe Weider and myself to appear, but this was not to be. As this was a big national night time TV Show, and Tom Snyder was a popular broadcaster, the Arnold and Sergio verbal showdown was seen by millions and the live audience really got into the action. The two giant bodybuilders debated back and forth their own physical merits and at times it got quite heated. With all the hype this show produced I was determined my Arnold/Sergio challenge would go ahead as scheduled.

With all that had gone into the Arnold/Sergio challenge, I knew it would be disastrous for it to not go exactly as planned. I spoke to Sergio then came back to Arnold, directly after Andy had finished speaking to him the first time, and told him that Sergio had agreed that the prize money could be split two ways, so regardless of the outcome, both contestants would receive $2,500 dollars. As well, I offered to pay all of Arnold's expenses including his round-trip flight from California to New York and a $100 dollar food allowance per day. Arnold told me he was worried he would not get fair treatment from the judges so, to assure him everything would be fine, I told him there would be three judges, one each from the AAU, IFBB and WBBG, along with an applause meter, which would score in favor of whoever received the loudest cheers. So I figured if it was the money Arnold was concerned about, he needn't have worried, as he would be guaranteed fair payment, and based on my selection of judges, fair treatment. Arnold told me that with the money on offer, and the way I had structured the judging panel, he would be there. He never showed. Without explanation he simply left us hanging without one half of our advertised main event. And to justify this to the many fans who had bought tickets, I had to say something in *MTI*. Because Arnold did not attend I simply said he had lost by default. That is all I ever printed on the matter. I made money on the show, but the audience did not get the Arnold/Sergio challenge they expected and I felt extremely bad over this. Arnold had not kept his word and I would not hear from him for two years.

In 1976 I ran my first WBBG Pro show in Los Angeles. At this time I received a most unlikely call: it was Arnold requesting an urgent meeting. He said he would bring Franco Columbu and that he had some important business to discuss. I considered this request strange since we had not left on the best terms two years earlier, but agreed to meet him and Franco for breakfast at the Century Plaza Hotel, where my wife and I were staying. At the time Arnold had been retired from bodybuilding for two years, after winning his sixth Mr. Olympia in 1975 and was enjoying the good life.

At breakfast, which lasted around two and a half hours, Arnold and Franco ate like they had never seen food before – they ate at least three large breakfasts each. I found this quite amusing until I got the bill, which I had offered to pay: $300.00 dollars, just for breakfast! I ate an average sized meal, about $20 dollars worth. During breakfast our conversation turned to bodybuilding promotion. Arnold told me that he was not happy with the coverage European bodybuilders were getting from Weider. He had with him a big bundle of pictures and articles he had apparently written on, the latest bodybuilders from Europe, and asked me if I would run them in my magazine. I said "sure, only to glad to help Arnold." At one point in our conversation, my wife got up to go to the ladies room. At this time Arnold leaned over to me and spoke of having had over 1000 sex partners since he had arrived in California. For whatever reason he told me this I remain unclear, since our discussion had been business-related up until that point. During the time my wife was absent Arnold spoke at length about his sexual conquests. When she returned he got back to business.

After breakfast Arnold gave me the inch-thick package of photos and articles and promptly left. I too was just about to leave when I saw a blue document poking out from the stack of pictures. After looking closely I discovered this to be a summons to appear in court. Claiming to know nothing about the challenge between him and Sergio, Arnold, as I later discovered, wanted a million dollars from me, as I had made money on the show. He sued me for using his name without consent. This blatant lie infuriated me. From the hotel I immediately contacted Franco and asked him if he knew anything about this. All Franco said was that Arnold laughed like a madman all the way home after our breakfast together, like he had received the greatest pleasure in the world. Franco gave me his word that he knew nothing. Arnold had pulled another of his pranks: he not only had me pay for breakfast but also served me with a summons. This was the last thing I expected from Arnold after spending years offering him opportunities and promoting him. And, after all, at the time of the planned Arnold/Sergio challenge Arnold was far from the international superstar he became. Up until then he had really only appeared in a few muscle magazines and was known mostly among bodybuilding fans, not general audiences as he later would. His real fame came after he appeared in Pumping Iron, the 1976 documentary that would promote bodybuilding as sport in its own right.

His claim that I used his images and name to promote my 1974 Pro Mr. America without his knowledge was a complete lie and I welcomed our day in court to disprove this ridiculous claim. After all, we had one critical piece of evidence that Arnold had failed to consider: the phone conversation between Arnold and Andy, which was fully documented and presented as proof of Arnold's willingness to compete in this contest. It clearly showed he was prepared to compete against Sergio at the 1974 Pro Mr. America. The court case, held at the Supreme Court, Los Angeles, was long and drawn out and Joe Weider was behind Arnold every step of the way. In fact, Arnold used Joe's lawyer and Joe paid all of Arnold's legal fees in a case that would not be settled until 1979. My legal costs were enormous. Every time I brought my witnesses from New York to California, the case was postponed. This happened four times, which cost me thousands. In the end the judge told me that we would have to settle the case, as we were getting nowhere. He told me if I did not settle I could lose a fortune. My lawyer, Barry Lane, also advised me to settle, as my legal fees alone would be more than any settlement figure. Then the judge went to Arnold, as he dealt with us one at a time in his chambers, and told him that I had a good case and to take whatever he could get from me. I was stubborn and did not want to give Arnold a penny, because as the judge had said, I did have a good case. I knew I was in the right, but Arnold, with Weider's help, had better representation and the financial means to drag the lawsuit on, which cost me hundreds of thousands in defense. The case was eventually settled by order of the judge. In the sealed settlement, Arnold got $100,000.00 dollars from me. He wanted one million.

Arnold and I did not meet again until three years later at the AAU Mr. America in Atlantic City. As my wife and I walked into the hall I saw Arnold out of the corner of my eye and quickly walked in the opposite direction. He walked straight towards me, I moved to the right. Just when I figured I had successfully avoided him, I felt a big hand on my shoulder. "Lets be friends again," said Arnold, a wide smile stretching across his face. I told Arnold that I could never be his friend after what he did to me, after dragging me through court and denying that he accepted to compete alongside Sergio at my Pro Mr. America. "Arnold, I helped make you famous," I said, pulling away from him. "I put 19 pictures of you in one issue of Muscle Training Illustrated alone, well before Weider ever published anything on you." He apologized and told me that when he sued me he needed the money. I told him I had nothing more to say and left. As my wife and I walked away, Thelma said, "Wasn't that a nice gesture Arnold made." I simply said: "no, screw him." His double-crossing cost me dearly, financially and emotionally, and I never wanted to deal with him in any shape or form ever again. But the world of bodybuilding back then was a small one and we would meet again under different circumstances.

In 1994 it was arranged for me to present famous talk show host Regis Philbin with an award for being the World's Most Physically Fit Television Announcer on the Nationally Syndicated Regis Philbin and Cathy Lee Gifford show. At the time, the WBBG was giving out many special awards to top entertainment-industry people, and Regis, having begun lifting weights at 13 and in tremendous shape for the award presentation, was a most worthy recipient. When I contacted him to give him the news he was delighted and said he would call me when the time was right to give him his award. A couple of weeks later he called and gave me the date: July 22, 1994. When I arrived just before 8.00am at the ABC Television Network in Manhattan, everyone in the greenroom told me Arnold was there. I did not expect this. As I sat there reading my newspaper with my son Mark sitting next to me, and the plaque I would present to Regis at my feet, Arnold walked in and the first thing he said to me was, "Dan, is that you?" Turns out he was there to promote a new movie he was working on. I hadn't seen him for at least 13 years. I ignored his question. He repeated himself: "Lurie, is that you?" I turned to him and said: "Arnold, aren't you ashamed to even talk to me after what you did?" Again he responded with what he had told me back at the Mr. America in Atlantic City, years earlier: "Dan, I needed the money then." I told him I had three words for him: "give it back." Arnold went on first that morning but, as I was later told, spent much of his time asking everyone what I was doing there.

Dan Lurie: Heart of Steel

He thought I was there to expose him for what he had done to me. And that was the last I saw of Arnold. I went on to present Regis with his award and said nothing about my dealings with the man who had tried to destroy me years earlier. As far as I was concerned the case was closed.

Arnold, Dan and Franco in 1969.

A lot has been written about Arnold over the years. Since I had firsthand experience dealing with him over many years, I feel I am qualified to offer some accurate insights into his character. Arnold was a man with a contrasting personality: he could one moment be your best friend, the next stick a knife in your back, as I had discovered. At first Arnold seemed as charming as could be, but I eventually found him to be sneaky and untrustworthy – I once called him a slimy skunk on national news television when he first ran for Governor of California. It could be argued, and many people would agree with me here, that Arnold uses people to get his own way. To this end I feel he had a good teacher in Joe Weider, the man who encouraged him to sue for anything.

Despite what happened over the years between Arnold and I, I [me,] still spoke nicely about him in my magazines. In the December 1984 issue of *MTI* I ran a retrospective pictorial to celebrate his onstage achievements. In 1981 I put him on the cover and inside featured a story on his life and acting career. In this issue we referred to him as a bodybuilding "God". He was also cover-man in August 1984, January '86 and October '91. Arnold's achievements as a bodybuilder are largely indisputable and before his arrival the iron game held little interest for many people. With his heroic movie roles where his muscles perfectly accentuated the testosterone-charged action roles, of which he was ideally suited to, and commitment to bodybuilding promotion with his yearly Arnold Classic bodybuilding championships, Arnold has more than achieved a major place in bodybuilding history. But to know a person fully you need the full picture and my views in the chapter, though some may not like them, do give insights into Arnold's history and form a big part of my background in the bodybuilding business. So they must be told.

Chapter Nine:

The Greatest Gift of All: Family. Everyday Life for Dan the Man

While I have been blessed with many wonderful friends, opportunities and experiences throughout my life, nothing has given me more satisfaction and happiness than my family. My wife, Thelma, five children, 15 grandchildren and seven great grandchildren have kept me grounded and everything I have done in my life has been done with them in mind. It has been said that behind every successful man is an equally successful woman, and for me this saying is true. Over the years my decisions have made me healthy and successful and have cemented my place in bodybuilding history. While some of my choices have been good, others were bad. Marrying Thelma on that snowy winters day, February 1, 1947, was the best decision I ever made. Sure life has its ups and downs, but thankfully ours has been one of continued happiness and joy. Through the good and bad our love has endured and on February 1, 2008 we celebrated our 61st wedding anniversary with close and extended family and friends.

Throughout our marriage Thelma and I have been blessed with five wonderful children who have all brought incredible happiness into our lives. Most of my businesses have been run as family affairs: Thelma's happy face, charming nature and sharp mind were a big part of the longstanding success of both *MTI* and the WBBG and my first-born child, Mark, was critical in the running of my shows and in arranging the layout of my magazines. As an expert photographer and skilled in a great many areas besides, Mark would take many of the photos that appeared in my bodybuilding magazines and would be one of the top organizers and directors at WBBG contests. My daughters Andrea, Shelly, Sandy and Jill have, through their constant love and support, helped me throughout my business and personal life. Later in life, their children brought me much joy and some of my grandkids have become integral forces in my current activities in the industry. My grandson, Ian, currently serves as a director and international liaison for our newly created not for profit organization aptly named, "The World Fitness Guild". I would have to say the combined efforts of all my family members have made a winning team that has helped me to achieve all that I have.

I truly believe that we are put on this earth to help other people and to make a difference in the lives of others. Without my family behind me and without the opportunities I have had to provide the best possible life for them, I could not imagine what things would have been like. Without special people to share your life, what is its purpose? I often considered this question as my life has unfolded. When making any kind of business decision and in experiencing victory, however large or small, I was always thankful that after everything was said and done my family would be there for me with their love and support. Always at the front of my mind was, and is, the belief that without family-based stability, life would be extremely shallow.

My contests and other business interests took up a lot of my time over the years, but my family have always come first. Time with them was considered a priority whenever business came up, and, wherever possible, I would include them. From my days on the Big Top television show, where I would bring ice cream home every weekend and enjoy time with my wife and children, to my contests and magazines where they would all have roles to play, my bond with my family has been the secret to my success. Often Thelma would tell me that I was spoiling her and the children. Looking back I guess I did, but remember I grew up in the Depression, a time where my siblings and I had very little other then the love of our parents. The time and money I have spent on my children is, I suppose, kind of a reaction to the poverty I knew during my younger years. I did not want them to experience anything close to the poverty I experienced.

Life as a husband and father began for me when I first met Thelma in 1946 outside East Flatbush, Brooklyn entertainment spot, Club Elegante, a familiar haunt on Ocean Parkway and Avenue J, a fun place where they served non-alcoholic drinks and provided a variety of games such as ping pong and skill-bowling machines. At age 23, I was not short of female attention. I was in top physical shape and had energy to spare. Two years earlier I had won America's Most Muscular Man for the third time and was now running my barbell business and managing the gym I owned on Pitkin Avenue. My physique reflected all the physical work I did daily to maintain my barbell business - this involved packing heavy barbell equipment for shipment to customers - along with the years of weight training I did.

Because of my physique, women would often turn and stare, probably because they were curious more than anything else. Thelma was the same; only with her there were immediate sparks, from both sides. On the evening we first met, my friends and I piled into my little car and headed from Canarsie to the brighter lights of Brooklyn, something we would often do, especially on warm summer evenings. On the evening in question, myself, Artie David and several other friends drove to meet some girls at Club Elegante. Artie and I had been close friends since we were 13 and sold Bungalow Bars at Rockaway Beach together. We were now young men who were more inclined to seek bright lights of the big city and female company.

As I parked my car near Club Elegante, I discovered it would not fit into the only available parking space within walking distance. As I maneuvered the car backwards and forwards, I found I needed a few more inches to fit into the space. Watching us from a park bench a short distance away were three girls. "Hey, girls. How about pulling your car up about a foot or two so I can park too," I yelled. Giggles were all I could hear. So after seven attempts to park the car and finally making it with mere inches to spare, I walked over to them. "Are you sure that is not your car?" I asked jokingly. More giggles. "Where do you live," I continued. "Across the street," Thelma joked. "That's a cemetery over there, you all look half dead. I'll bet you're from Pitkin Avenue Brownsville," I replied, as I sat down next to Thelma. That remark hit home and sure enough Thelma and her friends were from the Bristol Street and Pitkin Avenue section of Brownsville. Twenty-two-year-old Thelma and her friends, Shirley and Jerri, said they were from Brownsville and had taken the five-cent subway ride over to Ocean Parkway. With the ice suitably broken we all got talking and after we boys bought the girls soda at the club and played a little table tennis, which conveniently lengthened our discussion time, I drove everyone home, planning it in such a way that my last stop would be Thelma's house.

An Early Date: Dan on a photo-shoot date with Elaine Kusine, a well-known New York model, and Ms. Subway. Elaine attended Tilden High School with Dan.

We must have spoken for over an hour in the car that night. She told me she worked as a buyer at May's department store and that my best friend Artie had already asked her out that evening. I do remember Thelma being a beautiful looking young lady and naturally charming that night. But I was a little down, knowing that Artie would be dating her the following evening. The next night Artie and I double dated with Thelma and her girlfriend Shirley. Of course Artie had asked Thelma first so I took the girlfriend. Artie and Thelma sat in the backseat of my car, but after a while it became obvious to Artie that Thelma was paying more attention to me than to him. As I said before there were immediate sparks between Thelma and I and I had only taken her friend, who I had ignored on the drive as my attention had been focused on the lady in the backseat, out of respect for Artie, who had asked Thelma first. What Artie finally said would lead to what I had secretly hoped would happen that night: "Say Thelma. Would you rather go on this date with Dan?" "Yes!" she replied. "That goes for me to," I could not help saying, as if such a comment would get her from the back to the front seat faster. "Okay then, let's switch," Artie suggested. For the next six months I saw Thelma every night, and not long after this we married.

Back then communication was more of a problem compared with today's age of cell phones and e-mail, and we couldn't always talk because Thelma's parents did not own a phone. This did not bother me because just seeing Thelma was enough and every evening after work I would jump in my car and drive from Canarsie to Brownsville – about four miles - and park across the street from her third-floor, walk-up apartment. After tooting the horn a few times, Thelma would look out the window and wave goodnight. I'd wave back, start the car, and head back home to bed. Thelma's family name was Rothman. Her mother and father were not the wealthiest but were very loving and raised their daughter with good values that would eventually be passed down to our own children. Thelma's father, Isadore (Izzy), ran a stationery and candy store while her mother, Adell, was always busy caring for Thelma and her sister, Sylvia. One thing I loved about Thelma's father was that every time we picked him up from work he would always reward me with a giant chocolate malted thick shake loaded with ice cream, which he sold at his store; that along with the fact he was a very nice man who treated me like a son. After a few weeks of dating, Thelma's family accepted me and after three months we were engaged and had set a wedding date for February 1, 1947.

The In-Laws: Izidore and Adell Rothman with Thelma's younger sister Sylvia (on left) and Thelma.

The wedding was a large affair for the times: we had a caterer who served all the hot dishes - a big sit-down dinner for over 100 family and friends. It was quite large with all the trimmings, but the wedding reception menu itself was not all that fancy, though I always kidded that I overpaid. The bill was three dollars per person including tax and drinks. Artie David was my best man and we all had a great time.

The morning of our wedding day was business as usual for me. Before dressing for the big day I was doing what I normally did at that time of the day: I packed barbells in my parents' basement.

I might have been getting married, but business duties still called. I often joke to Thelma that the reason I married her was because of what happened that morning. I was stacking metal weight plates eight feet high and putting the bars in the center of each plate, preparing them for distribution. The working conditions weren't the best and the concrete floor was often quite slippery, adding to the fact that there was little room to move anyway. Halfway through packing one barbell, I suddenly slipped and one of the 10-pound steel plates fell and landed on my head. As I lay there hoping like crazy that the damage was not too serious, which fortunately it wasn't, although some might argue with me about this, my thoughts shifted to the wedding. Now I have heard all kinds of excuses for missing the big day but this one would have been just a little too hard to believe or accept. So I just cleaned up, put on my suit and kept what had happened quiet. And today when we talk of the big occasion all those years back, what I sometimes say to Thelma is: "Sure I married you, but I was hit on the head with a barbell plate and didn't know what I was doing."

Sore Head Dan? Dan and Thelma on their wedding day: February 1, 1947.

Just before our wedding a big snowfall hit New York City, and this made us extra happy to head to the South to sunny Florida for our four-week honeymoon. Our honeymoon destination, Florida, was ideal, but the living arrangements proved less than spectacular, at least for a newlywed couple. A few years before, a friend and professional associate of mine, Dr. Frederick Tilney, casually told me as I was leaving after doing some business with him, that if I ever needed some place to stay he had a room for me at his home in Miami. Earlier in my career I stayed with Dr. Tilney for a few weeks. At the time I was a bodybuilding competitor, not very sophisticated in the ways of the world and any room looked good to me back then. So I decided that Miami would be a wonderful place to take Thelma on our honeymoon. She had never been to Florida and looked forward to being a houseguest of my good friend Dr. Tilney. My father was also helpful in lending us newlyweds his DeSoto car, so with transportation and lodging suitably arranged Thelma and I figured we had it made. Well, at least this is what we thought.

Several days before the wedding it snowed quite heavily, but my father's old car seemed capable of handling the increasing build up. But as we headed south we discovered the storm had hit right down the coast of New York and southern communities were simply not equipped for heavy snows. The snow had been plowed from the north, but snowplows were scarce below Philadelphia and the white stuff began to get pretty deep on the highway. Thelma and I did not realize that the snow was building up on the underside of our car until suddenly we were up to our seats in the stuff. So heavy and deep was the snow that it finally pushed the wooden floorboards of the DeSoto up and into the front seat. And with the floorboards came a foot and a half of snow. We laughed about this sudden surprise, which didn't dampen our spirits in the least for it made us relish that Florida sunshine even more as we passed Daytona Beach and headed deep into the southern part of the sunny state. But we were not clear just yet and the surprises would continue.

When we arrived in Coral Gables, a friendly Dr. Tilney greeted us and showed us into his guestroom. To say the "honeymoon suit" was not exactly how I had remembered it would be an understatement. It wasn't the room that had changed, but me. Thelma was speechless when she saw that the room, about the size of your average bathroom, was part of the garage. Any thought of a romantic night was out of the question and our host understood perfectly when I told him privately that I had better try to find something a little more like the dream-palace Thelma had imagined.

The Handsome Couple: Dan and Thelma, moments after tying the knot.

The local Chamber of Commerce directed us to a beautiful private home in Coral Gables, which we rented for $25 a week. Now we were talking. Thelma and I loved it so much that we spent a whole month there – all for only $100. The great thing about this arrangement, for me at least, was the fact we got to pick as many oranges and grapefruits as we could manage, from the many trees surrounding the property. After our honeymoon, complete with an endless supply of good food, and luxury living, we got down to the business of being husband and wife and the first thing we needed was a good car.

The Greatest Gift of All: Family. Everyday Life for Dan the Man

Over the years, Thelma and I have owned many nice cars, the most memorable of these being the first respectable model I was fortunate enough to buy: a shiny new 1947 powder blue Buick convertible, bought a couple of months after our honeymoon. I say fortunate, as automobile companies had stopped producing cars during World War II so there was a severe shortage of good civilian transport right after the war. At the time, Thelma and I were living with her parents on Bristol Street and they had no garage, so I just parked the Buick out on the street, something I would never do today. It is a wonder it never got vandalized or stolen even back in the 1940s even when such activities were not as common as they are today. Back then people, even kids, respected the property and rights of other people much more. That car lasted us many great years, until we traded up. In some ways this vehicle solidified our bond as husband and wife. It was something we owned together and marked the beginning of our new life together.

The following year we began searching for a home. We limited our search to an area of Brooklyn near Brooklyn College, which was geographically the best area for me as my businesses were in this district. We found just the right house, one Thelma and I fell in love with, at 1192 East 51 Street between Avenues H and I, not far from the club where we first met. Even though we both liked it we could not buy it. We viewed this house several times and each time Thelma became more attracted to the idea of owning it. But each time she would get back in the car and say with a sad smile: "Dan, it's such a nice house. It is just too bad we can't afford it." One evening we stopped to take a final look at our dream house on East 51 Street, before we left to look for something more affordable. It was brand new and hadn't been sold so we peered though the windows for a better view inside. "Say, I wonder if this old key I have here in my pocket would fit the lock," I said, removing the key and presenting it to Thelma with much pride in my resourcefulness. "Dan, are you trying to get us arrested?" Thelma responded, horrified at what she thought was carelessness on my part. "We can't enter someone else's home." "Oh come on. We won't get arrested," I teased. Thelma's curiosity finally got the better of her and she said okay, "let's do it." I put the key in the lock and turned. Much to her surprise the door swung open. "Oh my, Dan. It worked." "Go ahead, take a look inside Thelma," I said half pushing her toward the entrance. "Go ahead, no one's going to bother you. This is your house!" Naturally Thelma was very happy. The house she had dreamed about for weeks was hers and she got to work examining the place from top to bottom. To this day she has never gotten over the fact that I had put a deposit on the house that afternoon before swearing the real estate agent to secrecy. It was his key I happened to have in my pocket that evening.

We spent many pleasant years and made many good friends in that house on East 51 Street. While we lived there, four of our five children were born - my son Mark, our eldest, was a baby when we moved in. Andrea was the first born, followed by Rochelle, so named in memory of my mother, then Sandy. A funny thought came to me after our youngest, Jill, was born: the first letters of our previously born children in order of age spelled MARS (Mark, Andrea, Rochelle and Sandy). What are the chances of this, I thought? Our announcement of Jill's birth caused something of a sensation among our friends, as word had gotten around that we had already made it to Mars, and we were now on a trip to Jupiter with the naming of Jill.

Lady of the House: Thelma Lurie at her other dream house in North Woodmere, Long Island New York.

The Greatest Gift of All: Family. Everyday Life for Dan the Man

Our Long Island Home

Our present home was a dream in every way, but our expanding family meant we had to move into something much larger: our second home in North Woodmere, Long Island. Moving into our 1st home was no problem. I had always been a saver so had the down payment money when it was needed. With the birth of Jill, and the mortgage on this home being paid off, we made our move to North Woodmere to a large 12 bedroom estate where my children could each have a room of their own. Out of respect to the profession that had given me so much, and with no reference whatsoever to myself, I called this home "the house that a dumbbell built". After we moved in I added an ear-shaped swimming pool and built a full-sized mirrored gym for my friends and I to train in. Along with my family, this house was my pride and joy. My only regret is that it didn't stand on a hill surrounded by several acres. After all, a high colonial with tall Georgian columns is imposing and needs an equally magnificent setting. My family and I spent many happy years in this home, and it provided ample room for the many activities and interests my children had.

Once we moved into this house we got to work molding it to our requirements. First of all I transformed an addition into a beautiful drawing room for entertaining. The 12-foot tall, built-in ceiling-high bookshelves and woodwork were custom made for the room by a local cabinet shop. My muscles came in handy, as I became my own contractor and added the wing, but I did hire people to lay the slate floor and cover it with hardwood. Since I was also in the sauna business at the time, we had several of these added, and all of them were separated from the drawing room by a wall of blue and white-leaded stained glass showing two huge peacocks, one either side of a carrara marble fireplace. At one point I considered putting a bowling alley in the basement and had made arrangements to have a pinsetter added. Then Thelma and I talked it over and decided that since neither of us bowled and our children were nearly grown it would have been a waste.

As you might have guessed, the drawing room was the central point for family activities. My favorite piece of furniture there was the baby grand piano. I love music and especially love to sing and when our children were younger we would all get around the piano and sing our favorite songs. I would often sit alone in the evenings and play song-after-song from paper piano rolls and sing along with the music, my untrained baritone voice penetrating every room of the house. My voice was untrained, but it was good and loud. I guess this came from years of hawking ice cream and soda on boardwalks and in theaters, and from my time in the Public School chorus at the age of 12. As a child I would love to sing and as I entered my teenage years, would listen to the opera on Saturday afternoons. I was told my voice sounded like a young Mario Lanza, who, along with Al Jolson, remains one of my favorite musicians. As a youngster I never took any formal singing-lessons, as my parents could not afford between 50 cents and one dollar per lesson, but if I had taken these lessons, along with extra voice and dictation training, I believe I could have made my living in the music business. Instead of doing this I would go on to sing the National Anthem to open my bodybuilding shows and Hall of Fame dinners, and to entertain my children, and later, grandchildren, at family gatherings. Where once I would entertain my family and whoever else would listen with my singing, such times are now strictly saved for a select few, and, of course, the bathroom.

Operatic Great: Dan flew to Tokyo, Japan, with international Opera star, Jan Pierce.

Clock Collector: Dan with one of his prized timepieces.

Along with the drawing-room den, where I did a lot of my singing, we had three other dens around the house. After our children had grown and left, Thelma and I had more room than we really needed. One Den upstairs, first transformed into a greenhouse where Thelma once raised marvelous, exotic houseplants, was used for my bodybuilding-related business. It was like a little oasis for me, complete with a big desk where I could work quietly. In this room I also kept such peculiar treasures as a large mechanical lion, a huge giraffe and two mechanical lovebirds that cooed and hugged one another. Other than their novelty value, these curious pets were wonderful to have around when my grandchildren visited: they delighted in playing with the large, exotic toys in my upstairs den. While the formal living and dining rooms were nice when entertaining, we never had much use for them otherwise. We'd rather sit in one of the dens than on the French provincial furniture. But the living room did provide a rather nice setting for some of my prized clocks. For instance, the French clock covered with gold leaf was made for and inscribed with the name Napoleon Bonaparte. Of all my fifty or more clocks, this one, the most valuable, would have to be my favorite.

The Greatest Gift of All: Family. Everyday Life for Dan the Man

Sometimes friends ask me: "Dan, where in the world did you get all of your clocks?" And that is the answer: in many parts of the world – England, France, Hong Kong and all over the U.S. A strange interest you might ask? It all began about 50 years ago when I bought one antique clock, then a second until I had gradually acquired quite a collection of these ticking treasures. I also read as much about clocks as I have time for. To me they are something alive. Their ticking is like a pulse beat and every hour, without fail, they talk to me with their chimes and bells. Sometimes a friend will ask, "What kinds of clocks do you specialize in Dan." I guess this is a natural question in our age of specialization and decentralization. Some stamp collectors, for example, buy only U.S. stamps, while others specialize in postage stamps worldwide. I often disappoint such aficionados when I tell them I love all clocks – French, American, English, German, porcelain, carved wood, and especially the ornate variety: the bronzes and those covered with gold leaf. 90% of my present collection is true antiques with those remaining being look-alikes.

I talk a lot about my clock collection because it is one of my loves and accordingly it belongs in my family chapter along with my wife and children, who remain the greatest love of my life. Clock collecting has also been a family activity, not really the buying part but more the enjoyment they provide - my children always loved the sounds they made and loved to learn about what made them tick, so to speak - their inner workings. My interest in clocks also explains another side to my personality, one that might put some light on how I think and operate. You see, I love detail and clocks are the most complex, intricate of things. They are reliable and constantly communicate to me in a variety of ways – their constant tick-tock is as regular and steady as a heartbeat, the music they make with their chimes as beautiful to me as any opera score.

Years ago I would have all of my clocks going and on time. At the stroke of the hour the whole house would be alive with the music of their chimes. My family and I loved to have visitors and the clocks were a great talking point. But on one occasion a guest could not see the beauty in my collection. In the late-1960s I hosted, at separate times, two rather large guests: bodybuilding champions Bill Pearl and

Boyer Coe, who both slept over at my house the night before they were to appear onstage. Well, it seems Boyer got the worst deal during his stay when he found himself sleeping in a room that housed most of my clock collection. Accordingly, every hour on the hour, the chimes would go off and poor Boyer would be shakily woken from his sleep. Finally, at two in the morning, he got up and turned all my clocks off so he could get some much needed rest. I discovered a rather quiet drawing room the following day, but he never told me about this until years later. Thinking back, Boyer's awakening might have been a wake up call for me because I eventually decided that going about the house each week to wind each clock with special keys or resetting weighted chains, was just too much work. Today I keep only a few of them going in rooms we frequent most. Besides, the deep-throated solemn gong of my nine-foot Black Forest grandfather clock is enough to remind anyone that I am a clock collector. Along with the clocks, our big North Woodmere home brought its share of challenges so we sold it in 2001. Today Thelma and I live in a three-bedroom condo in Long Island, New York, along with my remaining clocks and Thelma's plants.

Braving the Elements: Dan with daughter Sandy at their North Woodmere home.

The Greatest Gift of All: Family. Everyday Life for Dan the Man

Snowman: Dan hoisting the white stuff

The North Woodmere home will always remain a fond memory. I recall one time making good use of the ear-shaped pool and one of the several saunas I mentioned earlier. I was known at the time for my less-conventional ways of staying in shape – ultra high reps and endurance training for bodybuilding being an example. But one method had all of my family completely puzzled. I knew that if it was freezing outside and if you go out into the street with just your bathing suit on you are going to freeze to death. But I discovered that if you entered the sauna for about five or ten minutes and raise your body temperature, going outside afterwards would produce the most wonderful feeling of vitality, which I believe boosted my immune system. But it all depended on what temperature you set the sauna on. I usually started with 180 and then bumped it up to 230, and as you can imagine, it becomes very hot after a while and you sweat a lot. Well after ten minutes of being in the sauna I would open up the door and go outside where, in winter, it was below freezing. After being in the sauna it felt like a warm breeze hitting me. It just felt great. What I would then do is chop a hole in the frozen-over pool before ducking myself in for ten or fifteen minutes. Of course people thought I was crazy. Here I was shoveling snow away from the pool in freezing conditions in my bathing suit. But I was not stupid and would only do this after being in the sauna for ten or so minutes. When I entered the pool, my whole body became numb for two to three seconds. And after this period it left me with a nice, warm feeling. It was amazing. But one time it did not go exactly as planned. When the local newspaper learned I was doing this, they wanted to interview me. They wished to take pictures of me shoveling snow and enjoying my healthful dip. So they called me and we made arrangements to meet. The following day when the news people arrived, they came early and I had only just gotten into the sauna. And as luck would have it, and to make matters worse, the sauna's fuse box shorted out and did not work. They expected me to be all ready to chop the ice and jump into the pool as they arrived with their cameras. So here I was freezing, just having climbed out of a sauna - that did not work - after only one minute or so. I didn't want to let them down so I had to do everything including shovelling the snow and jumping into the pool in my swimming trunks. This time I really was freezing. It nearly killed me but they got their photos and story.

Come on in, the Water's Fine: Dan about to take the plunge.

The Greatest Gift of All: Family. Everyday Life for Dan the Man

Snow Squats: how Dan keeps fit

Human Snowplow: Dan clears the way.

Dan Lurie: Heart of Steel

Now that the children are grown, Thelma and I travel alone but always enjoy having at least some of our kids and/or grandchildren with us when possible. Back in the day, we were inveterate flea market visitors and there is nothing we liked more than haggling in the bazaars of the world. We also loved meeting new and interesting people and experiencing new cultures. One of the highlights of our travels was a visit in 1977 to Monte Carlo, where we met and spent some time in serious conversations with the Prince of Monaco, Prince Rainier III's, people where we discussed the possibility of holding a WBBG Mr. Universe or Mr. Olympus competition in Monte Carlo, a beautiful spot. At the time, the authorities were quite interested, but nothing came of it. Other travels have taken us to the most distant places and provided experiences we will never forget. Around 28 years ago, Thelma and I broke new ground and traveled with friends to Taiwan, Singapore, Hong Kong, Japan and Thailand.

Enjoying Life in Style: Dan holidaying with his wife Thelma and daughters (left to right) Andrea and Jill.

Classy Car, Classy Lady: while staying at the Carlton Hotel in Cannes, France, 1975, Dan's wife Thelma spotted a car and asked Dan to buy it for her. "It was cheaper to put her near the car and just take her picture," said Dan. "I saved a lot of money."

Thelma and I would always take the children on our travels. In fact, we made it our policy never to leave them behind. With them we traveled to Caracas, Rio, Acapulco and Puerto Vallarta many times, all of the islands of the Caribbean, Alaska, North Africa, Israel, Greece, Italy, France, Spain, England and Canada. Traveling to these destinations involved 50 or more cruises, our preferred method of travel. One of the more memorable vacations my family and I took was to Hawaii. We managed to get a lovely complex of apartments right on the beach and would go horseback riding every day. All five of our children, Thelma and I galloping on horseback along the beautiful Hawaiian shoreline remains an experience I will never forget. Another vacation experience I also remember fondly was one of several times we went to Acapulco, Mexico. We enjoyed this particular vacation so much we extended it by two weeks. Initially though, the hotel was fully booked. They recommended a small place down the road, so we took our chances; we did not know what to expect. Well, the managers of our first hotel must have confused their recommended spot with some other place because this 'small apartment' had over ten floors and a private swimming pool on the roof. We had the master suite with a living room, den and three bedrooms. Talk about home away from home. We were in paradise. Every morning one of our daughters - they would take turns - would print up a menu and we would get breakfast in bed. And to top it off, the rate was only half that of the fancy hotel. Another of our favorite family holidays was our yearly Easter vacation at the Fontainebleau Hotel in Miami Beach. Our Christmas Chanukah vacations were equally wonderful. Of all our vacations together my family say these two spots were their favorites.

The Loving Couple: Thelma age 85 and Dan age 86 at a recent wedding. This picture was just taken on May 23, 2009.

The first vacations the children, Thelma and I took were in the 1950s. At that time I was Sealtest Dan, The Muscle Man, and was asked to do appearances in-character all over the U.S. One time, owner Ray Parker invited me to perform at his Concord Hotel, the Waldorf Astoria of all vacation places located near Kiamesha Lake, not far from Monticello

The Greatest Gift of All: Family. Everyday Life for Dan the Man

in the mountains of New York. This expansive retreat, over 5,000 acres in all, included an 18-hole golf course, 30 full-sized tennis courts and an amazing ski lift which took guests all the way to the top of its surrounding mountains. The Concord had a nightclub that held over 3,000 people and every night featured some of the biggest names in show business. My family loved all of this and the fact it served three meals a day of all you could eat. In later years, after all my children married and had their own children, giving lucky me and Thelma 15 delightful grandchildren, we all began celebrating Thelma's and my wedding anniversary at the Concord. For ten years I would hire a large bus and on the Thursday evening drive all my family to a motel near the Concord, reservations for the 10 rooms having been made in advance. The next morning we would all have breakfast at a nearby diner before checking into the Concord by 10.00am, Friday. We would then holiday for three days. Since our party was around 35 people, we needed 10 rooms and even though Ray Parker always gave me a generous discount, Grandpa Dan paid for everything. Great times!

As my children grew, so did their ambitions. They have all achieved a great deal in life, and continue to amaze me with their talents and skills today. As my right hand man, Mark is one of the hardest working people I have known. From my contests, where he would set up all of the onstage lighting, arrange the competitors and ensure the smooth running of each show, to my magazines and barbell company, where his roles were also performed to perfection, he has never let me down. My magazines were also well illustrated due to Mark's photography skills. And exercise equipment was well constructed thanks to Mark's engineering expertise. He would even help to build the saunas I went on to market and sell. Mark also had a licence to show theater movies and would set up productions for us all to watch as a family.

My four daughters established good careers for themselves while raising three children each. Andrea became a schoolteacher, Shelly and Sandy partnered up to start their own company and Jill became a travel agent. Jill also loved to write letters and poetry. As a 25-year-old, she wrote me a beautiful letter, which expressed her love and which meant more to me than all the world's riches.

Dan Lurie: Heart of Steel

Father and Son: Dan with a newborn Mark Lurie in 1947

Mark Lurie, age 61

Daddy, how do I tell you the love that's been growing? For 25 years, Daddy still growing - Getting stronger each minute, like a balloon pumped with air, ready to explode. The balloon is my heart, the air your love. As a child Daddy I was afraid. I loved you but I was afraid. You were so strong and powerful, and I so little.

You were stronger, stronger than any man. Mr. America runner-up you were. But I see the pictures and hear the stories and feel as though I knew you then. I feel so proud of you.

Strong arms, strong legs, massive chest, soft heart - That's you Daddy. That's what I love about you the most, your heart. Always so giving. So much love to offer, so much joy and fun to share. There is nothing you could not do Daddy with your amazing mind. I've got my dreams, my rainbows, my suns and my moons invested in you Daddy. My world, my whole world.

You could be a conqueror, a star, a husband, a father and you are all these things and much more to me. The cold wind may age your bones a bit and the carousel of time may revolve and tarnish your hair to grey. You may lose your physique and gain some wrinkles, but these changes I will fail to see. Nothing could ever mar my cherished visions of you, for I love you Daddy. You will always be my Mister America.

Jill Lurie, 1986

Thelma herself was and is a very talented lady. Not only did she do most of the work raising our children, an amazing task itself, she became a well-known horticulturalist. She knew botany inside and out and had an encyclopedic knowledge of a wide range of plants as well as how to care for the many she kept at our home. Thelma would also help me run my contests in an administration role.

On February 1, 2007, Thelma and I celebrated our 60th wedding anniversary with a surprise ceremony and mystery two-day honeymoon, arranged by our children and grandchildren. After six decades of marriage, our bond as husband and wife was as strong as ever, and to share such a special time marking our life together with those closest to us, was the greatest gift. So as we once again walked down the aisle, this time under a flowered canopy and accompanied by a rabbi at our daughter Andrea and son-in-law, Michael Herman's, estate in Hewlett Harbor, I reflected on our many wonderful times together and silently thanked God for the blessing he had given me. After we exchanged our vows, there was an eruption of confetti and many there broke into a family dance to "Hava Nagila" a traditional Hebrew song of celebration. As customary, Thelma and I enjoyed the first slow dance to one of my all time favorite songsters, Al Johnson, as he sang the beautiful Anniversary Waltz. What a great start to what would prove the most enjoyable evening: a picture slideshow with over 150 old photos capturing special moments in the life of Thelma and I put together by Mark and his wife Beth, a lovely dinner facing the skyscrapers of Manhattan from the Waters Edge restaurant on East River, Long Island, and a family history trivia contest and delightful magic show held at the same restaurant, courtesy of daughters Shelly Lurie, Sandy Carl and Jill Kucker along with her husband Stephen.

The Girls: (left to right) the five women in Dan's life: Jill, Sandy, Shelly, Andrea and Mama Thelma.

The Greatest Gift of All: Family. Everyday Life for Dan the Man

The Happy Couple: Dan and Thelma attending the Concord Hotel New Year's Eve Ball.

After we cut the wedding cake and said our farewells to family and friends, Thelma and I were escorted by limousine to our honeymoon suite at Manhattan's Park Central Hotel. The perfect occasion was topped off with breakfast in bed the following morning. Lunch was served at the famed Carnegie Deli. I could not have asked for a more perfect way to celebrate 60 years together: doing what we love best, enjoying the company of family and friends and having fun in one another's company. May we have many more years of happiness together and enjoy the blessings life had provided for us.

Since marrying Thelma, I have experienced the best life has had to offer. I owe a great deal of this to her. At first we both had very little money; we grew together and worked hard to succeed in life. Over this time we both learned many lessons together and all of them would ensure a long, happy marriage. One of the secrets to a good marriage, in my view, is to never go to sleep mad at each other. Over the years Thelma and I may have had an occasional disagreement, but we never had a fight and harmony has been one of the keys to our happiness. Another key to our long marriage has been fun. Thelma and I never took life too seriously, though the nature of my work was often stressful and very mentally and physically demanding. But I would leave the stress at the office and always considered family time sacred, an opportunity to connect with my loved ones and forget about outside commitments. Respect and trust have also been important. Ask anyone I have dealt with and they will tell you the same thing: my wife and children came first. This choice, I believe, is based on the great respect I have had for Thelma over the years. I have also trusted her judgment in many matters, a decision that has helped me in both business and life. Our years together have been good ones because we both understand how important enjoyment, respect and trust is. No marriage can successfully survive without these.

Business and Pleasure: Dan mingling at one of his WBBG events with legendary bodybuilder, George Eiferman, and his constant rock of support, wife Thelma.

Chapter Ten:

People

Like most sports, bodybuilding is filled with interesting and famous personalities, and it seems to attract more than its share of colorful people. During my 70-year involvement in bodybuilding, I have personally had the pleasure of getting to know most of these interesting people and this has provided me with many exciting moments in a sport I loved right from the start. And the great thing about bodybuilding is that it attracts many who use it to improve their health and physical fitness, not only just to get onstage and pose their muscles. These people include sporting personalities from other areas, actors, politicians and television hosts. I have met my share of them too.

One such person from the bodybuilding and strength world that immediately comes to mind for his great strength and heart is Joe Greenstein, the "Mighty Atom". Though small in height at around five feet four inches tall, and perhaps 150 pounds, Joe was a good example of size counting for much less than most people think. The average person, who is not familiar with bodybuilding and the development of physical strength, usually regards a big fellow with muscles as much stronger than a smaller, well-developed man. Joe Greenstein shattered this myth again and again in his own remarkable style.

Dan Lurie: Heart of Steel

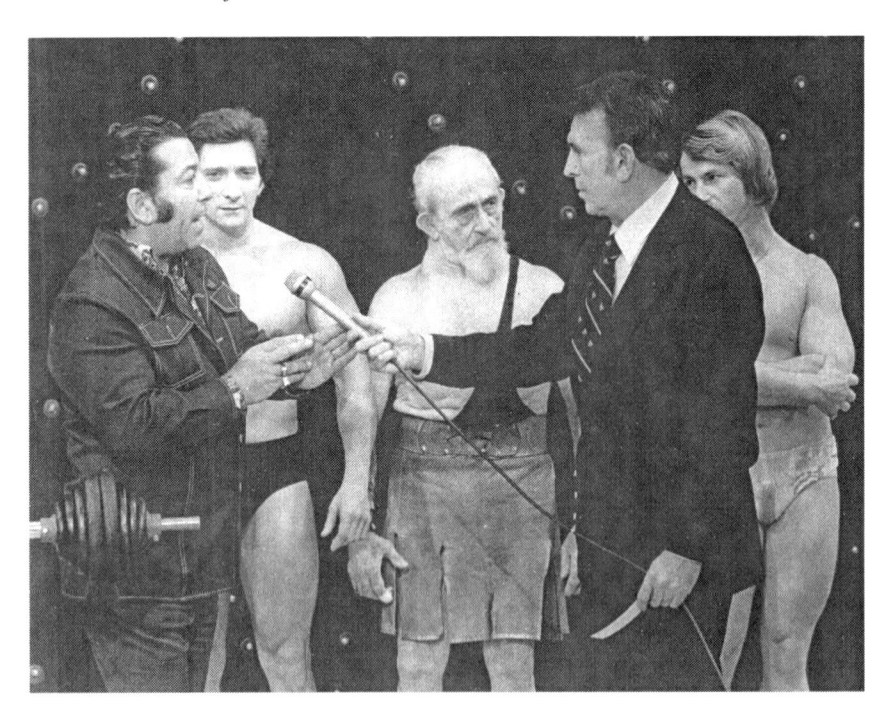

Man of Strength: Dan presents Joe "The mighty Atom" Greenstein to Dennis James' Cerebral Palsy Fundraising Show audience.

As one of my closest senior bodybuilding friends, Joe was like a father to me. In fact, during the last five years of his life I spent more time with him than his own children did. We traveled together and put on shows in high schools and he treated me as one of his own. For this I will always be extremely grateful and honored. Born in Poland in 1893, and coming to America as a poor immigrant like so many others of polish stock during that time, Joe was accustomed to paving his own way, with his own bare hands. He supported himself and his family with a medicine show where he would attract crowds in Atlantic City, but mostly in Coney Island, with his feats of strength, before selling the audience special soaps and lotions.

A rare combination of scholar, muscleman and showman, Joe was as well rounded as they come. He spoke seven languages and knew the scriptures, and he loved to give family counseling to couples with marital troubles. He was also very proud of his Jewish heritage, always wearing his Yarmulka, a skullcap worn by Jewish males during prayer and religious study. Known throughout the world as a man of strength and scholarship, Joe Greenstein was given the keys to the city of Tel Aviv and more than 20 U.S. cities, an honor fitting for this man of many talents.

Since my main interest was strength development along with bodybuilding, Joe's muscle power impressed me. To give you some idea of how strong the Mighty Atom was, I saw him bend steel bars with his bare hands and drive nails into two-inch boards with his palm, many times. Joe's strength was without question physical, but he also had great mental powers that enabled him to perform feats of strength that would break lesser men. He would look at a piece of steel and say to it in his mind, "You are just a flimsy piece of metal. But I am Joe Greenstein and I am going to bend you with my bare hands." And he would! It was as if he was willing the steel to bend. At first I thought there must be some trick to all this, so I tried it myself. The steel cut into my hands and I had to stop because of the pain. Now, once you have begun to bend steel you cannot stop, because it's almost impossible to begin again. Joe would bend the steel in one motion as he resisted the pain in his hands. I later learned he would use his mind power to block the pain. The same was true of driving nails into wood with his palm. I was afraid to do this, figuring I would drive the nail right through my hand.

Many times I watched Joe Greenstein wrap his chest with a chain and then break it. He once explained to me that it was actually pneumatic pressure that did it and that the chain had not been tampered with as many thought it was. To perform this amazing feat Joe would first inhale as much air as his chest could hold and then, with his near-perfect muscle control, transfer the air to his stomach by expanding his diaphragm. His stomach would swell as if he were pregnant. With the air gone, his chest would deflate. Only then would he wrap the chain tightly around his chest. Then, with a sudden movement, he would re-inflate his chest and the pneumatic air pressure would so strain the chain that the weakest link would spread apart causing the chain to fall from his upper torso to a heap on the ground. You may have seen Hercules in the movies, but Joe presented a real-life version and no theatrical tricks or special camera angles were needed for him to perform his muscle magic.

Dan Lurie: Heart of Steel

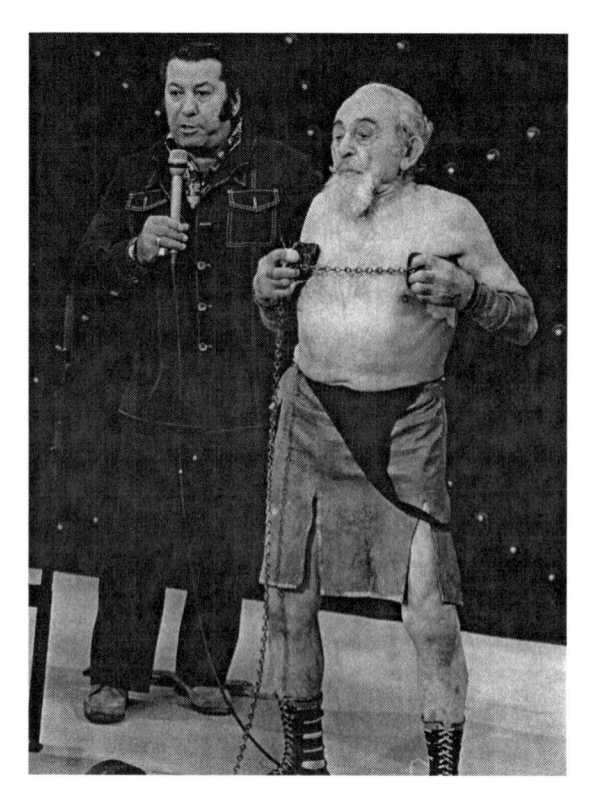

Breaking the Chain: Dan presents the Mighty Atom's famous chain-breaking exhibition.

Another time Joe, yet again, demonstrated to my absolute amazement his incredible strength and mental control. It happened one day while Joe and I were having lunch in Brooklyn with champion wrestler, Billy "Superstar" Graham. We three had been in my office having a discussion and stepped next door for a quick sandwich in a restaurant I owned. I would let the people I liked eat there for free and Joe and Billy were regular customers. There they would often arm wrestle. One time Joe was needling Superstar by telling him that he could hold him back with one finger. We all laughed because Joe was in his 80s at the time and weighed all of 140 pounds. Billy Graham was around 35 years old and stood about six feet three inches tall at a weight of over 270 pounds, complete with 22-inch arms and a tape-snapping 60-inch chest. He had a great physique. As a wrestling superstar noted for his physical rather than technical abilities, Billy was also extremely strong.

"Billy, you try to walk toward me and I will hold you back using only one finger," Joe said with a twinkle in his dark eyes. "Now, Joe," Billy replied, trying to show great patience with the older gentleman, "I don't want to hurt you." "Don't worry about hurting me, young fellow," Joe retorted. "Just try to walk." Mighty Joe then quickly stepped in front of Billy Graham and put his index finger across the bridge of the big man's nose, on the point where it joins the skull. Looking Billy directly in the eyes and leaning toward him slightly, he planted his feet on the linoleum tiles and never moved an inch. With great effort Billy tried to push forward, but could not. He grunted and strained and pushed, but he couldn't move an inch. Red-faced and breathing hard, he finally gave up. I was amazed and figured there must have been some kind of trick to this. I suggested a rematch with a twist. "Billy, you hold Joe back the same way," I offered. "Sure, Dan," Billy responded, before lifting his huge right hand and placing an index finger the size of a small banana on the bridge of Joe Greenstein's nose. Joe laughed, looked Billy in the eye and almost walked through him. After several more tries to stop Joe, Billy gave up. He was as confused as I was and could not figure out how Joe did it. We never found out and had to chalk it up to Joe's great strength and mental control. Billy is the second 'Hymie' in my life, a term I call him out of affection. He is a good and warm, close friend. You will hear more about him in this chapter.

Following his wife's death, Joe Greenstein slipped into a deep depression. Often he would talk about death and then one day, during an interview he and I were having with a *New York Post* reporter, Joe reached into his trouser pocket and took out a small bottle. He spoke about missing his wife so much and that he planned to end it all by drinking poison contained in that bottle. The reporter and I both gasped and I began to talk rapidly to change his mind. Joe remained disconsolate, but put the bottle away. After that, he often took out the bottle in my presence and spoke of killing himself. "Joe," I would say, "You are the Mighty Atom, Joe Greenstein. Are you a man or a mouse? Do you want people who knew you to say: 'Joe must have been crazy to kill himself.' That's what they are going to say. Do you want that?" "No, Danny, I don't want my friends to think I was crazy." So, he would put the little bottle away again.

Joe never used that poison, if it really was poison. He died of cancer a few years later in 1977, at age 84. A fighter to the last, Joe continued to entertain with his strength. One of the last times we appeared together was on Dennis James' Cerebral Palsy Television Show where Joe performed some of his last public shows of strength. The Mighty Atom, known all over the world, will be remembered by many, but especially by bodybuilders and strength athletes. He proved the power of mind over muscle.

A Close Bond: Dan and Joe Greenstein shared a bond as strongmen and friends.

One of wrestling's biggest names, Superstar Billy Graham, competed in my 1975 WBBG Pro Mr. America and came seventh, winning best-developed arms. At his very best he looked like a Greek God and had a fantastic physique. In fact, when he trained with Arnold back when the Oak was starting out in the U.S., everyone looked up to Superstar as being the strongest man at Gold's Gym, California. He also trained with me in my Lynbrook, Long Island gym, and I gave him his own key. Most mornings I would be there to watch him train with massive poundage's. He would often bench press over 500 pounds and threw the 100 pound dumbbells around like they were toothpicks. Before then he lived in Dallas, Texas, and planned a move to New York. So my son, Mark, and then son in law Scott Epstein, a wrestling promoter who also helped me to promote some of my WBBG events, found him a place to live in Long Beach, Long Island. And that is where he stayed for about six months before he became a wrestling superstar. Then he was on the road all the time. We remained good friends and, today, all I have to do is call Billy and say, "Is this Hymie?" and he will know who is speaking. He wrote me a very nice tribute for my recent induction into the Jewish Sports Hall of Fame. What he said really touched me and brought back fond memories of our times together:

"Congratulations sir for being inducted into the National Jewish Sports Hall of Fame. Your commitment to the world of bodybuilding is unmatched. I will never forget the countless hours of gut wrenching training I have done under your watchful eye. Your enormous knowledge of the iron game is unsurpassed. Without a doubt, you Dan are a living legend in bodybuilding, having been on the cutting edge of training techniques and nutritional information that helped create many top stars that became legends themselves. I can't thank you enough for the training knowledge you passed on to me. There is no question that your mentoring helped me to attain the greatest physique in the history of professional wrestling. Your friendship and mentoring is something that is priceless."

Superstar was one of the nicest talents I worked with and had the pleasure of knowing. Actually Hulk Hogan and other pro wrestlers would try to imitate the Superstar, which goes some way to showing how influential he was as a wrestler. Billy Graham is to my mind the greatest wrestler ever. He set the standard and all the others followed. My wife and I loved to watch him defend his title back when wrestling was big like boxing and I will never forget sitting ringside at Madison Square Garden watching the Superstar in action as he defeated opponent after opponent.

In the early 1970s I published a wrestling magazine, *Wrestling Training Illustrated* (*WTI*), and got to know all of the top guys and several of them were inducted into my WBBG Hall of Fame. One time I had Billy Graham give a speech before the great Steve Reeves was to be inducted.

Billy was the greatest, most exciting speaker I knew and his speech that day remains the best I ever heard. "Like a God descending to Earth" was how Superstar described Reeves' appearance on the bodybuilding stage. Superstar idolized Steve Reeves and spoke of how he admired him all throughout his life.

Wrestling's Best Honored: Superstar Billy Graham is inducted into the WBBG Hall of Fame in 1977. Steve Reeves (left) looks on.

I mentioned my ex-son in law Scott Epstein and how he helped to bring Superstar Billy Graham to the East Coast. Scott edited my wrestling magazine, *WTI*, was associate editor of *MTI* and *Hot Rock Magazine* and, at one point, vice president of the WBBG. I became friends with Superstar Billy Graham not long after Scott met him at my 1975 Pro Mr. America in New York City, a show Scott was helping me to promote. Hot property in the wrestling world at that point, the Superstar was promoted in *MTI* and *WTI* whenever possible and he was featured on the cover of the first two issues of *WTI*. These issues sold like crazy because at this time

Superstar was just beginning his rivalry with Bruno Sammartino, a feud that would become one of the biggest in pro wrestling history, and the fans were attracted to this new flamboyant star with the massive muscles. In fact, *WTI*, as a new wrestling magazine set record-breaking sales for those first two issues and today they are collector's items.

All in the Name of Sport: Superstar Billy Graham battered and bruised on the cover of the maiden issue of Wrestling Training Illustrated.

Bruno Sammartino was another wrestler I admired and, in 1976, he too was inducted into the WBBG Hall of Fame. When he first came to America from Italy he didn't speak much English but we eventually came to know one another quite well. Later on he told me that although he could not speak English at the time, he used to watch me on the Big Top Circus Show every Saturday. Bruno was a very nice guy and very powerful.

Dan Lurie: Heart of Steel

With the Classy one and the Atom: Dan with wrestling legend Classy Freddy Blassie (second to right), Scott Epstein (immediate right), Mark Lurie (immediate left) and Joe Greenstein at the 1977 WBBG Pro Mr. America.

The Legend: Bruno Sammartino regularly appeared in Dan's *Wrestling Training Illustrated*.

A wrestler I managed for many years was Ivan Putski, "Polish Power" as he was known. He would come to all my bodybuilding shows and he himself was a very powerfully built guy. I remember going out to dinner with Ivan after one of my contests and we discussed bodybuilding. He followed bodybuilding athletes like they were his idols - a true fan. I oversaw his training for many years and he gave me a lot of credit for helping him build his physique. When we did television shows, Ivan would give me recognition for guiding him to success and for inspiring him right from the beginning of his career.

Another bodybuilder I promoted was Tony Atlas, a massive guy with a great personality who also became a popular wrestler. He never called me Dan. He would call me "Mr. Lurie". Tony and I did many shows together. We went to schools and sporting goods stores to give posing displays and strength exhibitions. It would pay for me to bring Tony along to my promotional events, as this would help me sell a lot of equipment and he would benefit from the valuable exposure he got. The crowds loved Tony Atlas. On August 25, 2007, Tony Atlas along with 14 other greats was inducted into the WBBG International Fitness and Sports Hall of Fame. At this event Tony and I greeted each other with a huge bear hug. In all the years I have known Tony I have always called him the Ugliest Man on Earth…out of true love and respect.

Joe Bonomo was a good friend with a fine physique who inspired many people to take up bodybuilding. And like Joe Greenstein, "Superstar" Billy Graham, and Bruno Sammartino, Joe Bonomo was inducted into the WBBG Hall of Fame. Joe was a stuntman for Universal Studios in Hollywood in the 1940s and played many parts as a strongman in the movies. In later years he was a manufacturer's representative, selling and demonstrating bodybuilding equipment. Joe was very successful because he learned that marketing is not all about selling products and making money, but how close you are to the buyer. His outgoing nature and friendly manner caused him to quickly become friends with those he dealt with. He also entertained on a lavish scale at his home and on his beautiful boat and I recall enjoying many of these occasions.

Dan Lurie: Heart of Steel

Wrestling legend Tony Atlas body-slamming fellow legend Hulk Hogan!

Joe was one of the first to hire me to model for his bodybuilding courses, which he sold by direct mail in the 1940s. I was around 18 at the time and he paid me two dollars an hour, and I was very happy to pose for his pictures to get the publicity. He published a line of diet books, as well, and later when I had a gymnasium near the New York Coliseum, he was a regular member. A hip injury from his youth would sometimes bother him, so he loved to come in for a massage. The Bonomo name was known not only in bodybuilding, but also to the millions of annual visitors to Coney Island, as it was there that the Bonomo family ran their Bonomo Turkish Taffee business, known up and down the boardwalk for its sweet treats. Joe and I would get together often. I would meet him in Beverly Hills, California, and we would go to a well-known restaurant called Chasen's, where all the local movie stars ate, and he would pick up the bill. He treated me like I was his family. Joe died in 1978, in Los Angles, California, aged 77. He had left his mark on the entertainment industry by acting in 32 movies along with playing stunt-double in nine. I will also remember him as being a fine representative of the physical fitness lifestyle and a fine man.

Champions All: Joe Bonomo (second to right) with Dan, bodybuilding great Chris Dickerson and Joe "The Mighty Atom" Greenstein (immediate right).

Born Angelino Siciliano in Calabria, Italy, 1893, Charles Atlas might be the world's best-known bodybuilder. He built his bodybuilding empire, and his reputation, on two words: "Dynamic Tension". His bodybuilding course, ghost-written by fitness expert and dear friend of mine, Dr. Frederick Tilney, asked the bodybuilder not to lift weights or do push-ups to develop muscles and strength, but simply to exercise one muscle against the other. Atlas' course was nothing more than isometrics, as we call them today. Frankly, I consider this taking the easy way out. The only way to develop muscles and strength is to tax those muscles to make them respond and it takes a lot of sweat to do this. Isometrics are nice and they do help if you are confined to a cell in a prison camp and can't otherwise exercise.

Dynamic Tension does have some merit and in its time brought a lot of attention to the role exercise can have on boosting self-esteem and improving health and well being, but most serious bodybuilders used strenuous, full-range-of-motion exercise to build their muscles. Though none of this prevented Charles Atlas' name from becoming a household word throughout the U.S. during the 1930s, '40s and '50s, and even into the 1970s. It is likely that more people back then could identify Charles Atlas easier than the President of the United States, with the possible exception of Franklin D. Roosevelt. But even the great FDR - who was elected to an unprecedented four terms in the Whitehouse - had a shorter tenure than Charles Atlas, who ruled the popular bodybuilding field for three decades and is still spoken highly of today.

Almost everyone 50 years or older with a basic understanding of health and fitness remembers the full-page ads in the men's magazines and comic books showing a thin young man on the beach having sand kicked in his face by a big, burly fellow, while his girl helplessly looks on. The caption reads: "I was a 97-pound weakling". The ad, which showed the "skinny" man's transformation from zero to hero, to where *he* was doing the sand-kicking, also included a photo of Charles Atlas as a muscular bodybuilder and a statement that he owed his title "The World's Most Perfectly Developed Man" to his system of Dynamic Tension. The ad offered the same opportunity to the reader and a coupon was attached. This advertising approach worked wonders as many young men bought the Dynamic Tension course in the hopes that they too would build a body like Atlas to do a bit of their own "sand kicking". As much as I disagreed with Atlas' ideas on strength and health, I respected him greatly as he did stir up a lot of interest in a little-known activity called bodybuilding, which led to it's widespread acceptance as an excellent way to improve health and fitness, which gave people like myself careers in the industry.

Charles Atlas was one of the judges at my 1945 Mr. New York contest. I admired him so much that I had arranged for him to be inducted into the WBBG Physical Fitness Hall of Fame in September of 1972. Unfortunately he had to decline because of business responsibilities in Florida. He died less than three months later on December 23. I was the only one from the bodybuilding field present at his funeral at the Rockville Centre, Long Island, where I gave his Hall of Fame plaque to his sons. They were happy that their father had been honored in such a way, a fitting tribute to a life spent helping people get into shape. Among my many memories of Charles Atlas is talking with him at his home in Point Lookout in Nassau, Long Island. We would run along the beach together and he always treated me nice. Throughout his life, Charles helped many thousands to build their bodies. And he was definitely onto something with his approach. For one thing it was a lot easier to ship paper courses of the Dynamic Tension Approach than to pack and cart heavy weights. Clearly Atlas was a smart man. He was also a gentleman.

I mentioned that Charles Atlas won the title of "The World's Most Perfectly Developed Man". Well he gained this title from a *Police Gazette Magazine* contest run by Bernarr Macfadden. I know this story because I knew Macfadden personally and was, for a few years, associate editor of his magazine, *Physical Culture*. The *Police Gazette* depended heavily on photographs, so Macfadden decided to run a photo contest open to all readers. Contestants would simply send a photo and the best would be given a physique title. Charles Atlas won the first of these contests, "The World's Most Beautiful Man" in 1921. The following year he won Macfadden's "World Most Perfectly Developed Man" and his title was officially awarded at Madison Square Garden.

Bernarr Macfadden, called the "Father of Physical Fitness" in large part because of his famous books and magazines, was, along with being a supporter of bodybuilding as a means to achieve health and fitness, a millionaire when I knew him in the 1940s. At the time I met him he was 77 years young and still in top shape after decades of devoted weight training. He owned the Deauville Hotel in Miami Beach, Florida, and later ran for governor of this state. Macfadden also owned a chain of restaurants in the West specializing in health foods. The gimmick that made these popular was his insistence that the person eating the meal pay what they thought it was worth. Of course all his meals were healthy and in keeping with his views on health, Bernarr would found many "healthatoriums" in the Eastern and Midwestern states, places that offered educational programs such as "The Physical Culture Training School".

I remember walking along Broadway in New York City with Mr. Macfadden, then in his 80s. He always took giant steps, although, at around five feet six inches he was not particularly tall. "Please, Mr. Macfadden, do you have to take such big steps?" I would plead with him. "After all, I'm not as young as you are and find it difficult to keep up with you." This would please his ego and he would smile. I also recall Macfadden was so pleased to be selected as an honored Chairman at my 1945 Mr. New York City bodybuilding show that he later sent me a $1,000 donation. Quite often he would take me to lunch at the New York Athletic Club in Central Park South. He would talk on many different subjects and we spoke for many hours on health and fitness. He was a dynamic man. To give you an idea of just what kind of man Bernarr Macfadden was, he once parachuted from an airplane when he was in his 80s just to show that parachute jumping was not harmful to the heart. He had never done a parachute jump before, but this one got his point across. In his later years he became quite eccentric and began burying his money in cash on his estate in upper New York State. I'm not sure whether his heirs ever found the money, but I heard the property had been dug up in a number of places. He also attempted to found his own religion, "Cosmotarianism", based on his physical culture ideas. He felt this new belief would enable him to reach age 150. Some people thought some of his ideas were strange but most will agree that he was a health and fitness revolutionary. I really admired him and consider him the first influential bodybuilding educator and trainer. He certainly influenced me early in my career.

Frederick Tilney was another man who influenced me with many of his views on health and fitness. Dr. Tilney was a very smart man who probably did more than any other person in the 1940s and '50s to promote the benefits of healthy living. Dr. Tilney was often described as the world's most forceful, dynamic and inspiring lecturer on the science of healthy living, and he authored hundreds of books, articles and courses and helped others develop their own careers in the health and fitness industry. He was a very powerful writer and in 1922, ghost wrote the Dynamic Tension routines that made Charles Atlas millions.

In the 1940s Joe Weider and I would go to see him for advice and in later years he would judge at my shows. I would call him up and he would come and MC for me as well.

Healthy Living Pioneers: Frederick Tilney (seated) and Dan.

Popular American weightlifting bantamweight Joe Dipietro was my roommate in Los Angeles at the time of my second Mr. America appearance in 1943. Back then the Mr. America also included competitive weightlifting, so bodybuilders and weightlifters would get to know each other quite well. Joe and I paid around two dollars a night for our shared room at the YMCA and became good friends. He was a dwarf of around three feet tall, and he was very strong. He weighed about 112 pounds and could press over 200 pounds – an extremely powerful man.

Joe grew up with a close friend in his hometown of Paterson, New Jersey, whose name he did not tell me right away. I didn't give this a second thought until Joe asked me take him to visit this friend during our stay in California. So I arranged a rental car and off we went. He gave me directions and I drove. I had no idea at the time but Joe's friend was Lou Costello from Abbot and Costello fame. When we met I was surprised to see this one-time screen legend. At first I thought he had infantile paralysis but it turns out he had rheumatic fever. They pushed him around his spacious new home in Beverly Hills in a hospital bed. From room to room he would go in his bed. Despite his condition, Lou was in great spirits that day. At one point I went to take a souvenir from the house and over a loud speaker came, "Put that down!" Lou had a control speaker in his master bedroom and listened into and could see what was going on in every room of the house. At this time I also recall his wife, Annie, busy in the kitchen cooking up a big Italian meal.

Lou's wife took Joe and I for a tour around the house. As we made our way outside I noticed the pool house had a giant fifteen-foot key on its twenty-foot roof. Very strange I thought. His garden was weirder still: as a joke Lou planted liquor bottles instead of flowers. As we toured the section I took many photos. I even had one of myself taken on the diving board pretending to dive into his huge pool. For me this moment will forever be combined with great sadness: beside the pool was a baby carriage and inside was Lou's baby son, Lou Junior, who was just days short of his first birthday. It turns out that a few days after we left, Lou Junior was again put in the same spot and had crawled out of his carriage into the pool and drowned. Later I developed the film. The haunting image of Lou Junior in his carriage is one I will never forget. The photo showed the carriage to be in the same position it was the day he drowned. People who knew Lou say he never recovered from the loss of his son. I spoke with Lou's daughter Chris a while back and she told me that a special memorial had been made for Lou in his hometown of Patterson, New Jersey.

Lou Costello will always be remembered for his acting talents. From the 1940s through the '50s Lou starred in nearly 40 movies. In 1959, just three days short of his 53rd birthday, he died of a heart attack doing what he did best: acting.

People

Lou Costello with his comedic partner Bud Abbot

Over the years I have met many great weightlifters. One man who ranks as one of the best ever is John Davis, the unbeatable African American heavyweight who dominated his class from the late 1930s through to the early '50s. Winning his first weightlifting World Championship in Vienna at the age of 18, along with five more of these titles, and Olympic gold medals in 1948 and 1952, made John the most respected lifter of his time. These achievements along with his time competing on Bob Hoffman's York lifting team for many years had built him a great physique that appealed to bodybuilding fans as much as his weightlifting accomplishments did to the Olympic sport's aficionados. In fact, Johnny did once compete in the Mr. America, in 1940, where he won the best back award and, around that time, had many pictures taken by my early photographer, Earle Forbes. If John continued to compete in bodybuilding I think he might have won the Mr. America because he was a Bob Hoffman sponsored athlete, and because he had a very good physique.

I mentioned earlier that weightlifting back at the Adonis Health Club with my coach Hy Schaeffer formed a large part of my early training life. It was at this time I competed with John Davis when he was just starting out. He won this contest, while I discovered competitive weightlifting was not for me: it took too long and I found it boring. I would meet Johnny again. In the '40s when my barbell business was in full swing, John would pass by my house at 1729 Rockaway Parkway every day in the trolley car he worked on as a conductor. As I sat on my front porch reading business correspondence on my little box, he would ring his gong bell as he passed and we would wave to each other. In the hot weather my shirt would come off and I would spend much of my time out the front after many hours of packaging and shipping barbells from my parents' basement. This went on for years. John and I shared a bond as weightlifters, as members of a brotherhood of iron. Johnny had a great operatic singing voice and there were times we would meet at Lon Hanagan's photo studio and sing together while Lon played the piano. I loved and admired Johnny Davis; he was always a true gentleman.

Many entertainment greats have been honored in my Physical Fitness Hall of Fame. Among these are former Tarzans' Johnny Weismuller and Buster Crabbe. Johnny Weismuller, the second man to play Tarzan in 1932 and star of the 1939 World's Fair Aquacade and his Tarzan successor Buster Crabbe, who also starred in the 1940 World's Fair Aquacade, and played Flash Gordon in the movies, were among my movie heroes so I was happy to induct them. They also proved the value of muscle and fitness as a film-industry asset, as both men achieved physical greatness due in large part to their physiques: Buster as a gold-medal winning Olympic 400-meters freestyle swimming champion in 1932 and Johnny as a five-time gold-medal Olympic swimming champion in the 1920s and '30s. These two had amazing physical development and helped inspire me to achieve my own.

People

Screen Heroes Inducted: Buster Crabbe (left) and Johnny Weismuller receive the keys to New York City, as arranged by Dan. Both were also inducted into the WBBG Hall of Fame in 1976.

Speaking of great screen-icons, Steve Reeves, best known for his role as Hercules in the movies bearing the same title is generally regarded as the first muscular big-screen action hero. Steve, his wife, Aline, my wife and I were good friends and we usually met for dinner whenever they were passing through New York City. Many times my wife Thelma and I visited the Reeves' marvelous ranch in the Valley Center, San Diego, area where they raised Morgan horses. The last time we visited, Mrs. Reeves, which is the way I always addressed her out of respect, prepared a delicious lunch for us.

Dan Lurie: Heart of Steel

At the Reeves' Ranch: Mrs. Aline Reeves (seated) and Mrs. Thelma Lurie feeding the Reeves' Morgan horses.

When it comes to food and the Reeves', I like recalling the time I met the couple in New York City, in 1977. The story: when the couple arrived I checked them into The Plaza Hotel and invited them to dinner. But they said they would prefer a sandwich instead and Mrs. Reeves said she loved chopped chicken liver. So we left for the nearby Stage Delicatessen, a world-famous deli often visited by showbiz people. Naturally they were made welcome, and we all had one sandwich each. The next day Earl Wilson's column in the *New York Post* carried the gossip that Steve Reeves was at the Stage and had eaten *six* corned beef sandwiches implying that he was a glutton. This upset the couple and me greatly, so I spoke to the manager of the deli, scolding him for giving this wrong information to the press. He was full of apologies and wanted to do something to make up for it. I told him Mrs. Reeves loved chopped chicken livers, so he and I arranged for a large platter of three or four pounds to be sent to The Plaza Hotel, where they were staying. I Luckily managed to have the hotel place a refrigerator in their room, and the chopped chicken liver and apologies were graciously accepted. The liver was enjoyed with crackers as a 'nightcap' each evening the Reeves' were in town.

People

Mrs Steve Reeves, Aline, is introduced at the 1977 WBBG Hall of Fame awards, where Steve Reeves was inducted.

One man who hosted Steve Reeves along with many others I had arranged for to appear on his popular television talk show was Joe Franklin. Joe was a close friend of mine who ran his highly rated Joe Franklin Show for 40 years straight, featuring over 450,000 guests during this time. With a style all of his own, Joe's good sense of humor, ability to make you feel special and, as shown by his interest in the talent I arranged for his show, appreciation for bodybuilders and bodybuilding, was a hit with me and we hit it off right away.

As his show was held daily in New York, it was the perfect way for me to showcase the talented people I worked with and it was virtually guaranteed that these men and women would receive tremendous publicity by appearing. In the many times I appeared on his show, I introduced to the millions who tuned in, greats such as Steve Reeves, Reg Park, Johnny Weismuller, Buster Crabbe, Jan Murray, Superstar Billy Graham, Chris Dickerson, and the Mighty Atom along with many other people including entertainers I would meet at my bodybuilding events held at the Concord Hotel. These people needed a break in the entertainment industry and I told them I could get them the exposure they needed. It was a chance for them to be seen and they loved it. I called Joe Franklin, Yussel, which means Joseph in the Jewish language. I would call him up and he would say, "Dan, I love you and I need you." Joe was famous for his professionalism and for being the first man to run a television talk show. It was always a pleasure to work with Joe Franklin.

Introducing the Greats: Dan introduces Steve Reeves on the Joe Franklin Show

Introducing Reg Park on the Joe Franklin Show

People

From Joe Franklin:

"I had the longest running TV talk show for over 43 years and over this time included on my show over 450,000 guests. Dan Lurie remains in my top dozen all time guests; he helped me to achieve top ratings. He brought to my studio Joe Louis, Johnny Weismuller, Buster Crabbe, Steve Reeves, Charles Atlas and many others. Mr. Lurie presented Jack Lalanne with the WBBG Hall of Fame award for his outstanding contribution to health and fitness. Dan Lurie was the very first muscleman on TV, in 1950 with the Sealtest Big Top Show. He paved the way for many to follow. Dan was a pioneer in holding bodybuilding contests, starting in 1944 with the Mr. Brooklyn championships, inspiring others to follow in his footsteps.

"My long time producer and sidekick Richie Ornstein sums it up: "Dan Lurie is the epitome of the beginning of the golden age of bodybuilding on TV and is responsible for the fitness craze that exists today along with the creation of advanced exercise equipment." Everyone from rich and famous, poor and obscure, police, fire fighters, actors, clergy and many others in every walk of life the world over had "Dan Lurie Barbells" in their hands at some time. God bless this wonderful man for sharing his knowledge and experience with us."

Joe Franklin

One of the best thrills of my life came while driving a rental car on Collins Ave, in Miami Beach, 1946. It was then I spotted in front of the Traymore Hotel my favorite singer of all time. I parked the car and introduced myself to him. I couldn't believe my eyes. It was Al Jolson "The World's Greatest Entertainer", and he was the world's first talking movie star in the picture, The Jazz Singer, made in 1927. We spoke for quite a while. He told me he also worked out and about his love for horse racing. He was very friendly. I recall he had a great tan and wore a black turtleneck shirt. After meeting Al Jolson, I was then under the impression that if I just parked in front of the high-class hotels, I would meet other famous movie stars. This was not the case. When I sing, I imitate Al Jolson doing April Showers, Swanee and Anniversary Waltz, which I sang at my wedding on February 1, 1947. My two favorite singers were Al Jolson and Mario Lanza, the great operatic tenor.

Dan Lurie: Heart of Steel

A Beautiful Voice: Al Jolson.

Dan and his Mentor: Dan with his bodybuilding
guiding light, Terry Robinson, in 1985.

Remember who got me into bodybuilding back in 1939? It was my old friend Terry Robinson. When Terry moved to Los Angeles, he worked as a fitness trainer for the movie studios and trained many top stars. Terry and Mario Lanza became close friends. Terry was the first one to get the telephone call on October 7, 1959, to say that Mario Lanza had just died from a heart attack in Rome, Italy, at the age of 38. Mario's wife Betty died five months later and Terry and Sylvia Robinson raised the four Lanza children. In 1993, one of the children, Marc, died of a heart attack at the young age of 37. Today, the three Lanza children are very close to uncle Terry and aunt Sylvia. Terry now runs the popular Century Plaza health club in Los Angeles. On March 9, 2008, he turned 92 years young. He is also an accomplished artist and his work is sold around the world.

The Great Tenor: Mario Lanza.

In the middle 1940s I became good friends with the World's Most Famous Boxing Announcer, Sam Taub. Sam had his own sports radio show and hosted me several times. Sam Taub did all of the blow-by-blow radio championship boxing fights. We both lived in Brooklyn and Sam took me under his wing. I made dozens of personal benefit appearances for many churches, hospitals, at dinners and youth clubs. We traveled with five or six great athletes in our group. One athlete was famous baseball legend, Jackie Robinson, who played for the Brooklyn Dodgers. Jackie was the first black baseball player to play in the big leagues, in 1947. By breaking the color barrier in baseball, the nation's pre-eminent sport, he courageously challenged the deeply rooted custom of racial segregation in both the North and South. In 1962 Jackie Robinson was eventfully inducted into the Baseball Hall of Fame. Jackie married Rachel Issum, a nursing student in USLA. He was extremely good looking and was always humble. He passed away on October 24th, 1972 at the young age of 53. I enjoyed my time touring with Jackie Robinson. What nice memories to have.

Baseball Legend: Jackie Robinson.

People

Dan and the Greats: a collage of Dan with many of the celebrities he has met and known. Jackie Robinson can be seen in picture 15, Bernarr Macfadden picture 11.

While attending Tilden High School from 1937 through to 1941, my Spanish teacher was Mr. Sam Levenson. I liked him a lot, but he flunked me in Spanish, my first year, however when I graduated Tilden I finally achieved the Spanish award. When I visited Los Angeles in 1943, Sam Levenson gave me a letter of Introduction to his friend, one of America's greatest music composers, Ira Gershwin, brother of George Gershwin and co-writer of Rhapsody in Blue. Ira told me he began as a cashier for his father's Turkish baths in Brooklyn.

About Sam Levenson: he wrote the best-seller ' Sex and the Single Child " in 1969 plus many other best sellers. Sam Levenson was an American humorist, writer, television host and journalist. He also appeared on The Ed Sullivan television show 21 times, a show he also had me appear on as Sealtest Dan, The Muscle Man. On one of Sam Levenson's television shows, I appeared with Rocky Graziano, who I had known for some time. We ate at the same restaurants in Brooklyn. Rocky, whose real name was Thomas Rocco Barbella, was considered one of the greatest knockout artists in boxing history: in his 83 pro fights, he had 52 knockouts. After this show, Rocky's young son Junior wanted to meet Sealtest Dan. The first question he asked was, "Daddy, can you beat up Sealtest Dan?" Without hesitating I said, "Son your daddy is much stronger than I and could knock me out with one punch." Rocky smiled. He liked my response. When they made the movie "somebody up there loves me", Paul Newman played Rocky. Rocky died on May 22, 1990 at age 68.

The second WBBG inducted Tarzan, Buster Crabbe, also served as a judge for some of the bodybuilding shows and competitions I ran at my old friend Ray Parker's Concord Hotel on Kiamesha Lake, New York. It was at the Concord that I first tried skiing, an activity that would allow me to literally run into another famous entertainer. My son Mark likes to ski and while watching him I began to think: *I'm an athlete and in excellent physical shape. Why can't I ski?* Before then I had always heard of skiers breaking arms and legs and decided to stay away from that sport partly for this reason. *Who needs it?* I thought. "If I break a limb, I will jeopardize my bodybuilding training," I would always say. But Mark's success on the slopes aroused an interest, then an urge to try a downhill plunge on those barrel staves.

The next afternoon I gingerly placed on my skis and had Mark give me a few pointers before I swooped down the small hill in front of the Concord Hotel. I had no trouble staying on my feet and enjoyed the exhilaration of cold air in my face and the feeling of great speed on the slope. My enthusiasm increased. And when my other family members headed for the indoor pool, I chose to continue skiing down that little slope. My form improved. My willingness to improve and to endure the conditions remained, so bright and early the next morning Mark and I quickly placed on our skis and decided to try the Big Hill. Not knowing much about trail conditions, I didn't realize that the early morning sub-freezing temperatures had turned that light, fluffy snow into surface ice. To slow or stop on such a surface the experienced skier has to snowplow, something I had not been taught.

I started down that hill and didn't get 25 feet before I fell. "Well," I said to Mark, brushing snow off myself, "I guess everyone has to experience a fall at some point." So, back on the skis I got and, after a short distance, fell again. Not realizing that the icy surface was doing me in, I picked myself up and continued. This time I stayed up and kept gaining speed. Halfway down the hill I spotted another skier right in front of me, going slowly and carefully taking his time. I kept gaining on him and, finally realizing I was going to hit him, braced myself and yelled. We both went down in a tangle of legs, skis, arms and poles. The other fellow finally freed himself from the tangle, struggled to his feet, and said: "What'sa matter with you. Are you blind?" I was strongly tempted to reply, "No, I'm not blind. I hit you didn't I?" But, I thought it better just to apologize and get off that hill. The other fellow was Buddy Hackett, who was headlining at the Concord at the time and who was an excellent skier. I hoped to meet him again under less strained circumstances and would like to have asked him if he remembered the blind man on skis who ran into him at Kiamesha Lake. Buddy, who passed away in June 2003, starred in many popular movies of the 1950s and '60s and was especially famous for his role in the 1963 box-office smash: It's a Mad, Mad, Mad, Mad World. I would say his meeting with me confirmed to him the truth of that movie's title.

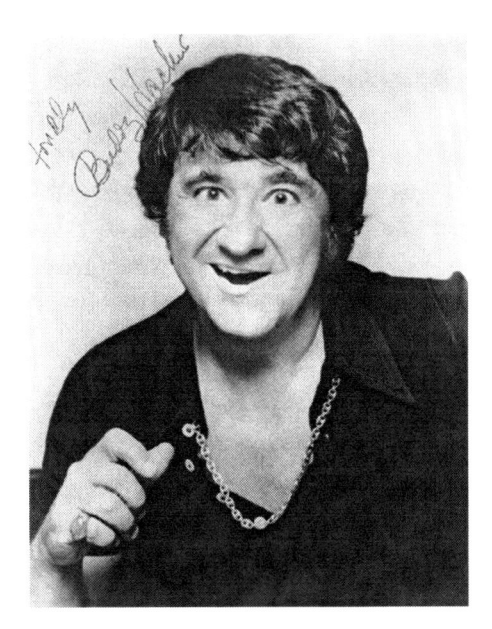

Dan Bumped into Him Once: Buddy Hackett, famous actor also known for his graceful skiing.

Sylvester Stallone is another actor who used bodybuilding to develop his image and he too was inducted into the WBBG Hall of Fame in 1977. Sly and his brother Frankie were members of my New York gym in the mid 1950s. Both were just kids at the time and had no real aspirations of fame and glory, but of course Sly went on to great things, becoming one of the movie industry's highest paid actors. When I inducted him, his brother Frankie told me that I kicked them out of my gym after one year. I responded by saying that I did not kick anyone out of my gym. It seems they both could not afford the $10 dues so they quit.

Another popular name in the bodybuilding profession is Jack Lalanne. Of smaller stature, but known for his great strength and his marvelous V-shaped torso, Jack is to my mind an incredible champion. Having been in the bodybuilding and physical fitness fields for many years, but never competing in national bodybuilding competition, Jack, who is still going strong into his 90s, was one of the first men to inspire me to extend myself in doing dips and push-ups. His own amazing success in the strength-feat arena can be partly attributed to his fine upper torso and light legs, a real advantage in doing dips and push-ups because you have a lot less weight to lift than a man with heavy, muscular legs. Inspired by Jack, I was able to win three world records: (1) The most number of push-ups in 90 minutes (1665), (2) The most number of parallel dips in 90 minutes (1225), and (3) a lift of 285 pounds with one hand overhead – all at a bodyweight of 165 pounds. The way I achieved the first and second of these records was to work with a partner. For every one push up my partner did, I would do two; for every two he did, I would do four, and so on in geometric progression. In this way I forced myself to keep up with him while doing many more push-ups and dips.

The Jack Lalanne spas, which were all over the U.S.A, were very nearly the Dan Lurie spas. Harry Schwartz, who set up and financed the chain in New York, considered two people to connect the spas to bodybuilding, to identify them with bodybuilders and the bodybuilding market: one was Jack Lalanne, the other myself. Both of us were well known, both television personalities, but at the time Jack had a small-screen exercise class that catered to women. This swung Schwartz's advertising agency to use Jack Lalanne's name on his spas because he figured they would attract more women. It was thought they would be more familiar with the Lalanne name because of his television show. In 1978 I presented Jack Lalanne with the WBBG Hall of Fame award for his outstanding contribution to health and fitness. He is truly one of a kind.

The man who could not afford his gym fees: Sylvester Stallone.

Fitness Pioneers Meet: Dan arm-wrestles Jack Lalanne while Steve Reeves officiates.

Vic Tanny is another well-known bodybuilding personality, particularly in the spa and gym industry. Vic was a schoolteacher in Rochester, New York, and his brother, Armand, another bodybuilder, was with the Mae West show. In the early 1940s, Vic quit teaching and moved to the West Coast to open a gym. He based the gym at Santa Monica Beach, California, and Armand soon joined him. In the 1950s he really expanded his operations. In addition to his gym, Vic built exercise facilities on the public beach: parallel bars, chinning bars and the like that attracted bodybuilders. They could work out on the beach for free, and they did, in droves. The area soon became known as Muscle Beach. It was years later that financial backers made Vic Tanny's name nationally known by building health spas bearing his name - the Vic Tanny Centers - across the country. It was after I won my America's Most Muscular Man titles that I met Vic at his gym in Santa Monica. He, along with all of the judges from the last of these contests, made out a citation and all signed it to show that I was the winner of America's Most Muscular Man. Vic's gyms were very plush with mirrors and carpets. Even my gyms were nothing fancy, the rugged type where people got down to the business of training. His were more upmarket. He became so big that half his managers were stealing money from him. In those days there were no real controls and staff would just put the money in their pocket and that would be that. Vic, who died in 1985, will go down in history as being the first big modern gym pioneer.

I mentioned that Armand Tanny was with the Mae West show. Mae West is also a member of the WBBG Physical Fitness Hall of Fame, and in 1975 was given the title WBBG Sexiest Woman of the Century. When I visited Mae West in her Beverly Hills apartment to present her with this award, we talked about Brooklyn, where she was born and first appeared onstage at the age of eight. Miss West, who achieved fame as an actress, playwright, screenwriter and national sex symbol from the early 1930s through to the late '70s, told me that she always received a warm welcome in neighborhood theaters, regardless of the crowd's ethnicity because she always did her homework and sang the audience's favorite song first: Italian, Irish, Jewish, Polish… and so on. Mae West reminisced about her father, Battling Jack, who was a weightlifter. As a girl, she always thought he worked in an iron shop because he would tell her that he was going out to "lift iron." Miss West's father, who used to rent horses and wagons from my Grandfather, Nathan Lurie, was a boxer and weight trainer too, so she seemed quite at home with the chrome-plated dumbbells I presented to her as an induction gift.

The second time my wife and I visited Mae, we spent about three hours with her. Miss West looked great, and at the age of 83, had hardly a wrinkle and the complexion of a teenager. She always ate health foods and exercised regularly to stay in top physical shape. Thelma and Mae became good friends because they both came from Brownsville and would talk about their experiences growing up there. Mae West died in 1980 at age 87, but by all accounts still possessed the beauty that made her famous, looks that earned her many accolades including the WBBG Sexiest Woman of the Century title.

Screen Icon: Dan would go up to see the WBBG Sexiest Woman of the Century, Mae West.

Along with bodybuilding and wrestling, I have always had a big interest in boxing. One boxer I didn't like all that much as a person but did admire for his excellent ring craft was Al "Bummy" Davis. I met Al when I first began training as a boxer at age 13 at Ferkies Gym, Brooklyn, in the mid-'30s - before my bodybuilding career took off. He was 21 at the time and over the three years I trained at Ferkie's I would watch him train whenever I got the chance. In his pro career he won 66 of his fights and scored 44 knockouts, many of these coming by way of his huge left hook. I sold soda and ice cream at the Canarsie outside boxing arenas during this time, so was able to watch many of Al's fights, and saw him knock out opponent after opponent. I was so impressed with his style that I began to copy it and eventually got so strong that, at 115 pounds, I managed to knock out a heavyweight fighter in the ring, with the same left hook he was famous for. I improved quite a bit just watching Al fight. Although I thought Al was a great boxer, I didn't care for the way he conducted himself as he was always cussing and talking himself up. In 2003, Al was listed in Ring Magazine as one of the 100 greatest punchers in boxing history. He died too young at age 27: he tried to stop an armed robbery at a bar on Remsen and Ditmas Avenue in Brooklyn, with his bare hands. He was shot, and died instantly.

Another of my Hall of Fame members is Joe Louis, the champion boxer who dominated the heavyweight division from 1937 to 1948, defending his title 25 times and facing all-comers. He was inducted into the WBBG in 1977 and it was a personal honor for me to meet this great man - one of the greatest heavyweight boxing champions ever - and his lovely wife, Martha, and to have him join the WBBG Hall of Fame. He was well liked in New York City by those who knew of him and saw him in the street and he never failed to stop and talk with his fans: a great man with a big right hand and an even larger heart.

People

Boxing Heavyweight Meets Bodybuilding Heavyweights: Dan with Joe Louis (left), Steve Reeves (center) and Serge Nubret at the 1977 WBBG Hall of Fame awards. Seated are Mrs Joe Louis (left), Aline Reeves (center) and Mrs Serge Nubret (Jackilyn).

Boxing Legend Inducted: Dan meeting boxing great Joe Louis, and his wife, Marva.

Sonny Liston was another boxing champion I admired and had the good fortune of meeting. When I met him in 1963, I was in Miami, Florida, and in very good shape. He was the Heavyweight Boxing Champion of the World and one of the most feared fighters of all time. When we met on the street near Bernarr Macfadden's Deauville Hotel, I had just come off the beach. At around 200 pounds solid, at age 40, my muscular bodyweight was approaching its peak and as I approached Sonny, a massive sight, he said, "Oh my God. I have never seen arms that big. Who are you?" We spoke for a while and he was very nice. Of course I was thrilled that a man of Sonny's stature was admiring my physique. He was just a massive, rugged guy, one of the biggest men in boxing.

Jack Dempsey, another great heavyweight-boxing champion, was a regular at sports dinners I attended. At these dinners we discussed boxing and he would reminisce about his days as Heavyweight Champion, where he dominated the sport between 1919 and 1926. At the time I was publishing my magazine, *Boxing Training Illustrated*, and Jack Dempsey would give me valuable input. Back then - in the 1960s - he was older than me and well past his prime but he still had a commanding presence.

Talking about Miami reminds me of my early bodybuilding days when I used to go there on business in the '40s. One of the regular entertainers there at the time was a young fellow, a comedian who would always poke fun at my muscles whenever he'd see me. I would then make fun at how skinny he was as he was well over six feet tall and only around 120 pounds. These regular, friendly jibes, eventually led to a friendship and his taking up lifting weights to build up his "skinny" body. I speak of the famous comedian Jan Murray, who became a good friend, and would present awards at my bodybuilding shows. In fact, his beautiful wife Pearl worked for me as head of a women's spa I owned for over three years. I would say to Jan, "You are in show business and need to look like you are a man, not like you are dying." Without my knowing he went and trained with Sig Klein in Klein's gym and built his body

People

to a respectable size, adding around 60 pounds. Jan awarded the winner's trophy at my 1948 Mr. Eastern America contest.

The third 'Hymie' in my life is Alan Burke, the well-known New York television talk show personality, who, from 1966 to 1969, pioneered the confrontational style of hosting where he would attack or insult his guests for the shock value it produced. We met in 1968 when he interviewed a group of bodybuilders and myself before one of my WBBG contests. I was warned that he liked talking down to his guests, but he was good to us and it formed the beginning of a friendship that has lasted many years. Alan hosted our Hall of Fame dinner presentations many times. He emceed WBBG contests and he even personally advised one of my daughter's and her husband in times of marital difficulty, which eventually helped them solve their problems. This, and his loyalty, has caused me to regard Alan and his family with great affection.

Dan Influenced Him to Build His Physique: comedian, Jan Murray.

Another entertainer I admired for his longevity as a performer and the wide range of roles he played on television, radio and the big screen was George Burns who, interestingly enough, became better known as an actor after his seventh decade. I inducted George as the "Sexiest Man of the Century" into the WBBG Hall of Fame at Caesars Palace,

Dan Lurie: Heart of Steel

Atlantic City, 1991. Mae West he wasn't, but I figured such a title would appeal to his sense of humor. At the time, George was 98 and still making his signature wisecracks. With trademark cigar and raised eyebrow, he was a big hit with everyone there that night. After he accepted his award we arm-wrestled, and he beat me.

A story George Burns would regularly tell during his many stage appearances concerned a contest his CBS radio show was running. When he and Gracie Allen first ran their George and Gracie radio show they were charged with finding a group to play this show's music. Having decided on two finalists they eventually chose a group called The Smoothies, headed by my old friend Charlie Ryan, and featuring his brother Little Ryan and sister Babs. The other finalist was an unknown singer. Both finalists wanted 300 dollars a week to perform. "As a smart businessman," George opted for the Smoothies for 300 dollars a week, as he would get three for the price of one. This unknown performer who missed out was Frank Sinatra.

Shock Value: Dan promotes one of his bodybuilders, Elliot Gilchrist, on the Alan Burke Show in 1975. Alan is standing mid-stage. Elliot began competing internationally in 1966 (1st place at the IFBB Mr. World) and continued competing into the 21st century (1st place at the NPC Southern States Master's 70-plus division)!

People

Gracie Allen and George Burns on CBS Radio.

Another Legend Honored: George Burns is inducted into the WBBG Hall of Fame as "The Sexiest Man of the Century".

241

Beating America's Most Muscular: George Burns
beats Dan in an arm-wrestling match.

Frank Sinatra

People

The Smoothies: (left to right) Charlie Ryan, Babs Ryan and Little Ryan

New York's Best: Dan awards John Flamino, winner of the WBBG best-built fireman competition. Pictured second to right is New York State Governor, David Patterson.

243

Dan hams it up on stage at his best built fireman contest!

One of America's best-known hosts and presenters is Regis Philbin, who has appeared on television since the 1950s and is still going strong today at age 76. I honored Regis in 1994 for being Television's Most Physically Fit Man in Show Business. As a lifetime devotee to the iron, Regis credits bodybuilding for the good health and fitness he has enjoyed throughout his career. I have known Regis for over 60 years. In fact, Regis' father brought him a 110-pound Dan Lurie barbell set when he was 16, and he never lost his interest in bodybuilding. He even kept a 310-pound Olympic Dan Lurie barbell set on his show to be used by featured bodybuilders and weightlifters. Over the years I would appear for Regis many times, often bringing bodybuilders I promoted to pose down for the cameras. I arm wrestled Regis in 1984 and, of course, he beat me - with two hands.

People

Best Presenter Meets Best Physique: Regis poses down with New York City's best-built fireman, John Flamino.

I mentioned my exercise equipment would be frequently used on the Regis Philbin show for years, but it appears this was not the only high-profile role it would play. One of the most popular actors of the 1950s and '60s and legendary public figure of the 20th century is Marilyn Monroe and it was interesting for me to note that she too may have used my exercise equipment to maintain her beautiful figure. Before she peaked as an actor, staring in the hit movies *Gentlemen Prefer Blonds* and *Some Like it Hot*, she lived in New York City and stayed at a rooming house, where she paid 10 dollars a week for room and board. I came across a photo that showed her room and a familiar sight caught my eye: after she had left her tiny room, her only possessions were a broken down suitcase and a pair of Dan Lurie dumbbells and sit-up board. The photo captured these. I never met Marilyn but would have loved to – her acting talent and exquisite beauty were mesmerizing. Her taste in exercise equipment was also to be admired.

Marilyn Monroe

One screen beauty I did meet was Susan Hayward. Susan was born on June 1930 in Brooklyn and acted in over 60 movies from the late 1930s to the early '70s; she won an Academy Award in 1958 for Best Actress in a Leading Role for her realistic portrayal of Californian killer, Barbara Graham, in *I Want to Live*. In 1944 I appeared on the famous W.O.R radio show, Hobby Lobby, hosted by Dave Elman and it was there I met Susan, at the time a pretty model and aspiring actress (it was her hobby). My favorite pastime was, of course, bodybuilding, and while it was arranged for me to lift 200 pounds overhead with one hand, something that was becoming a bit of a habit, Susan would speak about her acting dreams. I told her she could become a movie star if she put her mind to it. At the time we were both beginning our careers, two poor kids from Brooklyn. Our bond was immediate. Susan did go on to achieve acting success, and when Hollywood began a nationwide, highly publicized search for a beauty to play Scarlet O Hara in Gone with the Wind, she was considered along with eventual choice, Vivien Leigh.

Screen Beauty: Susan Hayward

Dan Lurie: Heart of Steel

Dan's Hobby: Dan appearing on Hobby Lobby.

Along with sports personalities and entertainers, I have met and honored many politicians. Senator Jacob Javits, a very famous New York politician, once ran for re-election by seeking votes from as many sportspeople as he could find. He found me and I was invited to sit with him for publicity pictures. During the photo session I had with me my wife and daughter, who also took part, and Javits and I hit it off very well. We became friends for many years and eventually I inducted him into the WBBG Hall of Fame. As I was about to induct him he said to hold off for the following year, 1978, because he had business in Washington. He died that year. To honor this great man the City of New York named a newly built convention center after him. At the 1986 opening I presented a plaque - that I had inscribed a year earlier with Jacob Javits' name - to his wife and family members. Javits and I had many conversations together and I remember him being very knowledgeable and charming.

People

Dan and the Senator: Dan presenting an award to Jacob Javits. Dan's wife Thelma is in attendance.

Press Pass: Dan at the 1986 opening of the Jacob Javits Convention Center, New York City. Many thousands attended this occasion.

Dan Lurie: Heart of Steel

The Javits Family: (Left to right) senator Jacob Javits's daughter, wife Marion, son Josh and his wife, at the opening of the Jacob Javits Convention Center, 1986.

(from left to right) David Dinkins, Dan and Abe Beame - Both Dinkins and Beame were New York City Mayors.

People

New York mayor Abe Beame was with me when I hosted Steve Reeves in 1977. Around this time I took Steve Reeves to Mayor Beame to have Reeves presented with the keys to the city of New York. When Joe Louis was honored, at the same time as Reeves, and the day after Abe Beame lost the election over Ed Koch, Louis, a small entourage and myself went to Abe's office. "Mayor Beame has cancelled all of his appointments" officials told us, but they happily welcomed us in. I said, "Tell Mr. Beame that I am thrilled to be here for him and Joe Louis has come all the way from Detroit to see him." So he led us into his office and said that as a kid he considered Joe Louis to be his idol. He was so happy to see Joe Louis. At only five feet two inches Abe Beame was of short stature, but was known as a powerful mayor who presided over New York City from 1974 to 1977.

David Dinkins, Abe Beame and Dan

Ed Koch, Mayor of New York from 1978 to 1989 is probably one of the best-known United States Representatives. A trained lawyer, Ed was well known for his attention to detail. He was also credited for returning fiscal stability to New York City after it was almost forced into bankruptcy in the mid 1970s. I used to run the best-built policeman, sanitation worker and fireman contests and would bring all the winners to Ed's office to have photos taken. I admired Ed, himself a bodybuilding fan.

Mayor Abe Beame with (left to right) Dan,
Buster Crabbe and Johnny Weismuller

Honoring the Mayor: New York Mayor Ed Koch receives a special WBBG award at City Hall. Here he is introduced to New York's best-built fireman, John Flamino (on Ed's immediate left). Also in attendance are Mark Lurie (left) and New York City's Fire Commissioner (right).

New Yorker Howard Rubinstein is one of the biggest public relations consultants in the world. He handled the Yankee Stadium and all the publicity for Madison Square Garden events. He also helped big movie stars and high flyers such as Donald Trump with publicity. As a man with much power, Howard could turn public opinion. One time New York's The Daily Mirror newspaper sought to help fight the war on drugs and enlisted Howard as a public relations man to support their cause. He had known me since I was a kid, so he called and asked me to come to breakfast with him to discuss the dangers of recreational drugs so people could get the facts from a health industry insider. He had come up with a slogan and asked me if it was okay to use what he described as a simple, but powerful message: "Dan Lurie says be strong and say no to drugs". They made up thousands of T-shirts emblazoned with this slogan and gave them out. Whether it did any good, I'm not sure, but it was nice to help in the fight against drugs, something I have continued doing in one form or another ever since. It was during this promotion I met Rudy Giuliani, who would become mayor of New York City in 1994. I did an interview with Rudy Giuliani on how he kept himself physically fit and I did some articles on him for my bodybuilding magazines.

Publicity Man: Howard Rubinstein

Dan Lurie: Heart of Steel

Dan and Rudy Giuliani.

On February 26,1946, I met one of the greatest political leaders of all time. It was during a business trip with Joe Weider - where we stayed at Dr. Frederick Tilney's home in Miami, Florida for two weeks - that I met a man who was to be honored at the Orange Bowl at this time, a fellow called Winston Churchill, Prime Minister of the United Kingdom during Word War II. As he left after making his speech and receiving his award, an honorary Doctorate in Law, he approached a box of around 25 celebrities and shook the hands of every one of these people. Dr. Tilney arranged to have me be among the celebrities. In meeting Winston Churchill I asked him how he was. He replied, "Well, thank you." I remember squeezing his hand and I could feel the great strength in his handshake.

I have been to Israel 13 times. Those who knew me best in Israel were the taxi drivers. They became my friends, as I would request certain drivers depending on where I was going. I would always call ahead to ensure I got someone I knew. Three times before leaving, I arranged through the New York City consulate to have awards made to honor outstanding dignitaries. I presented awards to Yitzhak

Shamir, who served as Prime Minister from 1983 to 1984 and from 1986 to 1992, Shimon Peres, former Israeli Minister of Foreign Affairs, and Menachem Begin, sixth Prime Minister of Israel and Nobel Peace Prize recipient. Of these three, Shimon Peres was, by his own estimation, an unlikely candidate. He was a big smoker. He asked me, "Why are you giving me an award? I am no athlete." But I did some checking and discovered that when he went upstairs from one chamber to another, he would take three steps at a time. Most people think two steps are pretty good. I said, rationalizing my decision to award him, "You take three steps so you must be pretty athletic," to which he replied, "How do you know I take three steps." I told him I had spies looking into such matters.

"I could feel the great strength in his handshake".
Great 20th century leader: Winston Churchill.

Dan Lurie: Heart of Steel

Big Steps: Dan presenting a WBBG Hall of Fame award to former Israeli Prime Minister and 1994 Nobel Peace Prize recipient, Shimon Peres.

Shimon Peres

People

Nobel Peace Prize Recipient: Menachem Begin

Yitzhak Shamir was small in stature, and the least athletic of the three, but at the time I gave him an award because the Israeli government, under Shamir's directorship, chose to use restraint as the Arabs heavily bombed Israel with rockets.

Leader of Men: Yitzhak Shamir (immediate left) is inducted into the WBBG Hall of Fame.

They knew more about me in Israel when I went there than I ever would have thought because they checked on me before I went. They knew so much about me; they knew my father was in the moving business. They knew everything.

Traveling the world presenting awards became a popular activity for me and in 1977 I ventured to Monte Carlo to present an award to Prince Rainier III, but on this occasion he could not accept due to business commitments. The secretary, who I spoke to couple of years before, discussed with me the possibility of running a muscle show in a palace named The Opera House. It was so gorgeous you could host royalty there, and they often did. I figured it would have been a perfect location to hold a contest. During my phone conversation with him he said, "Well if you are interested in discussing the possibility of running your show here, write to me." I said, "Write to you? I am looking at your palace from my window. I will be flying home in three days." "Well can you be here in one hour Mr. Lurie?" The secretary was so nice. He came from the Midwest. He arranged to have me taken around the city and to see the wonderful Opera House, from where I originally wanted to run a WBBG Mr. Olympus show. We eventually made arrangements to run the WBBG Mr. Monte Carlo International, but it never worked out. They wanted to extend negotiations and I wanted to have it finalized there and then. In 1990 I extended an invitation to Prince Rainier III for induction into the WBBG as Man of the Year and I understand he was interested, but he was very ill at the time and, again, could not accept.

I was in Venice one year with my wife and in order to get from Venice to the Lido hotel on Lido Beach, we had to wait for 20 minutes for a private hotel speedboat. We saw a woman on the boat who was very beautiful and my wife said, "It is Princess Grace." Shaking my head I told her, "Come on, what would she be doing here." There were four of us on the boat, my wife and I, Princess Grace and the sailor. I would have loved to speak to her but I didn't say a word. I didn't know at the time it was Princess Grace.

People

Prince Rainier III and Princess Grace (Kelly).

Dan with some other celebrities he has met and known.

Dan and entertainment industry great, Eddie Fisher

People

Dan with David Frost: famous TV personality from the McGinnis World Hall of Records and subject of the 2009 Oscar nominated movie "Frost/Nixon".

Standing by Her Man: Thelma and Dan in the company of Mickey Hargitay and French singer Denise Darcell - backstage at the Follies Burlesque.

Mickey Hargitay and wife Jane Mansfield.

With the Dom: Dan with the great actor Dom DeLuise

People

Dan with television and movie star Jack Albertson backstage at Jack's Broadway show. Jack attended Steve Reeves' 1973 WBBG Hunter College appearance; his role was to help hide Reeves in Dan's car prior to the event.

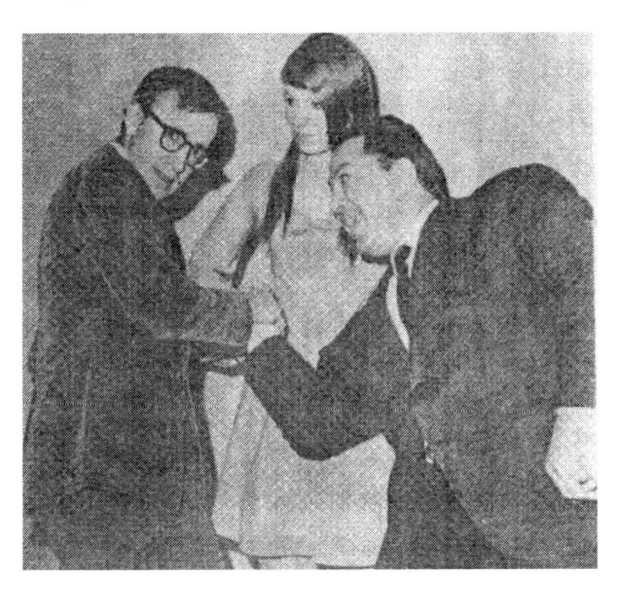

"Aren't you supposed to be a strongman?" Dan arm-wrestling Woody Allen in 1967

Dan Lurie: Heart of Steel

First Ever Screen Beauty: Dan with actress, Dagmar, first major female television star.

Cruising: Dan on an '80s cruise with Morty Minsky whose family owned the World Famous Follies Burlesque Broadway Shows. Dan and Morty remained good friends; Morty attended Dan's 60th birthday celebrations.

People

Dan and Walter Cronkite met at the Javits Convention Center opening in 1986. "Walter enjoyed keeping fit", says Dan.

As founder of the WBBG and its Hall of Fame award dinners, it has been my great pleasure to induct many great people into this distinguished group, many of which have been discussed in this chapter. Since it all began, a who's who of bodybuilding, sports, entertainment and politics has become part of the WBBG family. And the tradition continues! In 2007, 14 new inductees became members of the WBBG. Their tremendous achievements, and those of future inductees, will always be remembered through the WBBG Hall of Fame. Below is a complete list of all inductees. Congratulations to you all and thanks for the memories.

WBBG Hall of Fame Award Dinners

1968 Sigmund Klein

1967 Bill Pearl

1968 Ricky Wayne

1969 Boyer Coe

1970 Dennis Tinerino

1971	Sergio Oliva
1972	Reg Park
1973	Steve Reeves
1974	Peter Lupus Burt Reynolds
1975	Robert Redford Mae West Joe Bonomo Chris Dickerson Dave Draper The "Mighty Atom" Joe Greenstein
1976	Johnny Weissmuller Buster Crabbe Sergio Oliva Bruno Sammartino
1977	Steve Reeves Billy Graham Serge Nubret Sylvester Stallone The Greatest Boxer Joe Louis
1978	Robert Blake Clint Eastwood James Brolin Sen. Jacob Javits Jack LaLanne Jim Morris Bill Pearl Ivan Putski Chet Yorton

Special Awards to:

President Ronald Reagan

Three Prime Ministers of Israel:

-Yitzhak Shamir

-Shimon Perez

- Menachem Begin

Prince Rainier III of Monte Carlo

George Burns

Regis Philbin

Charles Atlas

Joe Franklin

Mayor Abe Beame, NYC

Mayor Ed Koch, NYC

WBBG Fitness and International Sports Hall Of Fame, August 25. 2007

Tony Atlas

Samir Bannout

Paul Bernstein

Leon Brown

John DeFendis

Kelly Everts

Bob Gajda

Warren Fredrick

Billy "Super Star" Graham

Anibal Lopez

Steve Michalik

Sergio Oliva

Harold Poole

Robby Robinson

In Memoriam Lifetime Achievement Awards
(presented at the August 25. 2007 WBBG Fitness
and International Sports Hall of Fame Awards)

Charles Atlas

John Grimek

Steve Reeves

Scribe Inducted: Ricky Wayne winning the 1970 WBBG Pro Mr. America. Wayne was also a famous bodybuilding writer.

One very famous political figure I got to know quite well was American President, Ronald Reagan: 40th President of the United States from 1981 to 1989. President Reagan represented to me the best of physical strength and endurance. As an avid follower of the great leaders of our time, men of strength and character, I decided to make a special award for the Most Physically Fit President of All Time. After much researching, I could only conclude that this man was President Reagan. Awarding him ranks as one of the greatest moments of my life.

Chapter Eleven:

The World's Most Physically Fit President Joins the WBBG

I go after the impossible. My dreams have always been big and I never place limits on what I can do. Mind over matter has always been my personal motto and this philosophy has helped me achieve many goals. So when someone tells me it can't be done, this is when I really get to work. The reward to me is in the challenge and this was certainly the case when, in early December, 1983, I sent a telegram to the Whitehouse's Presidential Office requesting a meeting with President Ronald Reagan. At this time I was known for honoring many celebrities for their health and fitness achievements, by inducting them into the WBBG Hall Of Fame. I had awarded those from many different fields – bodybuilding, wrestling, boxing, stage, screen and politics. Always one to aim for the very top, I decided to select for induction a U.S. President (to be inducted in person or in memoriam) who best lived the physical fitness lifestyle. After much researching, I came up with several names and at the top of the list was George Washington, Abraham Lincoln, Teddy Roosevelt and Ronald Reagan, all of them worthy candidates. But after researching their physical achievements, only one man came to the top of the list. That man was President Reagan. A two-term president who won in 1981 and again in 1984, President Reagan presented the perfect combination of good looks, vitality, strength and endurance, not to mention a consistent approach to exercise, a quality, I discovered, the other three lacked.

President Reagan continued training with weights while in office and had done this form of training along with a variety of other types of exercise including running, wood chopping and horseback riding, for over 50 years. All of this made him the perfect choice. Known as the "great communicator" Ronald Reagan was also a man of tremendous integrity and honor who appealed to people from all walks of life, qualities I also considered when selecting a Hall of Fame inductee. He once said: "I know in my heart that man is good, that what is right will always eventually triumph and there is purpose and worth to each and every life." This statement struck a chord with me and I knew as a president, and as a man, his human side always shone through, making him one of the most popular presidents of all time, and a man I longed to meet.

Arranging a meeting with the United States President was a major personal challenge, but I told my public relations man, Michael Beinner, that it would happen. His response was, "You are crazy, it will never happen. It does not work that way." I told him I had a way of doing things that just might get us a meeting with President Reagan. So I sent the President a telegram. Luckily, Whitehouse official and President Reagan's legal advisor David Waller, who just happened to be a runner, a recreational bodybuilder and reader of *Muscle Training Illustrated*, and who knew of my name in the industry, received it. David Waller was very happy with the idea of the President being honored with a physical fitness award from the publisher of the magazine he read. He told me they would be happy to get things rolling. So I had President Reagan's plaque made up before contacting him with the news that it would be presented at New York's Downtown Athletic Club, a very prestigious place where many awards would be presented to high achieving sporting individuals. From here the next step for me was to arrange a television press conference - for February 1984 - with the director of the Downtown Athletic Club, where we would invite the press and unveil the President's plaque. This went well and President

The World's Most Physically Fit President Joins the WBBG

Reagan was honored nicely, but when they aired it on television they used a little deception. They presented the unveiling as if the President was in the audience, taking part in the ceremony. He was clapping and applauding. He wasn't there at the time and this rankled me. I thought this was the wrong way to do things, but I knew bigger and better things were ahead. Remember, I have a way of doing things and I was determined to use my personal touch to publicize the President's achievements.

In late December 1983, while holidaying over Christmas and New Year with my family at the Concord Hotel, I suddenly received a call from my office in Brooklyn saying that they received a call from the Whitehouse wanting me to be there on February 16. *Wow, these guys don't mess around,* I thought. It had only been a few short weeks since I had first received the call from David Waller to tell me the induction was, in fact, possible. So after the unveiling and initial press announcement of President Reagan's award at the Downtown Athletic Club, which I had planned in between, there would be a proper meeting with the great man. I got to work preparing my speech and planning the visit, and after two months the day I had been longing for arrived.

The Excitement Builds: Dan outside the Whitehouse, moments before his historic meeting with President Ronald Reagan. Dan is holding Reagan's plaque.

Almost Time: Dan and President Ronald Reagan's aide, David Waller (right) - moments before Dan's meeting with Reagan.

The day of our historic visit began with Michael Beinner and myself flying out of New York to Washington D.C. After landing at Washington Airport we arrived, a short time later, at the Whitehouse where the President's officials warmly greeted us. Michael was as excited as I was to meet Reagan, as he too was a big admirer of the President. On our arrival, the first thing we were asked to do was meet with David Waller in his private office, before making our way to the Oval Office and our meeting with the President of the United States. Mr. Waller briefed us on what time we would be meeting President Reagan and how we were to address him. He told me he would speak first, before introducing me to the President. After he finished his briefing we made our way to the waiting area.

To meet the President of the United States is not an easy process. First of all there are well over 100 people who work in his department and

The World's Most Physically Fit President Joins the WBBG

to get an appointment you must be screened thoroughly by his legal team and undergo extensive briefing on what you can and cannot say and do. At the time of my meeting, the President had eight appointments a day and if you were lucky enough to make it through the Oval Office doors, you were restricted to one appointment only. There would be no second chance. So everyone who met with the President had to be sure that they had all their information in order so they could complete all their intended business, with no delays. As I waited with my purpose clearly in mind, people from international Jewish human rights organization, the Wiesenthal Center - named after Simon Wiesenthal, who was responsible for hunting down Adolf Eichmann and hundreds of other Nazi war criminals - had just finished their visit. The man who started this organization, Rabbi Marvin Hier, went in before me. Upon conclusion of his meeting he told me he was so nervous he forgot half the things he wanted to say. This made me nervous as I considered the possibility that I too might do the same. I tried to memorize my speech. Over and over it I went until I figured it was committed to memory. The excitement and exhilaration I felt moments before one of the biggest meetings I would ever have, scattered my focus, which made thinking almost impossible. I took several deep breaths and channeled my thoughts, picturing what I would say and how I would act. I held my speech notes tight as a precaution.

Finally it was time. On entering the Oval Office I was overwhelmed by the sheer size of the place. It was an otherworldly experience; I felt like I was dreaming. I had seen it - the most important office in the world - many times in pictures and on television, but nothing had prepared me for an actual meeting with the President there. The fact that we were to become a legitimate part of Whitehouse history was not lost on me as we made our way across the expansive room, past a beautiful stately grandfather clock to our right, to where the president was standing looking tremendous and powerful in his blue suit and tie. The President met me halfway and we shook hands. I told him I would give a little speech but first needed to put my glasses on. The President laughed and replied, "I understand what you mean. We all get to that age." His humour relaxed me as I put on my glasses and steadied myself, moments before the induction.

David Waller performed his introduction: "Mr. President, it is a pleasure to introduce to you Dan Lurie, publisher of *Muscle Training Illustrated*, and Michael Beinner." I began my speech: "I have something here that you are worthy of. Mr President, happy birthday, 73 years young. I am Dan Lurie, professional television strongman dedicated to bodybuilding for over 43 years, America's Most Muscular Man and record holder of 1665 push-ups in 90 minutes. The most important thing: I am a father of five children and eight lovely grandchildren." I continued, this time reading from my notes: "I am honored to be able to bring this award to you on behalf of the millions of bodybuilders and athletes around the world and the readers of *Muscle Training Illustrated*. You have inspired all American's young and not so young on how important it is to keep physically fit. Your daily workouts with barbells and muscle building machines certainly keep you in good shape. We all know how important exercise is. You have found the fountain of youth. After doing research work on all the presidents that have earned the title 'the Most Physically Fit President of All Time' only four names stand out. Six foot two, George Washington, who as a youth built himself a well-developed body. His love for chopping wood and the legendary coin tossing over the Potomac River is in all the history books. Abraham Lincoln was a strong wrestler as a youth and also a boxer. He also kept in shape by splitting over 4000 rails and he loved to do push-ups. Five foot ten, Teddy Roosevelt the 'Rough Rider'. His love for sports, hunting and exploring is well known. He was an extremely strong man." I pushed myself up on my tiptoes: "And six feet one inch President Ronald Reagan, at the young age of 73, keeps himself fit, strong and healthy and in top shape by exercising daily, chopping wood and horseback riding. I, Dan Lurie, publisher of *Muscle Training Illustrated*, and International President of the World Body Building Guild, present you the official title of the Most Physically Fit President of All Time this Thursday February 16, 1984. I would also like to induct you into the WBBG Hall of Fame, along with such greats as Joe Louis, Johnny Weissmuller, Buster Crabbe, Steve Reeves, Clint Eastwood and the Sexiest Woman of the Century, Miss Mae West. Mr. President, this is well deserving of you. It was presented in the Front Room of the Downtown Athletic Club. You really deserve it."

At this point I became quite emotional, as the whole experience was very intense and overwhelming. As a fellow American I was proud of President Reagan and all he had achieved and was impressed by the humility he showed in accepting his award. I fought to hold back tears. "The more I see you - you really do look young," I continued. "I have been in this field for many years." Also showing some emotion, President Reagan took the plaque. "Thank you very much," he said warmly. "I don't know that I am deserving of this but I am very proud." "I will tell you one thing," I said: "If you don't keep up your exercise I am going to come back and take the title away from you," much to the amusement of the President. It was hard to believe this man was 73, so robust and in such fine health. "You look great" I found myself saying. "Well I have to tell you I have never felt better," the President replied, a broad smile forming across his face. "Just keep on exercising, it is the secret to a long life, Mr. President. All I can say is God bless you, you are wonderful." The President thanked me once again before saying, "There is one record I will never try to break and that is 1665 press-ups in 90 minutes." "I never thought I would either," I replied. "As a youth, I had a heart murmur. One never knows. If you put your mind to it there is nothing you cannot accomplish. If you put your mind to it nothing can stop you. Just set your goals. And I am very proud of you and proud to be here today."

President Reagan then had his officials present Michael and myself with official Whitehouse lapel pins. I presented President Reagan with a portrait of him and myself that had been given to me by a friend of mine especially for the occasion. I felt this picture was most fitting as it portrayed the President as a strong, muscular and youthful figure, some of the qualities that convinced me to present him with his award. "I complained that the picture made me a little to heavy," I said mentioning a conversation I had with the artist. "Gee, you made the president look better than me." "Well he is certainly better looking than you," I said, giving the artist's response, which drew more laughter from the President. As he received his picture, he again thanked me and mentioned he would now be very hard to live with.

Dan Lurie: Heart of Steel

The presentation: Dan presents President Ronald Reagan with his Most Physically Fit President of All Time award and inducts him into the WBBG Hall of Fame.

Artist's impression: the drawing Dan presented to President Reagan.

Once all presentations were given, I suddenly thought of a way we could perfectly end the occasion. Since I was introduced as a professional strongman and most muscular bodybuilding champion, I figured it would be a great opportunity to have the Most Physically Fit President in United States history, test his strength against this most worthy challenger. "Since you are now the Most Physically Fit President of All Time, do you mind if we arm-wrestle, Mr. President," I asked. I quickly realized, after laying down the challenge, that the President might have, at that moment, questioned my sanity. I was almost expecting him to say, "Okay bring in the next character and get this guy out of here." His actual response was more to my liking. "Clear the desk," was his reply, as he strode towards the massive oak workbench. With an almighty swipe he pushed aside his phone and documents to make room for our match-up. "You know I am going to beat you Mr. President," I said, seating myself on a chair to the side of the desk. "I am only 61 years old." As we positioned ourselves on the desk, allowing enough room for the both of us to arm-wrestle - Reagan weighed around 185 pounds at six foot one inch and I was 220 pounds at five foot six - I asked, "Do you want the left hand or right hand?" President Reagan, sitting in his chair at the front of his desk with me to the side of the massive table, answered, "the right!" Well the right hand it was as we sat face-to-face, ready to get down to "official business". As we readied ourselves for our test of strength, official Whitehouse photographers scrambled around us to get their best shots of this historical match. "When I say three," I shouted. The room went quiet. It was on. "Three, go": I knew the President was strong as he had rough, calloused hands, the kind used to hard work, so I knew it would be no walkover. We struggled back and forth for around ten seconds, which seemed like a lifetime to me. President Reagan won. "I don't believe it, I don't believe it," I said standing to my feet. "I want a re-match." The President was all smiles: "he let me do that." In response to my request for a re-match he pointed right at me and said, "Okay, because you took a dive that time." "I didn't take a dive," I said as I moved back into position for our second encounter. Again the president won, this time in around 15 seconds. "I don't believe it, you are a great man," I shouted. "Thank you Mr. President." Arm wrestling the President was a surreal experience, the kind of an opportunity that only comes once in a lifetime. Having it take place in the Oval Office after official business, with both of us wearing fully buttoned suit jackets - which made the challenge much harder than I expected – made it even more unreal.

After our second arm-wrestling match we both walked towards the door I had entered less than an hour earlier and said our goodbyes. As President Reagan put his left hand on my right arm I told him, "You should be complimented on how you keep yourself." Then I did something completely unplanned. "I would like to kiss you if I can, because I am a kissing nut," I said. "Can I kiss you?" The President threw his head back in laughter. I then placed my left hand on the right side of President Reagan's head and kissed him on the left side of his face. This was a very emotional time for me. I am a loving person and my love and respect for President Reagan was expressed in that one kiss. "God bless you," I said as I left the Oval Office. "Be well Mr. President." I could see the genuine warmth in the President's eyes as he thanked me and smiled.

Since my arm-wrestling match with President Reagan was not planned, there was no media there to cover it. They had only their own camera people so it was kind of an inside deal. But two days later, on Saturday the 18th of February, and much to my surprise, an official Whitehouse photo of our match, complete with story, featured on the front page of the New York Times. In fact, I had to show my wife this item, to prove what had happened, as she did not at first believe me when I told her what I had done. "I just arm-wrestled the President honey." "Come on who are you kidding?" she responded. "I'm telling you I did. And not only did I arm-wrestle him, I kissed him." "How could you do that Dan?"

The New York Times was not the only publication to feature our contest. Pictorial footage of us arm wrestling was published all over the world. Our famous shot with Reagan pinning my right arm, a look of joy on his face, is now on display as a piece of Whitehouse history in the Ronald W. Reagan Presidential Library and Museum. Not long after my meeting with the President, I spoke to the photographer and he told me that day was one of the President's most enjoyable in office. Most of President Reagan's business was very serious, but our day was a day of fun and celebration.

The World's Most Physically Fit President Joins the WBBG

Ready…Go: the match begins.

Seen Around the World: Dan arm-wresting
President Reagan in the Oval Office.

Our first arm-wrestling match attracted so much attention it was only a matter of time before, to my mind, a re-match between the President and myself would happen. I certainly wanted this, as did it appear the President and his officials, and in July of 1984 I received another call from David Waller, informing me that the President would attend an Alfred E. Smith dinner in New York City, right in my backyard. "Could we arrange an arm-wrestling re-match?" "Of course," I said, not needing any encouragement. Mr. Waller told me this would be a perfect place for a re-match as there would be a very large crowd. They would arrange a table and at a pre-determined time I would yell out, "Mr. President. You are in my city now. You beat me twice but it won't happen again." It was again on. It seemed what I had first thought to be a once in a lifetime opportunity would, in fact, repeat itself. I couldn't wait, as it was great publicity for us both and, at the time, it was important the President, who was running for re-election, look to be very strong and in control. He was attempting to beat the one-time "World's Strongest Man", in the process, showing the courage, determination and strength he was known for.

One week later I received another call from David Waller saying the re-match was off, as the President would be wearing a long, white tuxedo and would not have enough to time arm-wrestle, then speak to the crowd. He assured me they would try for another venue. And so it happened: in August I received another call, again from the Whitehouse. I was contacted as I personally knew President Reagan and was a member of the New York Jewish community. They felt I was the best man to arrange for President Reagan's first ever speech in a Jewish Synagogue. In fact, this was the first time any standing U.S. president had made this kind of speech, making it an historical occasion. So Whitehouse officials wanted me to confirm how far the nearest Jewish temples were from JFK Airport, where the President would be landing on the New York leg of his campaign, to give his speech to this Jewish audience. I gave them the names of three temples quickly adding that I personally lived a short distance from all of them. The information I gave was forwarded to President Reagan's campaign people and of the three temples, Rosedale on Frances Lewis Blvd, the one I attended, Temple Orr Torah and Temple Hillel in North Woodmere, they chose Temple Hillel as it would seat the most people, had the best security measures in place and was closest to John F. Kennedy International Airport, a shorter distance for the President to travel.

Again I was delighted with the opportunity to meet the President, and to arm-wrestling him, only this time the showdown was planned. The script was almost identical to the first proposed re-match, the only difference being that I would shout from the audience, "Mr. President, you beat me at arm wrestling in the Oval Office, but you are now in my home town and in my *temple*. You won't beat me again." To make it official, New York Senator Alphonse D'Amato announced to the press that the challenge would take place on October 26, 1984 at Temple Hillel during the President's re-election campaign.

It was a rainy Friday morning when I arrived at Temple Hillel. As I entered the synagogue, President Reagan's security whisked me away to his aide's room, where I met my contact person for that day, who I discussed all the details of the challenge with. Because of the heavy rain, the President was one hour late. When he arrived, the pressroom was chaotic and the news people were in a state of panic. Everyone was yelling and shouting. It was made known that the President would need to be given a new speech. Due to his lateness they wanted to cancel the customary kosher lunch with temple spokesman rabbi emeritus Morris Friedman and his family, and Senator Alphonse D'Amato. The officials argued that they could not cancel the kosher lunch because, if they did, President Reagan would lose too many Jewish votes. After order was restored, the President made his way to the press gallery to speak. Tall and strong as I had remembered him from our first meeting in February earlier that year, President Reagan strode out to the podium wearing a traditional Jewish yarmulka skullcap and looking every inch the Most Physically Fit President of All Time as he was introduced by rabbi Friedman. As expected, the President came across as warm and compassionate and he lived up to his reputation as being the great communicator. Before Reagan's visit, Israel was experiencing problems with the United Nations, as the UN sought to expel the Jewish state. The President's words, comforting and empowering, found a place in the hearts and minds of those in attendance that day. "If Israel is forced out of the United Nations, the United States and Israel will walk together," he said, much to the audience's approval.

Getting Ready: President Ronald Reagan (left) readies himself to speak at the Temple Hillel on October 26, 1984. Rabbi Morris Friedman (right) introduces Reagan.

The large temple room was filled to capacity and, from where I sat in the crowd up front and to the left of where the President stood, I was very much aware of the table and two chairs that had been strategically placed a short distance from the great man. I was given instructions to wait for the word from my contact man, before standing and issuing my challenge. I waited and waited. All the while the President gave his great speech to a captivated audience. I knew the arm-wrestling match would be very popular. The audience were excited and energized by Reagan's talk and the prospect of one of their people locked in good-natured combat with the President would have caused a sensation, and won him many more votes I thought. After 20 minutes my man hurriedly made his way across to where I was. My heart rate must have doubled due to the anticipation and nervousness I felt. My muscles tightened and my nerves prepared themselves for the physical challenge ahead. "Sorry, but due to the President's lateness we have no choice but to cancel the re-match," said the disappointed-looking aide. President Reagan had two further speaking appointments that day and simply did not have the time to accept my challenge. After some discussion, they agreed to accept the challenge some other time. It never happened. But President Reagan did go on to win a second term, which made me happy. After all, this was election time for him and he had an extremely full schedule. All of his appointments were valuable, so I did not feel too bad about this missed opportunity.

At this time the President needed help to secure all-important votes and I gave all I could of myself. I told the media he was a very strong man with a solid character. But he was the oldest incumbent President ever and he was running for re-election. At the time people were saying that President Reagan was too old to run for re-election, that he did not have the endurance to continue in office. I knew that even though he was older than the other contenders, he was, in my opinion, by far the strongest. Presenting to the nation the fact that he was still fit, active and mentally and physically strong was my way of showing respect for him. Weeks later he was re-elected.

Alphonse D'Amato.

In 2004 I appeared on Fox 5 TV evening news, where New York anchor-reporter Linda Schmidt asked me whether I could set the record straight on what really happened in the Oval Office. In my relaxed home setting I made special mention of the fact I treasured the memories from that occasion, of President Reagan and his strength of character. I also made it clear that he did win the arm-wrestling challenge. But I did concede to letting him win just a little bit. The main reason for arm-wrestling the President was not to demonstrate or prove my strength. After all, I was in *his* office to present *him* with an award for being the Most Physically Fit President of All Time. Since our arm-wrestling match 24 years ago, many have speculated on what the result really should have been. Who should have won? Describing a photo taken at the time, The New York Times wrote, two days after the event, "it was a Whitehouse photo and no press photographers were allowed in…suspicious."

The fact that President Reagan beat me is irrelevant. I was there based on my respect for him, to honor his health and fitness achievements. I would never have gone to the Whitehouse to intentionally try to beat the President of the United States, as I had way too much respect for him. There is no question, though, that President Reagan was a true man of strength and a wonderful president. And I most definitely felt his great strength during our match. He pushed me hard and I had to work even harder to maintain any advantage. The President truly was strong. But what more could you expect from a man who trained with weights every night as he watched the news on four television sets, a man who pumped out reps of seated dumbbell curls minutes before attending official presidential meetings? The fact he was the oldest President in history to hold office while maintaining a schedule that would break lesser men, qualified him as the Most Physically Fit President of All Time. I am just honored to have played a small part in his influential life and to have promoted him as a President of great strength, endurance and character. Our historical arm-wrestling match remains one of my fondest memories.

THE WHITE HOUSE
WASHINGTON

March 6, 1984

Dear Mr. Lurie:

I just wanted to tell you what a great time I had when you came to the White House on February 16. You are indeed a challenging opponent and I really enjoyed our arm-wrestling bouts. Perhaps we can have a rematch someday.

I certainly appreciate the award which you presented to me. Please convey my gratitude to your colleagues for their part in this special remembrance. I'll try to remain worthy of your tribute.

With my best wishes to you and your colleagues,

Sincerely,

Ronald Reagan

Mr. Dan Lurie
Publisher
Muscle Training Illustrated
219-10 South Conduit Avenue
Springfield Gardens, New York 11413

P.S. I'll keep the caricature as a reminder of your personal friendship.

Letter from the President: President Ronald Reagan expresses his gratitude to Dan and shows interest in an arm-wrestling re-match.

In 1990 I wrote to President Reagan's wife Nancy at her home in Bel-Air, California, six years after arrangements had been made for a second arm-wrestling challenge, and four years before it was made known he had advanced Alzheimer's disease. She replied and told me the President wasn't doing that great. 14-years-later, on June 2, President Reagan died at the age of 93. As an influential figure in my life, and one of the greatest leaders of all time, President Reagan's achievements continue to inspire me today. As well as being impressed with his physical strength, I felt he was a very warm man, I felt comfortable with him. I will always fondly remember this great man.

Special moment: Lurie and Reagan embrace and kiss on the cheek!

Chapter Twelve:

Bodybuilding Champions

Over the years I have had the honor of meeting many of bodybuilding's great champions. Featuring these men and women in my magazines, honoring them at my Hall of Fame dinners and seeing them compete in WBBG contests remains one of the high points of my life. As well as working in the field for many years, I've also been a big fan of bodybuilding as the discipline and dedication bodybuilders apply to their craft is something I admire and the strength, development and artistic expression that is the end result of these champions' weight-training efforts is the very thing that attracted me to the sport when I was younger. Of all the greats I have honored and been associated with, it is impossible for me to single out any one of these champions as being the best of the best, as they all deserve the highest recognition and respect. It appears the respect I have for their achievements is mutual, judging by testimonials and feedback I have received from many of the men and women I have worked with over the years. At this point in my story I will highlight my involvement and friendships with several of these men and women.

Bodybuilding's athletes are often thought to be egoistic and so totally caught up in their own achievements that they have little time for anyone or anything else. I guess this mindset comes from the belief that bodybuilding is a self-centered sport, where success is largely determined by individual effort. Although parts of this are true, bodybuilders, like any other athletes, do need the support of fans, sponsors, promoters, exercise and nutrition coaches and publishers to make it to the top, and these relationships must be based on mutual respect. What follows will hopefully provide insights into another side of bodybuilding and what many of its champions are really like.

Steve Reeves

Meeting Steve Reeves for the first time in 1973 was the realization of a dream for me. I was always an admirer of his acting, the way he lived his life, and especially his physique, and I made it my mission to get him to the East Coast. He lived in California at the time and audiences from my neck of the woods dearly wanted to see him. Long before we met in person, I watched him perform in the Broadway show Kismet in the mid 1950s, a time when I was appearing on the Big Top Circus Show. At this time I was very impressed by his acting skills and of course knew of his success as a bodybuilder, but I hadn't planned to meet him at that stage. This would come 18-years-later and this is how it happened. I contacted Steve Reeves in 1972 - while he was on the set of one of his Hercules films in Switzerland - and arranged to fly him and his wife from California to John F. Kennedy International Airport the following year, where I would hold a press conference and he could meet his East Coast fans. After the conference he would appear on the Joe Franklin Show then at my Pro Mr. America the following day. He agreed. The day of his arrival came and I didn't know what to expect: would he be wearing a beard like in the Hercules movies or would he be clean-shaven as he was when I first saw him as a Broadway actor? He was clean-shaven and looked every inch the film star he was, a very good-looking man. We discussed beforehand the possibility that he appear at my 1973 Pro Mr. America at Hunter College and he accepted. So the date was set and the day had finally arrived.

The Hunter College appearance would be historical because it was the first time Reeves had appeared before a bodybuilding crowd for many years. When he became an actor he still trained hard with weights, but due to his film commitments he began to distance himself from the bodybuilding scene. His appearance at my show was like a comeback, a welcoming back to bodybuilding. He did not disappoint as he made a magnificent speech for the crowd and awed everyone with his presence. I inducted him into the WBBG Hall of Fame the following day, and again in 1977 with a WBBG lifetime achievement award for being the greatest bodybuilder of all time.

You are Very Worthy: Dan presents Steve Reeves with a WBBG lifetime achievement award in 1977.

For many years Reeves and I would meet whenever he came to the East Coast. Attending Broadway shows and eating out at restaurants together were nice times for us both. One time when he came to New York we had a snowball fight. He loved this, as where he came from it was usually hot and humid. We threw snow around like a couple of big kids and attracted much attention. When he used to visit our home, he would go up to our attic and put on my Sealtest strongman cape and it thrilled me to discover he had been a regular watcher of the Big Top Circus Show. His physique was admired because of its near-perfect symmetry and proportion: his arms, calves and neck were each 18.5 inches around and his waist was a mere 29 inches. He did not have the big, bloated look that typifies so many of today's bodybuilder's.

As we all know, Steve Reeves was the first bodybuilder to become a household name because of his acting abilities. In 1973, I, as mentioned, arranged for him to appear on the Joe Franklin Show. There he came across well and was a big hit with the audience. At the time he was working with Joe Levine, Executive of Embassy Pictures, and the man who brought the rights to all of the Hercules movies for the small sum of $50,000. People thought Joe was crazy and told him not to buy the rights. No one else wanted the movies. Fortunately for him the Hercules movies made a lot of money, giving him around ten million for every million he spent. At this time I was planning my Pro Mr. America at Hunter College and arranged for Steve Reeves to be the guest of honor. I approached Levine and asked him if he would like to help me with this production and he said no, not at Hunter College. My sadness quickly turned to joy when he told me Madison Square Garden was the venue he thought would be best; he wanted it to run on September 9, the date of his birthday. We agreed that along with my show, two Hercules movies would screen and Steve Reeves himself would appear, all at Madison Square Garden, New York's biggest venue! Unfortunately this plan fell apart and I had to go back to my original idea: Hunter College. But it all worked out in the end and Steve Reeves did appear at my 1973 Pro Mr. America. A side note: Steve Reeves' wife Aline worked for Joe Levine as his publicity agent and it was her job to escort Reeves around in Europe to promote the Hercules pictures. While he was in Europe with her they fell in love and eventually married.

Bodybuilding Champions

Snowball fight: Dan and Steve Reeves playing with snow on the cold streets of New York.

Dan Lurie: Heart of Steel

Dan with the Vice President of Embassy Pictures: After his meeting with Embassy Pictures Executive, Joe Levine

One of the things that impressed me most about Steve Reeves was his sincerity and humility. He was a genuinely nice guy who never let success go to his head. Steve was born in Glasgow, Montana, and later moved to California where he became one of the world's greatest bodybuilder's despite competing for a short period before becoming a famous actor. He died in May of 2000 and I will always remember him for his warmth and genuine personality, and as holder of the most beautiful physical of the 20th century. In fact, I once said during a Joe Franklin Show appearance: "Steve Reeves is the greatest name in the history of bodybuilding, and will be the greatest for the next 2000 years." We had some great times together. The following words he wrote I hold dear to my heart.

"The ones who live are the ones who struggle.

The ones whose soul and heart are filled with high purpose,

Yes, these are the living ones." - VICTOR HUGO

"Dan Lurie's active competitive sports life came shortly before my time, perhaps ending a year or two before I won the AAU Mr. America title in 1947. He'd already won America's Most Muscular Man three times, prior to the early 1940s. This was an extremely turbulent decade, when America struggled on a global scale, and - emerging from the conflagration - changed, and ultimately went in search of its new self. Dan and I both fought our individual ways into this dawning challenging 'atomic age'. I never personally knew Dan in the pre-atomic years, and yet we were contemporaries in the same sports field. But our lives paralleled as we made marks on the physical culture landscape, such as it was when bodybuilding was a misunderstood revolutionizing ideal. The decade was our mentor, being neither kind nor overly brutal on our persons.

"Later, in the early 1950s, again Dan and I would symbolically cross paths, walking the same New York City streets. Dan Lurie found himself trudging to the television studios of the period... oh yes, I remember the mighty 'Dan the Muscle Man' on the Seal test "Big Top". At the time I was busy pursuing my legitimate career in the theater on the Broadway stage, some years before I played the legendary "Hercules" of the cinema.

Yes we struggled in the same deep channels – and yet we did not know each other personally. Finally, in 1973 Dan and I met; and he would tell me how in awe of my influence on physical culture he was. So awed in fact Dan would enshrine me in his 'World Body Building Guild Physical Fitness Hall of Fame' and arranged it so that New York City presented me with the 'Keys to the City' . . . which was much appreciated."

"Fate had finally thrown us together as men of our times. My wife Aline and Dan's wife Thelma and we began to socialize, at Dan's home in North Woodmere, N.Y., with his five married Children and in-laws, and at my ranch in Valley Center, California. Who would believe this powerfully built man was an avid clock collector who owned more than 50 antique timepieces, all displayed in his luxurious home? As Morgan horses are my pride and passion this man was a person who viewed time as a collectable.

It was then I discovered my contemporary as a friend. Over the next years I would come to realize a fine personal relationship, seeing many Broadway shows together, sharing experiences at restaurants-including my favorite dinners of lobster and chopped liver."

Dan Lurie: Heart of Steel

"We'd both - many believed - exerted a profound influence on our sport. We had both struggled through our respective lives into success, each in his own area of interest-Dan a sports promoter, barbell manufacturer, publisher, and health equipment marketeer and myself into a lucrative acting career. I found myself slightly sorry for having missed this man during the early years, for our present friendships might have made our struggles a bit lighter had they existed way back when.

This husky fellow with his penchant for entertaining friends with singing and magic tricks has a sense of humor of great proportion. Dan is a very decent, family-dedicated Jewish man who would probably appreciate a little Jewish humor here:

"An elderly rabbi once impishly approached me, taking me by the upper arm (which was quite massive at the time) and wished me, "Muscletuff!" - his humorous adaptation of the Jewish 'Mozeltof' -a 'good health, good luck' wish.

Well, to you, Danny and Thelma, and the readers who will now know you through the pages of this book. . . live and be happy. . . "stay muscletuff."

Mozeltof!

Steve Reeves

Meet Mr. Reeves: the world's greatest bodybuilder, Steve Reeves, is introduced to nationwide audiences on the Joe Franklin show, 1973.

Sergio Oliva

One of bodybuilding's living legends and one of its biggest stars is the man they call "The Myth", Sergio Oliva. As winner of my 1972 Mr. Galaxy and '75, '76 and '78 Mr. Olympus contests, I consider Sergio to be one of my most successful bodybuilding champions. Regarded by many as the greatest bodybuilder ever, because of his genetically gifted structure, complete with the largest arms of his time, thighs that each measured more than the width of his tiny waist and a stunning V-taper that gave him the appearance of having perfect symmetry and proportion, Sergio simply dominated the competition. He also won Joe Weider's Mr. Olympia title three times. In 1974, one year before he won my Mr. Olympus title for the first time, I arranged for Sergio to challenge Arnold Schwarzenegger for the title of world's greatest bodybuilder at my WBBG Pro Mr. America. Both Sergio and Arnold accepted, but it was not to be. Looking back I have no doubt that Sergio would have won this contest convincingly such was his development at the time. For over seven years Sergio appeared in *MTI* advertising my Jet-707 protein powder and in fact used this product to help build his massive muscles. As a man, Sergio was respectful and courteous. He always showed great respect to my wife Thelma and loved my children as his own. He was always laughing and was so much fun to be around. In 2007 I honored Sergio for his lifetime achievements in bodybuilding at my WBBG International Fitness and Sports Hall of Fame awards and he wrote the following nice words before this event:

"Health, fitness, strength, entrepreneur, and the name Dan Lurie are synonymous. A pioneer of the sport who continues contributing to the fitness world; a champion himself and Founder of the WBBG - a true icon."

Sergio Oliva

The WBBG's Number One Star Attraction: Dan, and the man they call The Myth, Sergio Oliva.

Chris Dickerson

One man who became one of the greatest bodybuilder's ever and the first African American to with the AAU Mr. America, is Chris Dickerson. Chris also competed in the WBBG, winning the 1973 Pro Mr. America before enjoying a strong career in the IFBB as one of its most successful athletes and winner of the 1982 Mr. Olympia. I remember Chris as being articulate, intelligent and a real gentleman. He brought style to the stage with his posing skills and displayed his physique probably better than anyone else during his time at the top. I remember Chris always had an amazing singing voice: he trained as an opera singer and would open many IFBB events with the American National Anthem. One time in the '70s, I arranged for Chris to appear on the Joe Franklin Show with Steve Reeves. I urged Chris to sing on this show, but he was too shy and would not. I said, "Chris, it has been arranged for you to sing." But I was teasing. He replied, "I am not going to sing." I countered, "Yes you are." It was just a joke though. He did have a beautiful voice, but he will always be known for his physique. When he won my Pro Mr. America, I remember admiring his overall balance and presentation. Chris Dickerson is a worthy champion and a credit to the sport of bodybuilding. I inducted him into the WBBG Hall of Fame in 1975.

"Yes, I am proud I won that title. They were looking for the same criteria at the WBBG Pro Mr. America for each competitor. It was a good experience, right in New York City, so I did not have to travel for it. By the way, the Pro Mr. America trophy is the biggest trophy I have – it is huge: it practically hits the ceiling. I was also inducted into the WBBG Hall of Fame, which was another nice honor.

Dan Lurie was very loving and kind of like a father. Also he always wanted to please everybody. He wanted everyone to be happy. And he extended himself a great deal. He ran his shows and he did the best he could. He ran things a little bit on a shoestring, but he had his own magazine – he ran the whole thing like a little country store. God bless him. It was a family affair with his wife Thelma and son Mark in the office. They operated out of their Brooklyn office. It was unique."

Chris Dickerson

Promoting the Sport: Dan with popular WBBG athlete Chris Dickerson, taking bodybuilding to the streets of New York.

Boyer Coe

Another one of my greatest champions is Boyer Coe, who won my Pro Mr. America a record five times - from 1971 through to '75. Known for his great conditioning with some of the best calves and arms ever seen, Boyer also competed with the IFBB, winning - in 1981 - seven pro shows, more that year than any other professional bodybuilder in the world at the time. Boyer was always a straight talker, and always conducted himself with great integrity. The WBBG was all the better for having a man of Boyer's character in its ranks. Actually Boyer was so good as a bodybuilder that at one point other WBBG competitors feared competing against him. We used to have to hide him backstage, so no one would know he was there because, of course, once they saw him that would be it: they would not want to compete alongside him. To retain order at my shows I always had a habit of saying, as the contest deadline approached: "Is everyone here. In the next minute the contest will be over for you if you are not here on time." And competitors would be disqualified if they were not onstage at the given time. Meanwhile, I would have Boyer hiding behind the curtains and when the competitors walked out it would be like, "oh, Boyer Coe is here." I had to hide him to make sure they didn't leave. In the time I would say "one minute to go" out would walk Boyer and no one could back out. At other times I would have him stand on the balcony to watch the prejudging of the first show and at this time he would wear baggy clothing and glasses. Then when the contest was to begin he would come on down and arrive onstage last. I inducted Boyer into the 1969 WBBG Hall of Fame.

"I always found Dan Lurie to be a very likeable and down to earth guy. He was a family man and his family always came first. During the times I would come to New York, he had a wonderful lady that worked for him. His office and desk was always a mess, but she knew where everything was at and was able to keep the whole operation running smoothly. You could tell that he had great respect for her.

"From what I remember, his contests were pretty well attended and he did seem to draw quite a few contestants each year, so everyone seemed pleased with his efforts. I will say this, at least with me, he was a man of his word, and always did exactly what he said he would do."

Boyer Coe

Big Boyer: Boyer onstage after winning yet another WBBG Pro Mr. America contest.

Leon Brown

Leon Brown is one champion I have always been fond of. From Staten Island, New York, Leon began his bodybuilding career in 1966, placing second in the teenage short class at the WBBG Mr. Eastern America Championships. He achieved fourth place at the 1968 and '71 WBBG Pro Mr. America contests with his dazzling muscles, and this helped him to become New York's bodybuilding pride. Leon has competed as a bodybuilder for a total of 40 years, remarkably competing, since he began, every year other than 1976, '77, '82 and '85. Being a major bodybuilding star in Staten Island in the '60s, it was only natural that Leon and I would cross paths at some point. When I first met Leon he was a young man in his late teens. I instantly saw his potential and eventually he made his way into the WBBG and was regularly featured in *MTI*. It was in an early edition of *MTI* that I profiled Leon, listing his bodybuilding goals and predicting that he would some day become one of the East Coast's top champions. He never won a major professional title, but Leon had his share of high points: he narrowly lost the 1967 Eastern America to Frank Zane, beat two-time Mr.

Olympia winner Franco Columbu for the most muscular and best back titles at the 1970 Mr. International, an achievement he would repeat against big Lou Ferrigno at the 1973 Nationals. On June 30, 2007, Leon took part in my annual Long Island Checkers Championship's, carrying the American flag and showing his great muscles. He looked fantastic. Respected writer Charles Gains gave a good account of Leon's physical greatness and the kind of impact he made on the bodybuilding stage, when he wrote in his landmark bodybuilding book, Pumping Iron: "Somewhere toward the middle of it he slid into a back pose and jiggled it tense – trapezius, deltoid infraspinatus, lats, all the work-horse muscles of the back coming together suddenly like a click of a box and gleaming above his white posing trunks like oiled chocolate in perfect organized mounds. It was the kind of pose that a bodybuilder finds only once in a while – where everything is right and he reaches for it and hauls it down, and all the muscles fall into place like gears meshing." This perfectly describes Leon's posing style: fluid and flawless. Leon will be remembered for his great posing, bodybuilding consistency and as being one of the sport's truly nice guys.

Bill Pearl

A man who never competed in the WBBG, but who is probably one of the top three bodybuilders of all time, is Bill Pearl. Inducted into the WBBG Hall of Fame in 1978, Bill, who would have a big influence, through his training methods, on fellow inductee and WBBG champion, Chris Dickerson, demonstrated what a great bodybuilding champion should be: he was more than a worthy competitor and another who could have successfully challenged Arnold. He was a man who lived the bodybuilding lifestyle, rising at around 5.00 every morning to train. He also became a respected writer and bodybuilding judge. The year he was presented the WBBG Man of the Year award, 1967, Bill guest posed at the Pro Mr. America, held at the Roosevelt Auditorium, attracting one of the largest crowds we ever had. This was the first time Bill Pearl had guest posed in New York City and his physique was like nothing seen before. Remember, this was before Sergio and Chris Dickerson made their impact in the WBBG, and our crowds were simply not used to seeing a guy of Bill's size and shape. We were so impressed by Bill's sportsmanship and bodybuilding success that we asked him to write a regular column for *Muscle Training Illustrated*, which he did for several years.

Two legends: Dan Lurie receives a Champion Award while Bill Pearl looks on.

Bill turned pro at the 1956 Mr. USA Professional show and went on to win the 61, 67 and 71 NABBA Professional Mr. Universe titles. He is widely regarded as one of the first bodybuilding training and nutrition experts. Today they would call him a bodybuilding "guru". In all my dealings with Bill, I always found him to be the total professional. His impact on bodybuilding is immeasurable.

"When the final book on strength training has been written, Dan Lurie's name is destined to stand as an icon among the superstars. He has lived the life of a strongman/superstar/businessman for nearly 70 years. His story reads like a best-seller novel with as many twists and turns.

"Dan has gladly shared his wealth of knowledge on the fitness world with countless thousands over the years. The superstars of yesterday, today, and tomorrow owe him a round of applause for his tireless efforts to bring physical culture from a cult-like activity to a mainstream activity that is shared by the world. Everyone who loves the world of health and fitness cannot help but take their hats off to this living legend."

Bill Pearl

Harold Poole

Harold Poole will go down in history as being one of bodybuilding's greatest for several reasons. In the 1960s he was one of the first men to set the standard for the desirable balance of mass and shape needed to succeed at the pro level. His runner up positions at the 1965, '66 and '67 Mr. Olympia's were a world first as was the fact that he was, at age 21, the youngest man to have competed in this show, a record that stands today, and that he was the only man to have entered the first three of these events. Like me, Harold could not win the AAU Mr. America, but instead won the Most Muscular. But his time would come and in 1964 he captured the IFBB Mr. America and made history by being the first African-American to do this. It is my view that Harold was one of the few men to successfully bridge the gap between the mass and shape of Sergio Oliva and the flair, presentation and audience appeal of Larry Scott. Harold spent many years out of the spotlight, even after being inducted into IFBB Hall of Fame in 2004. I am happy to report that Harold is today – in 2007 - still training hard with weights. Harold won my first ever WBBG contest, the Pro Mr America in 1967 and was inducted into the WBBG Hall of Fame in 2007 - in the eyes of many he will remain one of bodybuilding's true greats.

Great WBBG Athletes Both: Harold Poole (left) and Leon Brown at the 2007 WBBG Hall of Fame awards - still looking great.

Anibal Lopez

Anibal Lopez has such a great physique that Steve Reeves himself once commented that Anibal was one of his favorite bodybuilder's. As one of the more balanced competitors in the WBBG, Anibal, with his God given talent, represented bodybuilding at its best. When it came time to choose a bodybuilder to illustrate my first bodybuilding instructional book, Anibal was an obvious choice, as he appealed to the average person. His body was admirable, yet achievable for many lifters. He is also a very inspirational man who still trains hard today into his late 60s.

"I always tell people that Dan helped me be known all over the world. As a kid I would watch the Big Top Circus show just so I could see that muscular man with his cape who resembled Superman. Little did

I know that one day I would meet him in person and he would help me become known in the world of bodybuilding. I became recognized when in 1978 I won his most prestigious title at the Lincoln center in New York Pro Mr. America. He sponsored me to compete in London at the NABBA Mr. Universe contest. I also had the opportunity to appear in several TV shows with Dan. This year on August 25, 2007, he is doing it again by inducting me in the WBBG Hall Of Fame"

Anibal Lopez

Three Greats Today: Warren Frederick, Chris Dickerson and Anibal Lopez (from left to right) in 2007.

Dave Draper

Mr. America, Mr. Universe and Mr. World winner, Dave Draper, was a man that left a lasting positive impression on bodybuilding. Called the Blond Bomber, Dave built a massive physique and was always in shape. When I first saw the pictures that Weider printed of Dave, he looked like a Greek God, tall and tanned. Even though he came from the East Coast, I never really had much to do with him, but I do remember he was a major Steve Reeves fan. When I honored

Steve Reeves onstage at my Pro Mr. America, Dave was so eager to meet the Hercules star and considered approaching the great man. But it was not to be because Dave was at the time pumping up to appear at this show and had oil dripping from his body. He told me he didn't want to meet Steve Reeves under those conditions. Like Reeves, Dave became one of bodybuilding's greats and as his 2007 induction into the prestigious Association of Oldtime Barbell and Strongmen suggests he will forever be remembered as a legend. I inducted Dave into the WBBG Hall of Fame in 1975.

Dave recently wrote me a nice testimonial before my induction into the 2007 Jewish Sports Hall of Fame.

"Dan Lurie is a survivor and hero of many tough worlds. He's a strongman, a muscleman, a showman, a businessman, an entrepreneur and a family man. He's no stranger to struggle and has blazed a path though rugged terrain with villains in the shadows. Villains beware. The East coast builds them strong. New York City with rebar and concrete."

In 2005 Dave wrote the following:

"Dan Lurie. The powerful and alluring world of strongmen and muscles was not built by one man alone. It wasn't Sandow only who constructed the foundations of might and it wasn't Grimek and Reeves only who introduced classic lines to the male physique. The world of muscle and might grew by word of mouth and by print, by momentum of popular interest and by the passion of its early champions.

"Dan Lurie is one of those champions. He lifted tons, exhibited a Mr. Universe physique, printed words of inspiration and information for hundreds of thousands and spoke to the international audience to develop and popularize physical culture everywhere. He did these things when the sport was an infant, a child, a robust young man and the towering giant it has become today. Long live Dan, one of a kind."

Dave Draper

Dan Lurie: Heart of Steel

The Blond Bomber: Dave Draper.

Warren Frederick

I have always favored balanced muscle mass on a competitor. If you can balance a great amount of muscle and still remain in proportion, this is ideal. Next to Sergio, and several others, Warren Frederick had this kind of build – huge, hard, rugged and almost perfectly balanced. His arms and legs were simply breathtaking and his posing was dynamic and powerful. The thing I liked most about Warren was his personality. A lifetime career in the U.S. Army Special Forces made him as a man of strength and honor and his devotion to his daughter and two grandsons is something I personally admire and can relate to. In the 1960s and '70s Warren was a regular *MTI* star athlete and made the cover in 1968 and twice in '74. 1974 was a big year for Warren, as he had just won my Pro Mr. America and was at the very top of his game. He is also a special part of the WBBG family as he was the only man ever to have won the WBBG Pro Mr. North America, which was held only once in 1972. I remember being amazed by the sheer size and vascularity of his legs at this show. Today, now retired from the military, Warren still gives bodybuilding seminars and is in good physical shape.

Steve Michalik

As a 1971 Mr. USA, '72 Mr. America and '75 Mr. Universe champion, Steve proved that he had all the talent to make it big as a bodybuilder and his training methods and expertise as a fitness educator have helped improve the lives of many. I met Steve when he was only 13. He showed great promise then and he would get even better. As his physique changed, I knew I had a future champion on my hands and started working with him on bodybuilding projects. He was featured regularly in my magazines and in advertisements selling my products. In 1972 he appeared in the pages on *MTI* posing with Lou Ferrigno. I remember thinking at the time that these two men would go on to create real waves in the bodybuilding industry, a thought that proved correct as Louie became a major TV star based largely on his physical gifts and Steve a bodybuilding champion and fitness expert. Steve remains a true bodybuilding ambassador through his continued involvement in the sport as an educator, trainer and author.

"Somebody told me that Dan lived in North Woodmere, the next town over from me. I couldn't believe it! It took me a couple of years to get enough guts to go over his house and ring his doorbell, but I finally did it. To my amazement there was Dan, bigger than life, standing at the door. Dan was everything I dreamed he'd be and more. He was muscular and powerful, and also kind and understanding. Dan didn't hesitate to invite me in. I told him of my ambition to become a bodybuilding champion and Dan was very encouraging. From that day forth, I always knew I'd have a friend in Dan Lurie.

"As our friendship developed, so did I. Dan and I worked on a number of projects together. I appeared many times in Dan's *Muscle Training Illustrated* magazine. Additionally, Dan has always been a leader, not only in the health and fitness arena, but also with civil rights and drug abuse. I worked with Dan setting up forums and seminars for seniors regarding exercise and nutrition. We set up bodybuilding contests in Harlem and posing exhibitions for the deaf. We were also involved with underprivileged children and Dan was also an advocate for women's rights, encouraging them to stay fit and exercise.

"Before Joe Weider and Schwarzenegger, there was Dan Lurie. Dan is a pioneer in the sport of bodybuilding and has always fought to bring respectability to a sport that few knew or cared for. Through his contests and publications, Dan brought innovative and fresh ideas to the sport. Dan was the first to make barbells and dumbbells available to the public. He opened the first bodybuilding warehouse where everything from supplements to gym equipment could be easily found. To this day, Dan continues to work tirelessly to bring new ideas to bodybuilding in an honest and sincere way. Dan was great to work with. He respected his bodybuilders and was always friendly and encouraging. He is an honest man with a high level of integrity. You could always trust Dan to keep his word and do everything he said he would.

"Dan always treated his athletes in a fair manner with the utmost respect. He was always ready to lend a helping hand. That's just the way he is.

The wonderful thing about Dan was that he was always approachable. An athlete never felt there was a class distinction between promoter and athlete. Dan was the promoter, but he was first and foremost a friend."

Steve Michalik

Bodybuilding Champions

Mighty Steve: Dan with Steve Michalik at the NABBA Mr. Universe bodybuilding championships.

Dan with Steve and women's bodybuilder Gladys Portugues, the wife of actor Jean-Claude Van Damme

Bill Grant

The winner of the WBBG 1972 Pro Mr. America, Bill Grant, is still actively involved in bodybuilding as a contest promoter, trainer and educator. He was known for his great abdominal and biceps development, along with his dry conditioning which gave his muscles the look of marble. Bill proved that the WBBG was totally fair organization that did not discriminate. In 1972 Big Lou Ferrigno was one of my rising stars and many felt that - based on his involvement with me - he would easily win that year's Pro Mr. America. But Lou, who came in out of shape, didn't know a massive ripped Bill Grant would appear and lost to Bill. Bill proved himself to be a great champion and one of few men ever to beat Lou Ferrigno in bodybuilding competition. After this contest I flew Bill to the 1972 WBBG Pro Mr. America contest, held that year in California. He won. In 1974, I sent him along with fellow bodybuilders Warren Fredrick, Boyer Coe and Kelly Everts to the NABBA Universe in London. Bill's physique was so great I also put him on the cover of my special commemorative 1977 AAU Mr. America Contest magazine. Bill was a respectful man who loved his fans and represented bodybuilding in the most professional way.

"I think Dan Lurie was very good for the sport of bodybuilding as much as anyone else. For instance he used to be the Sealtest Strongman. He was very visible in the '60s, especially on TV. I think he represented the bodybuilding community very well and yes I think back in that time he was a good ambassador.

"I knew Dan Lurie back in the '70s when he had an organization called the WBBG. At that time he had a thriving bodybuilding organization with some of the most elite bodybuilders of our time being a part of it. There where guys such as Sergio Oliva, Boyer Coe, Ken Waller, Dennis Tinerino, Lou Ferrigno and of course myself.

"He used to have other big bodybuilding stars at his shows as well. Steve Reeves, Bill Pearl and Reg Park, these guys did not compete but they were a part of the event. Maybe most people don't know, but in 1972 I won the WBBG Mr. America competition. I also appeared on the cover of one of his magazines as well.

"As we all know, he was a big competitor of Joe Weider back then and Joe, I recall, was not very happy when he knew that some of his top guys where competing in a non IFBB show.

"I do have to say one thing; he was always nice and cordial to me - always. I remember after I won the America Dan promised to pay my way and Lou Ferrigno's way to the NABBA Universe in London in the next three weeks and he made good on that promise: he took care of me and Louie very well. I don't think most people know that Dan Lurie and Joe Weider used to be business partners years before the IFBB started."

Bill Grant

Sri Chinmoy

Sharing my interest in strength was Sri Chinmoy, a multitalented man who became a very close friend. Very few could come close to Sri in the strength department; he was another who used his incredibly strong will to win to perform strength feats, but above all else this gifted spiritual teacher and philosopher showed his great compassion for humanity through the many humanitarian causes he supported and established. In 2007, a few months before he died in October of that year, Sri was nominated for a Nobel Peace Prize and a decade prior was honored as a saint by the internationally respected Hinduism Today magazine. Sri Chinmoy: A great man who I was honored to have known.

My Dearest Brother-Friend Dan,

You are the bodybuilding pioneer. When this sport was still in its infancy, you had the vision of how muscular development could be the key to an entirely new level of physical perfection. More than half a century ago, you were the four-time holder of the "Most Muscular Man in America" title. You inspired thousands and thousands of young men to become strong and fit.

Dan Lurie: Heart of Steel

You carried this inspiration far and wide through your most informative and illumining Muscle Training Illustrated magazine, your distinguished World Bodybuilding Guild and many other striking innovations. So much of what we take for granted nowadays in the world of bodybuilding is based upon your ideas, your vision and inspiration.

I am so fortunate that for the last two decades you have so kindly, lovingly and self-givingly encouraged me in my own humble weightlifting adventures. I shall eternally cherish your most valuable comments, suggestions and insights.

Sri Chinmoy

The Dan Lurie Song, composed by Sri Chinmoy

Bodybuilding Champions

Sri Chimnoy performing a feat of strength, lifting Dan

Kellie Everts

In all my years of bodybuilding promotion I always gave credit where it was due. At a time when the public and other bodybuilding organizations ignored female bodybuilding, I saw the value in weight training for women, and the benefits of promoting the muscular female physique. In the early 1970s, very few women used weights to stay in shape and hardly any competed in bodybuilding. Of course that would all change but at the time it was, for many, not conceivable that a female bodybuilder would flex her muscles in competition. When I met Kellie Everts in 1972, she had been weight training since 1964. A young lady with a great physique, Kellie was as motivated to compete as any male bodybuilder I had worked with. I would promote her to the world and in doing this become the first publisher to profile a female bodybuilder. By 1974 Kellie was already known as a good female bodybuilder and one who opened the door for women's weight training, but she was not being taken seriously. The men's competition was regarded as the main event and women were added as an afterthought, a way to attract fans to the venues. Kellie had other ideas and, as a writer and competitor, has tirelessly promoted women's bodybuilding ever since. In 1974, I received a call from Esquire Magazine photographer Jean-Paul Goude, asking me who I would recommend as a subject for a 'Amazonian' spread he was planning. I instantly told him, "Kellie Everts is your lady." In my mind she was the only female bodybuilder around at the time. In fact she was the first real female bodybuilder ever, a fact not lost on me when I put her in my December 1974 *MTI*. This was the very first article any muscle magazine had done on a female bodybuilder up until then. After this time, Kellie often featured in *MTI* and in my contests. She guest posed at the 1975 WBBG Body Beautiful contest at Hunter College. Alan Burke was the announcer that night and Kellie looked stunning as usual. In 1974 I sent her, along with Bill Grant, Warren Frederick and Boyer Coe, to the NABBA Universe in London where she represented America. As a bodybuilder, and in her various career paths, it seems controversy would follow Kellie throughout her life. To my mind, one thing is for sure: she was the first female to break through to make women's bodybuilding widely known to mainstream audiences.

"Dan Lurie is a very fine person. I admire him greatly for his courage, panache, show business savvy, business acumen, the love he has for his family, and his gigantic, good heart. I admire also his publicity skills; he had everyone beat in that area. His involvement with celebrities like President Ronald Reagan speaks loudly. Dan has persevered and today he is as great as ever and re-building his bodybuilding empire."

Kellie Everts

The champions featured in this chapter were all at one time respectively the best bodybuilders in the world, and their achievements should not be forgotten. Over the years I have given recognition and publicity where it was deserved and I have good memories of my time with those I have honored and featured in my magazines. The sport of bodybuilding has experienced a transformation and now it is bigger than ever. But is it any better? While some would say bodybuilding has progressed, and I can't argue with that, others would say that it has spiralled out of control. I see merit in both arguments. Bodybuilding has become big business and the physiques have gotten bigger. But except for a few of the top guys competing today, I feel bodybuilders lack the quality they had back in the 1960s and '70s. Today there is too much of an emphasis on drugs and many of the physiques have become overdeveloped as a result. The bodybuilders I worked with, including all of those profiled in this chapter, competed in what I feel was the true Golden Era. These were times when physiques resembled sculpture and were as distinctive as they were balanced and aesthetic. I salute these men and women for the look they presented. I hope to see this type of physique dominate professional bodybuilding once again.

Chapter Thirteen:

Dan Lurie Says, "Say no to drugs"

One of my more popular quotes has been "HEALTH IS YOUR GREATEST WEALTH". I often use this phrase to sign off on my letters and for many years it has been a big part of my business philosophy. It remains the reason why I originally got into bodybuilding, and for promoting a healthy body and mind, weight training and its accompanying good eating practices and promoting of a positive outlook cannot be beaten. Making the most of what God gave us by maintaining a good appearance through bodybuilding is something I have always preached in my magazines, and to anyone who will listen. The process of pushing our body to the limit through weights to create something that is attractive and healthy is what, to my mind, the sport is all about. That is what greats like the early 20th century strongman Eugen Sandow, who is widely regarded as the first bodybuilder ever, presented best: muscle, fitness and health. After Sandow's death in 1925 came a great number of physique stars all honoring his legacy through their efforts to build the natural physique. There was Sig Klein, Bernarr Macfadden, George Jowett and Earle Leiderman, champions who paved the way for bodybuilding, as we know it today. But along the way things became murky. Due partly to the competitive nature of several top weightlifting champions of the early 1950s, lifting weights

Dan Lurie Says, "Say no to drugs"

purely for health and personal achievement slowly but surely died out. Drugs - pure testosterone injections initially - were introduced to the sporting world, and they forever changed bodybuilding's destiny.

"Health is Your Greatest Wealth": Dan at his best in the 1940s and '50s.

Back in 1938, when I first began lifting weights in my parents' basement with that little 100-pound barbell on that rickety old bench, I would never have imagined the direction bodybuilding would take. Back then bodybuilders usually worked incredibly hard for their gains and the thought of using any kind of chemical to increase results just didn't enter their minds. Weight training then was all about building on the potential we had naturally, and the kinds of gains we did achieve were long lasting. For bodybuilders who came after me, that was all about to change.

Although scientists in Nazi Germany had discovered steroids in the early 1930s, they were not at first used for sporting purposes, but experimentally through the first human trials conducted by the

Nazis during the Second World War. This included the alleged experimenting on prisoners of war in an attempt to treat chronic wasting and on German soldiers to boost aggression. In the 1950s they were used to treat illnesses such as chronic wasting conditions and to stimulate bone growth, puberty and appetite. But in between times other uses were found for testosterone. So impressed were the Soviets by the amazing effects on recuperation and growth this new German "technology" was having, that they began using testosterone for sporting purposes directly following the war, all in an attempt to prove their communistic superiority to the world. And it worked… at least as far as sporting success went. When Russia dominated the weightlifting event to walk away with most of the medals at the 1952 Olympic Games in Helsinki, Finland, and the 1954 World Games in Vienna, some people put their success down to synthetic testosterone use, which, as is now known, was true. They were on anabolic drugs and it showed in their results.

On the Bob Hoffman-headed American team to the World Games was a man called Dr. John Zeigler, who later found the Russians were, in fact, using testosterone to boost their performance. A scientist and a physician, Zeigler, who was the American weightlifting team doctor and good friends with Bob Hoffman, figured he could seriously help the chances of the U.S. lifters if he could successfully encourage them to take steroids. In 1954, Zeigler, who was then receiving testosterone for experimental purposes, was experimenting with these drugs on burns victims and even appendectomy patients to determine their recovery rates. At this time he was also giving testosterone to trainees at his gym, as well as injecting himself, but the overall response was not as effective compared to what would be expected from an experienced athlete. He needed experienced lifters to fully assess testosterone's effects. This same year, he began giving testosterone to some of Bob Hoffman's weightlifting champions, including John Grimek, which was thought to be the first time these drugs were used in the U.S. for strength purposes. John Zeigler went on to develop the first anabolic steroid, Dianabol. By 1958, steroids were produced in greater numbers by pharmaceutical firms and their use spread from there. Now their use is out of control.

Back when it was first introduced to American lifters, testosterone was taken mainly to improve performance and strength, but it was also discovered to have a pleasant side effect: muscle growth. Athletes then began taking it to build muscle, rather than to get stronger. It is no act of chance that the champions of the 1960s and '70s all of a sudden were 30 to 40 pounds larger than those of the 1940s and '50s. Since pharmaceutical firms were distributing steroids by the late '50s, the public now had access to a wider range of these drugs. And the bodybuilder's physique reflected this new addition to its muscle-building bag of tricks.

In the 1940s I was considered large at 165 pounds of solid muscle, though I was smooth and small compared to today's standards. My fellow competitors like Jules Bacon and Frank Leight were also considered large for their day, although they would be classed as small compared to the physiques of today. In fact, it is not uncommon to see competitors today walking onstage at five foot seven and 250 pounds of well-conditioned muscle. In my day this was unheard of, as even men standing around six feet tall would be considered large at a mere 200 or so pounds. For example, the five foot eleven Frank Leight, who beat me to win the 1942 AAU Mr. America, competed at 209 pounds of smooth muscle. He was considered a large bodybuilder for his day. Another York man, Steve Stanko, at the same height and 220 pounds, was a veritable monster. Today men of a similar height weigh at least 260, and many are around the 280 to 290 mark. In a majority of cases you cannot say that training and nutrition alone will add 50 to 60 pounds of solid muscle over and beyond what would be expected naturally. Most bodybuilders of the 1940s and '50s trained extremely hard and ate mega-amounts of protein and carbohydrates, and reached their natural potential. Now physiques are like science fiction creations. Science has taken over and bodybuilding is no longer an honest activity. Sad but true.

Dan Lurie: Heart of Steel

Muscular...Naturally: Dan posing in 1941, one year out from his first Most Muscular title.

Of course I am talking as one who lived in the "good old days" but if you really look at it objectively, where have drugs taken bodybuilding? Since the 1970s there have been many reported cases where steroids have played a role in serious health problems and even, in some instances, death. This is not to mention the psychological problems they cause. Now, many will say that there are no proper statistics to show the exact extent of the problem, but if you open your eyes it is plain to see. Being close to the action, I have first hand knowledge of the dangers of bodybuilding drugs. In fact several of my top champions have come out and admitted to me personally, and to the media, their experiences with steroids. Associated drugs that are also used to produce that naturally unobtainable ripped, dry and huge look include Human

Growth Hormone and Insulin, and these are also used widely by the competitors of today to build and shape muscle.

Two of my greatest champions were wrestler Superstar Billy Graham and bodybuilder Steve Michalik. Both these men built terrific physiques and were among the strongest men of their time, but their progress did come at a cost. Steroids almost claimed their lives. Billy Graham is an old, old friend of mine and he will tell anyone who listens about the dangers of steroid use. He got himself into such bad shape, that in 2002 he needed a liver transplant. He came so close to death. Like so many bodybuilders and strength athletes of the 1970s on, Billy abused these drugs to the point where they ruled his life and almost cost him it. Because of his 25-year involvement with steroids, Billy needed fusion of both his left and right ankles and a hip replacement along with a new liver. He lost four inches in height because his bones became so weak through continued steroid use.

In the early 1970s, before he became a wrestling superstar admired the world over for mat skills, Billy was an avid bodybuilder and to build his physique he experimented with steroids, which were legal at the time. As is often the case with bodybuilders, he figured more would better. He was one of the best-built athletes around before he touched steroids and did not have to go that route. He got caught up. He got sucked in.

Steve Michalik is another bodybuilder I worked closely with who used steroids. By the time Steve began experimenting with these drugs, he had already won 22 bodybuilding titles including Mr. America and Mr. USA. He had developed a very impressive physique naturally. But as with Billy Graham, Steve wanted a fast route to greater success. He chose to do it with steroids. He began abusing them and eventually became so ill that he almost died.

Steve says that he continued to take them because every time he came off he felt bad. This is how addictive they were. Finally his system broke down and he was forced to stop. Steve then spent many years campaigning against steroids and he would educate people on their negative consequences. In all the years I knew Steve, I found him to be brutally honest about his drug use, but it disturbed me to see this great champion using these drugs. His attitude changed. He became more aggressive in a negative way. In a 2004 interview Steve said that he regretted his steroid use but that "back in the '70s no one knew about the side effects or the possible future problems associated with using them." "Doctors administered them to us and they worked. As you got bigger, your responsibility to self lessened. With this lessening of responsibility, came a cocky attitude about side effects and a dumb sense of immortality," explained Steve. "When you finally came back to your senses, and became yourself again, you look back at what you did and what you became. After that, the only good thing to do is try to make up any damage you may have committed to yourself and others. My way of trying to undo my mistakes is to help others."

But Steve is realistic and knows the problem of drug abuse in bodybuilding will not go away any time soon. He says, "I think in some weird way, anabolic steroids have evened the playing field in bodybuilding. In my day, if you were not genetically gifted with a great bone structure and muscles that could grow beyond their natural capacity, it would have been impossible to win even the lowest level of competition. In the early days we were an elite group that had the potential from birth to achieve greatness. Anabolic drugs seem to have changed all that. Steroids provide the physically challenged an opportunity to at least compete."

Steve recently told me that he is all for providing education so people can make informed choices about steroid use. "Because of the pain and suffering I endured, I feel obligated to make others aware of the dangers of anabolic drugs. On the other hand, if you are determined to achieve a level of greatness equal to or greater than what is being presented today, it is impossible to do so without them." Here Steve is simply saying that they are a reality in today's competitive sporting world and that their use will aid performance. Of course this is all true and that is why many athletes risk their health with drugs, to chase glory. But they almost killed Steve. People need to ask themselves, "Is it all worth it?" I have often said that bodybuilding should be fun, first and foremost. Bodybuilding needs to work around our lives, not the other way around. Bodybuilding should be a lifestyle that is health promoting, not health destroying. But since professional bodybuilding today is what it is and the public expectation for massive freaks exists, things are unlikely to change anytime soon.

Bulking up The Natural Way: Dan, as Sealtest Dan, downs a glass of milk with his co-star, and former Ms. America runner up, Jan Crocket.

During my 70-plus years in bodybuilding I have seen the damage steroids, growth hormone and insulin can do. It often takes an experienced eye to see the bigger picture when it comes to drugs in bodybuilding. Even Joe Weider recently said that he was heartbroken to discover that steroids had made their way into bodybuilding and that he wished there was no such thing as anabolic, performance-enhancing drugs in sports. My good friend Marvin Eder also has a strong anti-steroid stance. In fact, Marvin, who is one of bodybuilding's true champions and top Mr. America competitor of the 1950s, a man whose strength and physique were truly ahead of their time, has been silent in the media for many years due to his disillusionment with what bodybuilding has become. He recently told me that steroids have, in his view, ruined bodybuilding. And whatever Marvin, who completely naturally, regularly chinned with 200 pounds attached to his waist for over eight reps and had a most outstanding physique says about bodybuilding is worth listening to in my opinion. "Health was never divorced from my training. I would never under any circumstances consider the use of any kind of artificial drug to stimulate my muscle growth. What's going on now is a nightmare, an obscenity. And in a way I hope the whole thing just disappears, that it would be wiped off the face of the earth, but it is just getting worse and worse all the time.

"Eventually these people will suffer. You cannot do that without destroying your body. Eventually they come down with other forms of disease. You can't pour artificial testosterone into yourself and growth hormone, and God knows what else, without upsetting the natural homeostasis of your body. You will suffer from it. I really don't care what their goals are. You want to get muscular and stronger, workout hard and look after yourself like I did."

Men of power: Dan with the powerful one, Marvin Eder, at the Oldetime Barbell and Strongman awards, 2005.

To be fair, Marvin Eder was in his own genetic class. Had he used steroids, I'm sure he would have become one of the most massive men ever seen in bodybuilding. Other competitors were not so willing to take the natural route. When one guy took them and got great results, everyone else would follow him. The temptation was too hard to resist for most bodybuilders. Now all professionals are on them.

When I first began competing there were no steroids or other bodybuilding drugs and the effort needed to get into top shape was obvious. We trained incredibly hard every day, in some cases for hours on end for the results we got; and we felt better for it. There were no bodybuilders being carried off stage or whisked away for medical treatment hours before pre-judging. I believe that ethically we were doing the right thing. The playing field was more naturally level and guys were expected to work their bodies to the limit and eat wholesome foods all year round. It truly was a lifestyle. Now the chemical warfare, as it has been described, appears to have turned bodybuilding into a race to see who can take the most steroids. Many would say that the increase in drug use among bodybuilders is a sign of progress. I would say that progress should be measured by a person's ability to outsmart the opposition through advancements in training and eating, not by taking the easy way out through drugs. When will it end?

I mentioned that anabolic drugs first made their appearance in the 1950s when York athletes took them to gain the edge over their rivals. Since then it has expanded big time. Steroids are basically lab-made forms of the naturally occurring male sex hormone testosterone and artificially gave athletes mega-doses of the very thing needed to build massive muscles. Over the years, the different combinations of steroids, each made for a specific purpose, have grown. Each also comes with their share of side effects and when it comes to bodybuilding, users usually stack several types of steroid, which adds to their effectiveness, and damaging effects.

One of the big dangers of steroid use is that their negative effects may not be seen until many years after the athlete has taken them. You might feel strong, powerful, massive and full of confidence at the time of taking them, but years later there may be a hefty price to pay. Medical illness is so commonly associated with steroid use that taking them is like gambling with your health. Lyle Alzado, who used to buy exercise equipment from me when he was starting out as a weightlifter and football player, blamed them for the brain cancer that ultimately claimed his life at age 42. Lyle, who played football at the highest level for the Oakland Raiders, took massive doses of steroids and he seemed to grow larger and larger every time I saw him and I saw him often and noticed the changes. When he first started coming to my fitness store in Queens, New York, he was a very skinny teen. Within a year he had put on 50 pounds of muscle and not long after this became one of the world's strongest men. Suspicious? Not long before his death he wrote a book where he explained that steroids ruined his health and that he regretted ever having taken them.

Steroids' influence on personality and behaviour can cause severe mood swings. The user can go from being depressed to feeling extremely irritable to feeling like they are invincible. Extreme aggression is common. I have seen it first hand. Steroid users often get very angry. They fight with their partners and have fistfights with their friends. They actually become different people and it is almost like they are drunk. They often wake up the next day and do not know what they have done.

Even though steroids are thought of as an aggression drug, many men who take them also experience feminizing effects and decreased male sex function, which includes reduced sperm count, impotence, development of breasts, shrinking of the testes and pain while urinating. At their worst, steroids have been shown to cause liver and kidney damage, elevated cholesterol and clotting disorders and they can lead to weakened tendons, which must go some way to explaining why so many of today's guys are getting injured. Another big problem with steroids is that they are addictive. Once the guys go on them, getting off can be next to impossible. This probably explains why the men who shared their experiences in this chapter kept on going until it was too late, and they were forced to stop. When a regular user stops taking steroids, they can get withdrawal pains as their body becomes used to the drug's empowering influence. The psychological process of seeing all those gains disappearing is also a major reason why bodybuilders stay on them for so long. Even though they know these drugs are bad for them, they simply cannot stop. And that is when you might experience the advanced medical problems listed in this chapter. It is the irresponsible, abuse of steroids that causes their major side effects and problems. Superstar Billy Graham himself said, after experiencing all of his medical problems, that despite the heavy price he paid for using steroids he would do it all again to experience the rewards associated with being massive and strong. My advice is simply never to start in the first place. If you are on them get off now before it is too late.

Dan Lurie Says, "Say no to drugs"

Still Going Strong: Dan with weightlifting legend Tommy Kono (top photo) and 1943 Mr. America Jules Bacon (bottom photo) in 2005 - men who did not rely on steroids.

I feel that anyone who begins taking steroids will experience some kind of medical problem. It is just a question of time. Steroid inventor, Zeigler, himself suffered from heart disease, a condition he partially links to his experimentation with these drugs. He died in 1983 from heart failure and in his final days he condemned steroids, saying in his introduction to Bob Goldman's famous book on drugs in sport, *Death in the Locker Room*, that "if it wasn't enough that we had to deal with drug addicts there are now healthy people putting themselves in the same category. It's a disgrace. Who plays sports for fun anymore," he said. Who indeed.

I am still amazed by the large number of bodybuilding athletes who take drugs when they may not even make it to the pros and even if they do, the chance of making decent money may only go to the top few guys. I can only assume that money is the only real motivation these men have for pumping their bodies full of dangerous drugs. Otherwise, what is the point? Why not just build muscle naturally? With their genetics I am sure the champions of today could build terrific physiques without drugs. Of course there has always been a fascination with being the biggest and the best. Even when the WBBG was in full swing, most of my champions were taking steroids. I knew this but was powerless to do anything. Besides, they were grown men, responsible for their own lives. I did make it known that I hated what they were doing whenever I could, but in the end I had to do the best I could under the circumstances. Yes my champions were all great competitors, but I do not approve of their steroid use. And I am not contradicting myself here. Champions are champions: it is one of the routes that are taken to become one that differs, not the overall mindset that governs their ultimate training outcomes. In fact, over the years, even when heading the WBBG, I gave thousands of talks to many different groups. Any chance I got I would, and still do, mention the harmful effects of steroids. Children especially should know the dangers of steroids. It saddens me to see that high school kids are using steroids to get bigger and stronger for sport. When I broke sporting records at Tilden High in the 1930s, I did so with heart and courage, not drugs. Today I tell kids that it takes these qualities to succeed and that they cannot expect to find victory in a bottle.

Dan Lurie Says, "Say no to drugs"

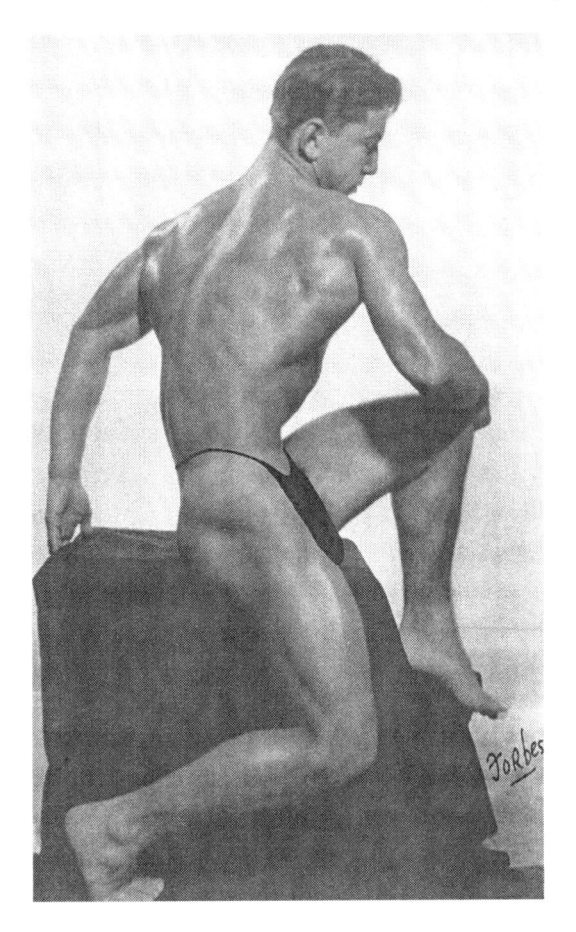

Great Physique, Built Naturally: a teenage Dan, just starting out.

In writing this chapter I spoke with a man I go a long way back with. A respected researcher on drugs in sport, Dr. Bob Goldman, like myself, is a strength record holder and began as a weight-training athlete. Bob is a fine representative of the benefits of weight training and has proven his natural strength by being listed in the Guinness Book of Records for several of his feats, including 13,500 consecutive sit-ups and 321 non-stop handstand push-ups.

Bob, who has studied the negative effects of steroids for over 30 years, believes these drugs can be very dangerous and strongly advises athletes against taking them. His view is that steroids do have a legitimate use, but should only be given to those who are genuinely hormone deficient. He says there are many side effects associated with steroid use including cardiovascular disease - a drop in the beneficial HDL's (High Density Lipoproteins) and an increase in the damaging LDL's (Low Density Lipoproteins). He also told me that the joints and ligaments of the body might get damaged because when the lifter is on steroids they are forced to lift too much weight compared to what the muscles can safely handle under normal conditions.

I have always felt that ethically the athletes of today are far removed from the training culture that we had back in the 1940s and '50s and of course this is to be expected: it is a different age. But does the rampant drug use that goes with these changing attitudes make it right? I seriously doubt it. Bob also feels the athletes of today are often into the quick win and will do whatever it takes to get there. He feels ethics today are "pretty sparse and pretty blurred." I have to agree with him.

I am often asked what separates those competitors of the 1940s, '50s and '60s who were steroid free from bodybuilders of today, who all tend to take the stuff. I think what it comes down to is work ethic and good genetics. Those who really stood out back then, men like Marvin Eder, were simply cut from a completely different cloth and their genetics separated them from other bodybuilders. This enabled them to make great, steroid-like progress with no drugs. These men also had an ability to work like you wouldn't believe. They were workhorses who would never slack off, never miss a workout and never doubt their ability for one moment. It seems people are always looking for an easy way in today's world. In my era there were no easy ways, but in the '60s steroids made rapid gains possible. Call me old fashioned, but I would rather put in 100 percent effort and work harder and longer without the drugs.

I am also asked if the physiques of today are any better than those of the 1940s, '50s and '60s. I believe not. For one thing they all seem to look the same. Place a bag over each of the competitors' heads in any given line-up these days and you will be hard pressed to tell who is who. When drugs weren't so common the men were easy to identify onstage. Now the look is overly large and in many cases bloated. There are some exceptions but they only serve to prove the rule.

The best physical specimen of all time would, for my money, have to have been Steve Reeves. He was never known as a drug user and I believe he never touched a steroid in his life, and his physique reflected that. It was perfect from all angles and showed no signs of steroid use, excessive bloating and extreme massiveness. Had Steve Reeves taken steroids, at his height and structure he would have tipped the scales at least 250 pounds and he was never that heavy. I personally believe that if the physiques of today were in the mould of Reeves, bodybuilding would be a better, safer sport.

"They Were Workhorses". (Left to right) An 18-year-old Dan with fellow workhorses: Paul Como, Barton Horvath and 1938 Mr. America Bert Goodrich. Photo taken in 1941, one year before Dan entered his first Mr. America contest.

Though bodybuilding has become an activity where steroids and other anabolic drugs are used to gain the edge, many people have made great efforts to inform the pubic on their dangers. In 1975, former NABBA Mr. Universe, Chet Yorton, who once beat Arnold in bodybuilding competition, formed the Natural Bodybuilders Association, and in that same year it become the first federation to test for steroid use among its athletes. I was at this first show, held in Las Vegas, and remember that all the athletes had to pass a urine test. The event was reviewed in *MTI* and at the time gave hope to those like myself who wanted to see the sport cleaned up. At this contest Chet gave an onstage speech where he said: "See friends, these are the real champions." I had to agree with him. Three years before this contest, in the February 1971 issue of *Muscle Training Illustrated* magazine, I was the first publisher ever to expose the dangers of steroids, right on the cover, on which the great Mr. America Chuck Sipes said he was quitting competition because he did not want to compete against steroid drug users. Inside he said that drugs were destroying musclemen. The entire editorial was dedicated to the dangers of steroids.

Telling The Truth: Bodybuilding champion Chet Yorton explains the dangers of anabolic steroids to Dan (left) and magazine publisher Robert Kennedy (right) at Chet's 1975 Las Vegas, steroid tested bodybuilding event. Dennis Tinerino was the overall winner.

Dan Lurie Says, "Say no to drugs"

I do not write this chapter as an attempt to claim any kind of superiority over anyone else or to condemn the champions of today. My views are my views and the guys of today will continue to do what they wish to do. I do so as a way to bring greater awareness to an issue that is all too often glossed over by those who claim to represent the best interests of those seeking health and fitness. It is hoped this chapter will help to convince people that bodybuilding drugs are not the answer. Train like the champions of old and do it naturally. Your body will thank you and you will enjoy a longer, more productive life.

"You will enjoy a longer, more productive life." Dan, at age 19: with his 1942 Mr. America awards.

Documented record of deaths from steroids: from 1975 to 2007

Bodybuilders: 1,289

Pro Wrestlers: 985

Athletes   21 and older: 1,374

                -Under 21: 364

Women   21 and older: 119

                -Under 21: 88

TOTAL 4,219

Source: US Dept. of Drugs and Alcohol.

For the past 27 years, 156 deaths resulting from steroid use are, on average, reported each year.

Chapter Fourteen:

Bodybuilding Pioneer

Bodybuilding to me is all about the training. Always has been. A hard, focused and intelligent approach to hoisting the iron is what it takes to build a great physique, possibly even a championship winning one. When I began weight training in 1938, my body showed little of the potential that would see me win the AAU America's Most Muscle Man title three times consecutively.. I was skinny, but had good shape. I remember training on an old bench with a 100-pound weight set and, for about a year, did many different exercises with this set, along with callisthenics-type movements, before joining my first gym. That first year of training was tough; there were few training manuals around, as bodybuilding had not become even remotely scientific and the gains I did make over that period came through experimenting with different approaches and careful monitoring of my training progress. I would note every improvement, however small, and adjust my training to stimulate further gains.

Back then a person usually trained for strength, and weightlifting was the number one iron sport. If you wanted to lift weights, simple: you joined a weightlifting gym. But for me weight training for strength was only one thing, and I loved to increase my lifts just as much as the next person, but building the body, developing it evenly with attention to aesthetics and proportion, was what I really enjoyed most. In the 1930s, this was not really something that was emphasized. People focused on the two big weightlifting movements, which were the snatch and the clean and jerk. These built size but not the kind of shape needed to win bodybuilding titles. And that is what I wanted: the big titles.

"I Wanted the Big Titles": A teenage Dan, dreaming of greatness.

At the time the men I looked up to were those who managed to build great shape along with size, while increasing their strength levels. Eugen Sandow and Bernarr MacFadden were two of the few who had achieved this kind of shape and who were tremendously strong for their time, but there were others who were ready to continue the legacy these men had left, through a more structured way of displaying the body to its best advantage. What we needed was a contest where we could show what we had worked so hard to build, and that is what we eventually got. The Mr. America competition was born and at last there was an event that awarded those who had the best-developed bodies, not only those who were strongest. But for the time being I slaved away in my parents' basement, developing my own ideas on training, methods and principals that would, in the years to follow, allow me to compete at the highest level and, further along, help others achieve their own muscle-building goals.

"Drop-sets", "rest-pause", "cheating", and "instinctive training" were among the many training principals I experimented with during the years prior to my first Mr. America showing. I discovered early on, through necessity, as my physique was not the best genetically, that in order to stimulate my muscles all these approaches would need to be used. So that is what I did. I attacked my muscles from all angles in every conceivable way. After joining Hy Schaeffer's Adonis Gym in 1939, I intensified my efforts and, because Hy emphasized weightlifting movements, used these too.

I truly believe my body would not have become as big and strong as it did, had I not taken a balanced, progressive approach to training, meaning I used many different exercises and tried to achieve greater intensity each time I trained. My early training was often hit or miss, but I eventually learned to add detail and balance to my physique through discarding what did not work and keeping what did. In the *late* 1930s, no one really thought too much about challenging the training methodology of the day. Most people trained with massive poundages on the Olympic weightlifting movements, an approach that generally involved a lot of pressing for very few sets. It really made a lot of sense to me to mix things up and try new approaches. If you train a muscle over and over using the same methods, what will happen? Eventually that muscle will become used to the imposed stress and refuse to grow further. It will adapt. This is one of the first rules of training for ongoing results: always seek to challenge the muscles in new ways. This is what I did and it paid off.

Dan Lurie: Heart of Steel

"It Paid Off": Dan, at age 18, after two years of bodybuilding training.

Bodybuilding Pioneer

My physique reflected the training knowledge I had gained through much trial and error. In the years to follow, others within the bodybuilding industry would come out with the same ideas that I had used in 1939, and bodybuilding would evolve into a major discipline, with its own set of scientifically based guidelines and methods. Complete bodybuilding systems would be developed and various trainers would claim authority over bodybuilding training methods and principals. In reality, though, training with weights and gaining muscle through progressive resistance had been done for centuries, well before I picked up my first dumbbell. It has been due to the combined efforts of people like myself, Bernarr MacFadden, Dr. Frederick Tilney and Joe Weider that it has become a system and a science in its own right.

The truth is, I was doing drop-sets and cheat-reps long before Weider packaged and marketed these, along with all the other "principles" he claimed were his. I have to give credit where it is due and Joe has helped bodybuilding to become the popular sport it is today, but to say he is the father of bodybuilding or The Trainer of Champions is quite incorrect. Sure he has helped, and his guidance has assisted many champions, but bodybuilding does not begin and end with his influence. Joe simply put his name on existing methods of training, dressed them up a bit, and marketed them as his own. One thing you cannot doubt is his promotional ability and enthusiasm - traits that helped push him to the top. Had I not chosen to pursue an acting career and run a chain of gyms, while further developing my barbell business along with starting a large family in those early years, and instead focused more on promotion, or even begun a magazine sooner, things might have been different. Who knows what might have happened. It all came down to a question of timing and Joe had that base covered; he hit the market when the world was ready for bodybuilding instruction and because of this, people came to believe he developed the whole industry. People must remember that there were many main players in the bodybuilding industry before Joe and these people should also be considered.

While Joe was steadily building his empire, I continued to train many great champions. The 1960s and '70s were real boom eras for the health and fitness movement and it was during this period that I advised many people - face to face and through my magazines - on training, diet and the finer details of pre-competition preparation. Champions would seek my advice and I was only too happy to help. I never lost site of the fact I was once in their position. I was one of them after all and always will be. Bodybuilding is a sport I loved as much as seeing my athletes succeeding, and nothing would make me happier than seeing the results of their gym efforts.

Perfecting The Form: Dan guiding WBBG athlete, Josh Rivera.

My most successful bodybuilder was Lou Ferrigno, who at age 16 was brought to me because he wanted to put on weight. In three years I managed to help him pack on over 70 pounds of solid muscle. Among other better-known personalities I have trained were bodybuilders George Eiferman, Warren Frederick, Freddie Ortiz and Steve Michalik along with wrestlers Superstar Billy Graham, Ivan Putski, Bruno Sammartino and Tony Atlas and gym owners, Tom Minichiello, Julie Levine and Joe Gold. I even helped to train Joe Weider from 1942 to 1948. This was at a time when we were good friends and would train together when we met up to do business, usually at my Clarkson Avenue gym in Brooklyn. I would push Joe to get more reps and I have to say he was an incredibly focused man. We even had photos taken posing together. Joe learned a lot from me during this time, and because of the progress I was making, he began regularly featuring me in his magazines. In fact, in the May 1943 edition of *Your Physique*, Joe printed the following:

"Then follows the exciting climb to the top of the ladder, where robust health, wonderful strength and marvelous muscles are his, and his to keep. No one can ever take them away. Such intangible possessions constitute the greatest wealth obtainable. Then he may glance backwards and visualize the ordinary individual he once was, and if this former self could stand side by side with his present self, no one would believe that the two were once the same person.

"The only way a check can be made is to compare a photograph of the fellow taken before he started his climb with a photo taken when he has reached the top, and now LOOK! Look at the transformation of Dan Lurie shown in connection with this article! Have you seen anything more impressive? It is actually hard to believe the ordinary chap who had been dabbling in light training and was photographed before he lifted a barbell, is one and the same, when compared with the massive strongman who posed ten months later; but these are bona fide proofs of an amazing result Dan Lurie obtained by adhering to proper training after he suddenly resolved to make the most of himself that one day, a few years back. Now, today, he is one of the foremost strongmen in the world, and possesses a most massive physique. Dan, we offer a salvo of salutes to you."

At the time Joe published this, we were training together and I was making my assault on the 1944 Mr. America; he was learning what it took to become a bodybuilding champion through my efforts in the gym. For all the drama that has happened between Joe and I, I still fondly recall the days we trained together, an era where bodybuilding was new and fresh, where we trained for the sheer joy of physical improvement.

Dan Lurie: Heart of Steel

Then there were the many thousands who never made it to the big time, but who did make great progress under my supervision. One man who made it big was comedian, Shecky Green, who was a headline act in Las Vegas for more than 30 years and will be remembered as being one of the world's most talented performers. Throughout his career Shecky battled weight problems, which affected his ability to perform. That was until he met me and lost 50 pounds using my *Instant Action Postitrain* approach, so called because I always believed that one should constantly advance forward in their training and with my system they could make noticeable progress in muscle size in mere weeks of following it. In Shecky's case it also worked wonders for fat loss.

From Fat to Fabulous: Dan with another satisfied customer, Shecky Green.

I also designed a complete weight-training program for another well-known actor, Yul Brynner, famous for his role in The King and I and The Ten Commandments. I recall that, under my guidance, he added a tremendous amount of muscle to bulk up for some of his later roles.

Bodybuilding Pioneer

Yul Brynner

A sharp eye for detail never leaves you and to this day I know what to look for in those asking me for training advice. I also train myself every day, mostly with bodyweight exercises, but also with lighter weights for very high repetitions. My rep ranges these days will often reach 100, but this has kept me fit and active at 85 years young. I can honestly say that today my energy levels and degree of motivation are as high as they have ever been, but you can't fight nature and my training intensity is way down compared to where it once was. Actually I give bodybuilding full credit for keeping me focused and alert. A recent medical test showed my health to be excellent and my energy is as high as ever thanks to the iron.

85.5 Years' Young: Dan doing what he does best; hitting the iron

My training philosophy has always favored higher repetitions and moderate weights to stimulate the muscles and develop physical fitness at the same time. To me, bodybuilding should be about building health along with the physique and I figured rather than do countless hours of aerobics, why not combine endurance with weight training. I was one of the first bodybuilders to popularize this method, and my appearance and the fact I was able to perform athletically at a high level, resulted. I also learned the importance of combining exercises in that first year of training. After taking the bar I would do one all-out set bench presses, re-rack the bar and quickly move on to floor press-ups to emphasize the stretch and more fully pump the muscles with blood. Most of my exercises would be done in this fashion as in doing so would allow me to accomplish two goals: I would improve my endurance to become fitter and healthier and I would shape my muscles better than I could with just one set of one exercise, with a minute or so rest in between. Later on other trainers would discover this method of combining two exercises into one and today it is called, among other things, super-setting. Again, many of today's most popular training principals and methods were actually used, and eventually pioneered by myself during my early years as a competitor. But I also give credit to those who came before me.

Progressive resistance, where the amount of weight lifted is increased progressively over a certain training period to force the muscles to super-compensate and grow, was an idea identified by Alan Calvert over 100 years ago. But before Alan, who, by the way, was instrumental in developing and distributing the first barbells with his founding of the Milo Barbell Company in 1902, took weightlifting, which was a pretty primitive practice at the time, and transformed it into a proper system with its own set of instructions, things were pretty basic. In fact, the practice of weight training goes back many years. Archaeologists discovered that barbells were used by the Egyptians thousands of years ago and the concept of progressive resistance, which lies at the heart of bodybuilding, is something that has been known of for centuries, ever since Milo of Croton, cited as the father of progressive resistance, began lifting a calf on his back to test his strength. As the calf grew, so too did Milo. This principal of overload, minus the bull, was to be used by myself, and every other bodybuilder of the early 20th century, and all of them since. Of course, when I began weight training at age 15, I had no idea of what all this meant. But it did make sense, so I kept doing it and in a short period devised my own ideas on training to become one of America's top musclemen.

All the principals I used in the late 1930s would be passed down to people who trained with me and who came to me for advice. People then came up with their own systems of training and today there are thousands of different approaches. It seems that every trainer or ex-bodybuilding champion has their own way of doing things, and this is great as it provides a greater number of options for those starting out. A good trainer, these days, should have a thorough knowledge of the different systems of training to effectively assist those seeking their guidance. Whether it be the Heavy Duty approach of low sets and all-out intensity popularized by Mike Mentzer in the 1970s and '80s, the higher volume system used by many bodybuilders of the '70s or the super-set/endurance method I pushed, every "way" has something to offer the trainee. Personally I think they all have merit and would consider any of them when training someone for competition, provided the bodybuilder is responding well to that particular method. There is more than one way to skin a cat.

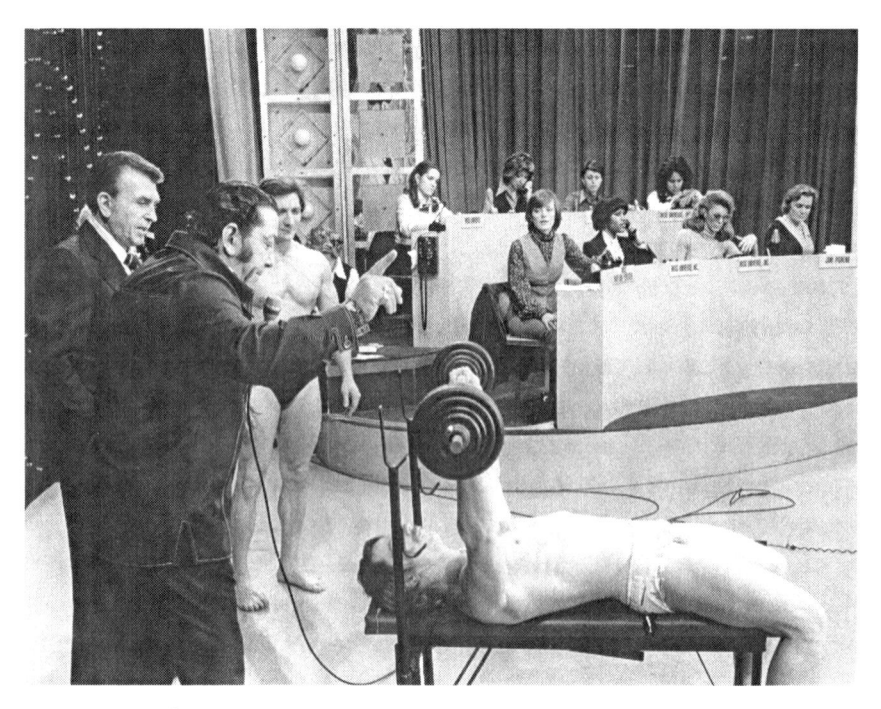

Dan The Motivator: Dan encourages "one more rep" on the The Muscular Dystrophy Telethon with Dennis James.

It wouldn't be until 1979 that I published my training ideas in a book. Before then many of my methods were taught to people the world over through my magazine, *Muscle Training Illustrated,* and the positive feedback I received daily from those who followed this advice prompted me to summarize my methods in my first book, *Pro Mr. America, Instant Action Positrain.* For me the key with developing any one of my champions was always to first assess them for weak body parts. If they were not proportionate, I would then aim to build up their weak areas before building overall size. As both a competitor and trainer, size for the sake of size has never been my goal. If a competitor were lacking in one area, I would recommend training specifically for balance. My approach was to emphasize the weak muscle group and cut way back on training stronger areas until everything was proportionate. Getting in shape through definition training was something I also pushed. I truly believed that a bodybuilder could continue to grow if they trained correctly, got enough rest and sleep and ate enough high quality calories. Always a big believer in bodyweight exercises - especially for beginners - I developed a plan that would combine these with the popular added resistance weight training movements of the day.

Sissy squats, one-arm floor dips, push-ups between chairs and step-ups using a chair were among the many bodyweight exercises I used. My theory here was that this approach in the early stages would accustom the body to training with resistance, while encouraging the flexibility, athleticism and technique needed to more effectively move the heavier stuff when the time came for that. The first phase would be five weeks of bodyweight exercises before engaging the barbell and dumbbell workouts that upped the intensity and really packed on the mass. More advanced trainees could go directly to the barbell and dumbbell workouts – barbells and dumbbells because I believed, and still believe, that these provide the necessary full-range-of-motion and gravitational pull needed to properly tax the muscles.

My system included my exercise-combination principal along with full-range-of-motion for all exercises, adequate rest and nutrition, consistency and a focus on training for balance. *Instant Action Positrain* was written with these ideas in mind and presented the training system that I had developed and used to get thousands of people the bodybuilding results they wanted.

To trial my approach I had several of my champions at the time workout using my ideas. Their results were spectacular to say the least, with all of them achieving their best possible shape and muscle gains. One of these men, Anibal Lopez, used my methods successfully to win the 1978 WBBG Pro Mr. America and Pro Mr. World contests. He looked fantastic in both contests. In fact, he had just come off his win at the Mr. World when we took the photos that accompanied the book's exercise descriptions. In these images he was the biggest and most ripped I had ever seen him. Anibal achieved such great results that he went on to win the 1980 WBBG Pro Mr. America and Mr. World competitions. Don Ross, who won my Pro Mr. America in 1977, was another who made great progress following my system. The results of his efforts also featured in *Instant Action Positrain*.

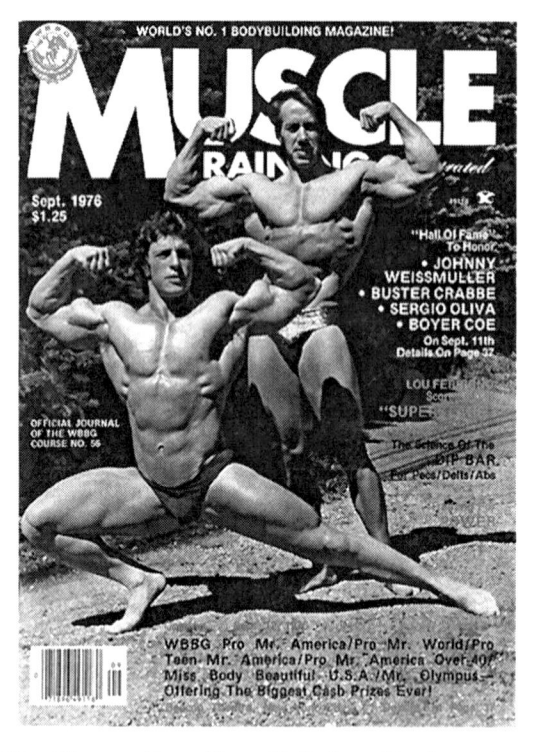

The Ripper: Don Ross (left, kneeling) on the September 1976 cover of *MTI*.

Along with using a targeted approach involving exercise combinations and bodyweight exercises, I also believe that we are all built a certain way so we should all find what works best for us. As I mentioned, higher repetitions worked best for me, but others might need heavier weights and lower reps to grow. That is why my system of training always ensured the trainee use a weight and rep range that suited them, so long as they trained for balance and maintained their health with endurance work.

Speaking of endurance, when it comes to getting aerobically fit, a person has to balance their cardio workload with weight training to get the best of all worlds: low body fat levels, good health and lean muscle. That is why I tend to favor low volume/higher intensity aerobics. A favorite cardio method of mine involves and apparatus that can be taken anywhere and used at any time. I like to call it the "magic rope" and I have personally found it to be the best way get into, and stay in shape. It's magic because you cannot see it. In fact, it does not even exist. I recommend initially using this "rope" mornings or evenings three to four times a week for a few minutes, before building up to 30 minutes or so. You use this rope by picking it up and beginning to skip as you would normally. Twist and twirl it over your head and continue skipping as it passes beneath your feet. Move your feet in different directions, skip backwards and even run forwards and backwards. They key, as with all of my recommended exercises, is to add a little more intensity to the movement each time you do it. You could increase the time or quicken the pace. Am I joking? Actually no. As crazy as it may sound, this exercise really works wonders. Having an imaginary rope means anyone of any age, size or shape can skip and the variations in hand movement and foot placement allow many more muscle groups to be worked compared to regular rope jumping. I began jumping rope back when I started boxing as a kid. All boxers will tell you, as I will now: jumping rope improves coordination, endurance and athletic performance probably better than anything else. Call me old fashioned but it really works.

People often ask me whether there are any secrets to building muscle and losing fat. I always reply that the only real requirements are hard work, a commitment to improving your physique and the right knowledge. In over 70 years as a trainer to many world champions and promoter of bodybuilding at the highest level, I have found many things to work well. Here is a list of what I feel every aspiring bodybuilder should know. Included are several principals that I learned when I was starting out and which are still in vogue today.

Training Minds Unite: Dan with the youngest ever Mr. America, Casey Viator (left, seated), bodybuilding genius, Arthur Jones (right, standing), and a dapper Sergio Oliva (easily identified).

-Be specific

The number one principal for getting in shape and staying that way is to follow a system that works for you based on your own requirements, not for someone with a different genetic blueprint. In order to fully assess exactly what is needed to reach your potential, it is important to try a number of approaches and record all results. From this information, build a program that works for you. You might need to train longer and harder, like me. Others might require less work to get the same results. In fact, for these people long sessions might work against them and result in over-training. One thing I have always tried to emphasize - for everyone I have trained - is specificity of training. Simply put, what works for me may not work for you. We all have different recovery abilities and genetic dispositions. To expect one program to work for everyone is like thinking we will all make it to the professional bodybuilding level if we follow the system a Ronnie Coleman-sized competitor would use.

This is not to say some systems do not work better than others. For example, eight to 12 repetitions for four sets per exercise are seen as an acceptable way to add muscle size. Here the workload and exercises used on a given day can be changed around to accommodate a lifter's unique requirements. This is something that all beginners should understand.

-Work smart

All the training knowledge in the world means very little if you fail to train in a safe, productive way. I learned early on that to stay active in the bodybuilding game I would need to stimulate my muscles to a certain point, and then ease off when required. Once again, the body requires high intensity as a stimulus, but also enough recovery time to complete the muscle growth process. The way I would train my muscles was in a controlled fashion, lowering for a two-count on the negative (lowering) part of the movement and speeding it up for a one-count on the positive (contracting, or pushing part). I would put my mind into my muscles and through this connection feel them working over a full range of motion. I like to call this "the mind/muscle link".

I would sometimes also use a little looser form to "cheat" the weight up to get past a sticking point, but even this, as paradoxical as it may sound, would be deliberate and controlled. For example, to increase the weight's momentum on a bicep curl, push the hips forward slightly when pulling the weight up. This will help you to achieve a peak contraction, something I would always aim for as a competitor, and even today. Another tip: to get a perfect peak contraction on exercises such as the bench press, bicep curl and barbell row, always keep continuous tension on the muscle and give an extra squeeze at the top of the movement. Contract hard, then squeeze. That little bit of extra tension is just the ticket to faster gains.

Another key to achieving great bodybuilding results is to set little goals, then work away at achieving these goals. I would have a diary and note all progress, and constantly reflect on where I had been and what was left to achieve. All my bodybuilding goals were attained this way and I urge you to do the same. As an example, you might aim to lose two inches off your waist in six weeks. You would write this goal in your diary, before selecting the best approach to achieving this outcome. Take a measuring tape and assess your progress every week at the same time and under the same conditions to achieve a more accurate measurement, and note the result in your diary. Using this method you will 1) know how well your approach is working and 2) have an ongoing source of motivation, which will help you achieve your goal faster. Train smart by setting goals, using the right approach for your needs, working the muscle in a controlled thoughtful manner and knowing when to ease off.

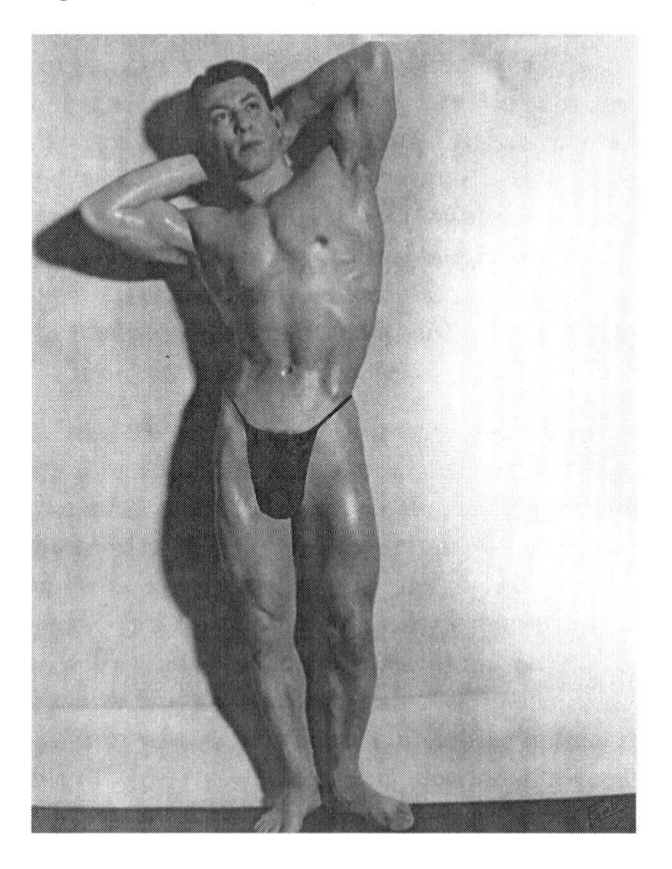

Set Your Goals: One of Dan's first physique photos, his progress made possible through goal setting and a willingness to follow through.

-Use intensity techniques to boost your gains

My program always revolved around the basic movements. When I was 16 years old there were no real variations to the basic three sets of 15 in the bench press and so on. Progressive resistance was a known concept, but it was not widely practiced. And people generally got it all wrong and did too much too soon and, as a result, many either reached a sticking point and progress for them stopped, or they became injured and dropped out. Because my goals were lofty and I wanted to become America's Most Muscular Man, I could not continue to do what I had always done. So as well as progressively increasing either the weights lifted, but usually the number of repetitions I performed in an add reps style - to be explained soon - I experimented with several techniques that have become known the world over as methods for increasing the intensity of a given exercise. The following four methods are what I did and what I recommend for intermediate to advanced bodybuilders.

End of set pausing

At the completion of a set, when no further reps are possible, simply pause for one to two seconds before banging out another rep. I usually recommend aiming for two to three pauses per set. One thing to remember: use this method and all other intensity techniques infrequently to stimulate gains while avoiding undue stress being placed on the system.

When we near the end of a set, the muscle fills with a waste product - a by-product of anaerobic metabolism - called lactic acid, which prevents further contractions. As a big believer in getting the most from a set, I would try to extend that set any way possible. Pausing is one method that worked well for me.

Super-sets

From day one I was a firm believer in increasing muscle endurance along with strength, power and, of course, size. Super-setting, which I called combined-set training, achieves all of this and can be used to increase the productiveness of your workout. To perform: complete, for example, one set of biceps curls and follow this immediately with a set of triceps pushdowns to work the bicep's antagonist muscles. This is a great way to get an overall arm pump and I could get mine up to around 20 inches using this method. Super-setting can also be used with individual muscle groups by simply selecting two exercises that work the same muscle and performing them back-to-back. Again, to stimulate gains use super-sets for one or two exercises in perhaps every second or third workout. Don't overdo it.

Drop-sets

Another way to increase muscle endurance and tax muscle fibers to the limit is through taking a weight that you can perform a good 10 to 12 repetitions with. Upon finishing the set, reduce the weight by 30 percent and complete another 10 to 12, reduce again by 30 percent and do as many reps as possible. Performing sets in this manner progressively overloads the muscles like nothing else and believe me when I say the pump is incredible.

I recall doing drop sets in the build up to my first Mr. America. People thought I was crazy putting myself through what appeared to be torture, but I continued to use this method in most of my workouts and the results showed. Today, drop-sets are common practice. Who would have thought?

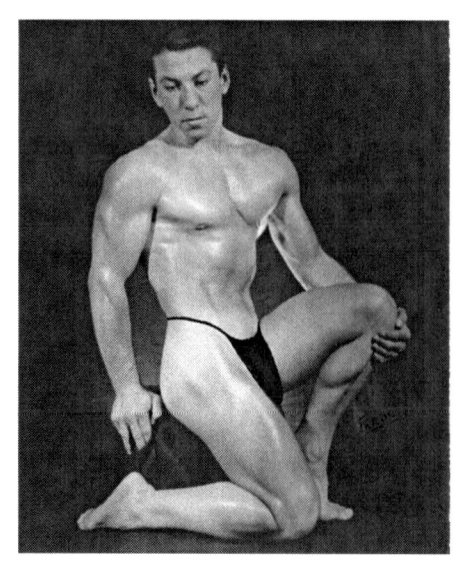

**Drop sets helped develop this physique: two
early classic photos of a teenage Dan.**

Add Reps

When starting out in bodybuilding I would always be on lookout for smart ways to train, since my life was busy with my barbell and gym businesses. I needed that extra time. Then I hit on an approach that increased the intensity of my workout and saved me time. I called it the Add Reps principal and it has enhanced my workouts ever since. It is probably the simplest principal in all of bodybuilding but one of the most effective, and very few people know of it. Here is how it works in its simplest form: when completing any exercise, and upon attaining failure, rather than rack the bar and add weight, simply add another rep.

The thinking behind this is that people tend to stop short of all they can do because they feel the weight is too light. They get caught up in adding too much weight, thinking that this will enhance their growth. What I have found is these people will usually opt for ultra-heavy weights in place of correct technique and, because of this, will hoist the weight up any way they can, risking injury and achieving substandard results in the process. By adding a rep you shift away from the 'more weight is best' mentality and concentrate on what you really should be focusing on: quality of movement. And you would be amazed at the intensity you can build by just adding one more rep rather than increasing the weight, which might break the flow of the movement, as you have to stop your set to adjust the weight, and might result in sloppy form as you may be pushing beyond your abilities. It is also one of the best time-effective ways to train.

In some cases I have had champions cut their sessions in half by just adding a rep here and there. We can exclude whole sets and the time it takes to change weights. I am not telling you to ignore the important goal of systematically increasing the weight. Rather, what I advise is to place less of an emphasis on this and more on grinding out that extra rep. When you feel your current poundages are no longer enough, then you can up the weight - but only when you can no longer get that extra rep, which included at the end of a hard set is, I would argue, as effective as doing another set.

For the more advanced, I recommend the add reps approach that really boosted my progress, which includes using several exercises along with the high reps. When I first started out, I began using this system, which I have now done most of my training life, with a partner. With my partner Marty I would do one rep and he would do one, then I would do two and he would do two – we would play follow the leader in this fashion right up until we could do no more. Then eventually I discovered a way to increase the intensity even more, by combining five exercises into one: the reverse curl, the curl, the back (behind neck) and front press and the squat being a popular combination. To do this I would start with one rep and my partner would do one and so on like before. But this time you do all five exercises back to back, achieving the desired number of repetitions for each before moving on. It's a killer. Even massive men like Harold Poole and Freddy Ortiz couldn't go over eight reps because they didn't train for endurance. It was a different type of training. I would go up to 10, while other athletes would stop at seven or eight. And one to seven amounts to 28 reps if you increase the reps with each successive turn, which is what we did. So if you keep on going you end up doing a lot of repetitions all combined from five exercises at one time. For the ten reps I usually did over five sets that would be 260 reps in total! I felt I got the best bodybuilding results doing it that way and you really do see how your body changes.

I would often train more conventionally, but with higher reps of course, and end each workout with my combined sets. They talk of supersets and giant sets, but this was truly an intense way of grouping your sets. Sometimes I would also do one mega set of press-ups to finish a workout - as many as I could - this time doubling them as I went: one, two, four, eight, continuing up to six lots of reps, which would be 53 reps in total. We got to the point where my partner would do one and I would double everything he did, as his endurance was not at my level. He did two and I did four. For a typical five-rep set I would be doing 31 reps in total. Nowadays I do a variation on this where the reps are not doubled for each "rep" but are done in a logical progression as explained earlier: one rep, two reps, three reps and so on. The same set of five that would give me 31 reps doubling the reps each time, would give me 15 reps and I usually complete 12 reps, which gives me 76 reps total.

The Man With the Arms: Dan with WBBG competitor Freddy Ortiz, and a fan.

I mentioned earlier the importance of increasing training weights every so often, but as far as I'm concerned this should not be your priority. Actually I never really increased the weight. I would just add one rep and keep going up. At the beginning I would add weight until I found I wasn't getting the results I wanted – adding reps I was sweating more and my muscles found it harder to work. I was building up endurance. Strength was needed but I didn't look for strength, I looked for the endurance. I recommend anyone try this and observe the results they get.

So the key for me at least was to use lighter weights and combine the exercises. I would also change my grip and do the movement in different ways to confuse the muscles for new gains. For example, I would reverse my hands when pressing dumbbells either overhead or lying on a bench. It worked wonders as it targeted a different part of the muscle. And I kept it light. I remember all the other guys in the gym were killing themselves with heavy weights. It wasn't necessary. At night I would take a 40-pound dumbbell and do 300 reps on pullovers, nice and easy. Just a light dumbbell, but the reps would be stretching your lat muscles and developing the back. I would alternate between holding the dumbbell closer together and doing do a stiff-arm movement with a barbell.

Push the boundaries training

One thing I have learned is you sometimes need to be a little unorthodox to get the best results. Do not be afraid to push the boundaries of training convention in a safe manner, as in doing so you will get further in your quest for massive muscles. Another thing I would do to get major pumps is set up little competitions with my training partner. In fact, the best pump I ever got was when I challenged my partner to a dumbbell press/pullover contest back in the mid-'50s. Here is how it went. I took a 50-pound dumbbell - if you decide to try this at home, you might want, or need, to use a lighter weight - and bench-pressed it once with my left arm and once with my right arm before doing one pullover. Meanwhile my partner did the same combination. We worked our way up from one to 28 reps this way, using the add reps logical progression method, and by the 20th rep it felt as if someone has stuffed molten larva under all of my upper body muscles. The pain was intense and the challenge was making it to 25 reps - we both made it, but it took at least ten minutes before we could continue the rest of our workout! We would also have competitions, where a couple of dumbbells would be passed back and forth. For each set, starting with one rep, we would do double the number of reps that came before until we could not achieve our pre-determined number of reps. Say you were curling two 20-pound dumbbells for one rep. Well the second set would be two reps and the third set would be four reps and so on. Passing the weight back and forth, from partner to partner, would encourage you to do more than you normally would as, if you are anything like me, you don't want to fail before your partner does.

Bodybuilding Pioneer

**Pushing the Boundaries: Dan's training principals
built massive muscles over a short period.**

-Increase the endurance

As you will have learned by now, I am big on endurance. Drop-sets, super-sets, you name it and I would do it. In my early years I would specialize in endurance feats, setting many world records along the way. Though it takes many approaches to build big muscles, and you cannot expect everyone to gain using the same methods, I always believed that to fully assess strength, you must test muscular endurance. If you think about it: with the right training most of us could probably do a pretty respectable squat or bench press for a single lift. Get the same person to do 100 squats with a fraction of that weight and you will truly see the kind of strength I speak of.

Building muscle endurance is also a great way to burn fat - it also helps to create muscular definition. Why do countless hours of cardio when you can blast your muscles with training that is specific to the muscles you are working and growth enhancing? Building muscle endurance is something I credit for helping me to work hours that would completely break a lesser man. Over the years there have been very few times where I have felt overwhelmed with my workload. I guess if you can do thousands of push-ups and dips in one sitting, the demands of everyday life pale by comparison.

The great Arthur Saxon, who once bent-pressed 385 pounds, wrote in 1906: "Genuine strength should include not only momentary strength, but also the far more valuable kind of strength known as strength of endurance. The man who can miss a night of rest or miss a meal without showing any ill effects or without losing any physical power, is better entitled to be considered a strong man than the man who is only apparently strong, who possesses momentary strength which is, after all, a muscle test pure and simple." Like myself, Saxon, who built a massive physique to rival Eugen Sandow, believed in developing muscle endurance along with extraordinary power. His many strongman acts where he, among other feats, snatched 195 pounds and lifted 448 pounds proved that his endurance training did not interfere with his single lift strength.

For building the legs

One body part I have seen lagging on competitors more than any other is legs. Bodybuilders seem fascinated with building up the chest and arms, but when it comes to getting massive thighs they will often do a couple of sets of squats and that's it. The single most effective movement I have found for developing thigh shape and size is – don't laugh - Ballet Squats.

To perform this movement I would have my athletes put their heels together with their left and right toes pointing out. Place your feet on an imaginary line and turn them directly outward; then squat down, keeping a nice flat back and looking up. In learning to do this movement you will lose your balance until you get used to it, but it develops your legs like crazy. I gave this advice to many of my champions and they grew like crazy. If a bodybuilder is weaker in their inner leg area, ballet squats are the ticket. I would ask whoever I was working with at the time, that if they are using 400 to 500 pounds on the squat and killing themselves, why are their legs not improving? "Why don't you do a simple thing with 100 pounds?" I would say. They would usually reply, "You must be kidding." "Believe me," I would respond, "When I get through with you, you won't be able to walk." Of course they all started out with no weight until they were able to do it with lighter weights. Then I would have them add 10 pounds, 20 pounds to work their way up. It takes time - about three or four weeks - just to learn how to balance your body. But what inside definition and outer quad sweep you get. What a burn!

Nutrition, Dan Lurie style

Nutrition is also a key when aiming to build massive muscles or to simply get in good shape. Over the years I have witnessed many mistakes made in this area. The good thing about bodybuilding nutrition is that it is balanced eating for total health. This means everyone can benefit from eating a balanced bodybuilding diet. To avoid common dietary pitfalls, such as too many or too few calories, the wrong types of food for building muscle or energy-robbing foods, follow these tips.

-Eat less starch and fewer sweets

One thing that impresses me about bodybuilding today is the nutritional knowledge the guys have. Back in my time, things were pretty simple. We ate our vegetables and meat and drank a load of milk to get as big as possible. One problem that many of the guys back then had, though, was getting enough protein. They compensated for this by eating tons of starchy carbohydrates like bread and potatoes, and this often led to the smooth look seen on many competitors from this era. These days carbohydrate timing and the ability to determine the quality of these nutrients and structure them into the diet properly has become a science. And the physiques are far more cut as a result.

What I would do to boost my energy levels and keep my body fat low was eat most of my starchy carbohydrates early in the day, as this would provide the energy needed to train hard during the day while ensuring body fat was kept to a minimum. Eating heavy carbohydrate meals at night is one of the worst things people can do if they want to lose fat, as the body at this point may store any surplus and this is usually stored in the fat cells, not the muscles. Eating sweets is one thing I would avoid when aiming to get into shape. And even though I would be given free ice cream during my Sealtest days, this was the first thing to go when I needed to lose weight. My advice to you is to limit your starchy carbohydrate intake to earlier in the day and eliminate your intake of sweets. In doing so you will have more mental and physical energy and your fat free muscular body will thank you.

-Use less oil when cooking

Whether it is training an athlete for competition or advising the average person on healthy eating I would also assess overall energy balance before cutting back on, or increasing, calories. If you are having trouble losing weight, and this is a problem experienced by over half the American population, you might find that excess oils and fats are a major contributor.

Oils add many calories without our awareness. With a bowl of ice cream or a hamburger it is obvious that we are taking in more fat than we need. But with oils, they can be added to nearly anything, almost as an afterthought, and this can become a habit. A tablespoon of oil contains around 130 calories and it is not uncommon for many who have trouble losing weight to use up to five of these servings per day on salads or vegetables and when cooking in general. That is 650 calories per day of fat! Another thing about fat: it does not have the same kind of positive metabolic effect that protein has, and is more likely to be *stored* as fat. Eliminating oils can drastically reduce your overall fat intake.

-Eat more protein

Protein works differently to fat. A pure, high biological value protein source such as egg whites or chicken actually stimulates the body to burn a greater amount of fat compared to either carbohydrates or fat itself, because it requires your metabolism to increase its energy output. Our systems must work harder to process protein and this increases the rate at which we burn stored fat calories. In fact, protein will boost the metabolism by around 30 percent compared with fat, which will only give a 10 percent increase. Protein, especially sources that contain the essential amino acids that the body requires from food directly, also builds muscle, as we all probably know by now. And given muscle tissue is more metabolically active compared to fat, the more muscle we have, the more fat will be burned at rest. To develop a muscular body with low body fat, it makes sense to include at least 30 percent of your calories in the form of protein.

-Eat plenty of fresh fruit and vegetables

Carbohydrate sources that I always preferred when getting in shape came from certain vegetables and fruits, not from starchy bread, pasta and the like. Fruits and vegetables contain valuable life-giving vitamins and minerals and boost overall health. I recommend those who want to lose weight and build a muscular physique consume at least 50 percent of their daily calories from them. It should be noted here that fruits also contain sugar so it is best not to overdo them when aiming to lose weight, but they are by far a better alternative to sweets. Fruits I recommend are peaches, plums, apricots, raspberries, watermelon and oranges as they are lower in the concentrated sugar found in bananas, pineapple, figs, apples, prunes and grapes. This is not say that all fruits are not beneficial in some way, because they are. Just ensure the majority of your intake is based on the low sugar variety if weight loss is your aim.

-Avoid overeating

A mistake bodybuilders made back when I was competing was to eat too much at one sitting. In their eagerness to pack on quality muscle, guys would pack away over 1000 calories at one time, something that would almost always add more fat than muscle to their bodies.

I could never understand the process of bulking up in the off-season. To me, adding fat does not equate to gaining quality size so I never did this and chose to stay in shape year round when competing. The key to getting in shape is as it was back then: eat smaller meals more frequently. For the bodybuilder wanting to gain lean body mass, around 3000 calories a day is usually the best approach, although more may be needed depending on the size of the person. If you divide the first three meals of the day into 700 calories with the latter three supplying 300 calories you will have your 3000 calories. This approach will ensure you are getting sufficient calories early in the day, where they will be used to build muscle in the gym sessions to follow, and a reasonable, though necessarily smaller amount in the evening to prevent fat storage. If you were to average them out to 500 per meal over six meals this would probably provide too many calories in the evening. Eating three 1000-calorie meals would, for each meal, take too long to digest, negatively impacting training intensity (you will feel more lethargic) and contributing to fat gain as well.

A good calorie converter book will give you an idea of what foods to include and where to include them to get the right number of calories, considering you will be taking in roughly 50 percent of your calories from carbohydrates in the form of fruits and vegetables, 20 percent from good fats and 30 percent from protein. Remember that these ideas are suggested with the bodybuilder in mind. If you are interested in just losing fat and looking trim, simply cut the calorie count by around 500, but keep the ratio of protein, fats and carbohydrates the same. Female bodybuilders, who are generally smaller than their male counterparts, can also cut back on overall calories to suit their needs.

-Avoid eating between meals

Once you have your meal plan in place, eating between meals will only add unwanted calories. What is perhaps most important about the dietary advice given here is that it should prevent you from snacking during the day, as when we snack it is usually with the wrong kinds of foods. I recommend spacing all meals about three hours apart, with no eating in between. As it takes at least one to two hours on average for a meal to digest, eating again at this stage can interfere with this process and the body will not get the nutrients it needs at the right times.

The thing that appeals to me most about weight training and eating for bodybuilding purposes is that it is a continual learning process. Methods I learnt from those who came before me when I was starting out, and those that were uniquely my own, are still used widely today, but there are also many new ideas being developed all the time. This is great as it is a sign of bodybuilding progress and proof that the sport is continually evolving.

The nutrition and training industries have become big business. I never imagined this would be so when I first begun. Back then many people lacked the knowledge on how to best achieve massive muscles, as formalized instruction was not as widespread as it is today. Thanks to great strides made by those with the passion and courage to pioneer new ways of training and eating - to break away from the way things were done - we now have a booming industry.

One thing that amazes me today is the quality of the amateur athletes, many of which would compare well with the professionals of the 1960s and '70s. Along with the infiltration of drugs, I attribute this partly to advances in training and nutrition. I look back and feel satisfied that I played a part in bodybuilding's evolution and look forward to further supporting the sport that has given me so much.

All the excitement within the industry, and progress made by the new bodybuilding methods and systems, motivated me to consider promoting again. I figured at my age and given my energy levels are still high, why not re-establish the WBBG and its Hall of Fame. On August 25, 2007, we did just that with the WBBG North America Bodybuilding and Figure and Fitness Championships and International

Dan Lurie: Heart of Steel

Fitness and Sports Hall of Fame awards, held in South Portland, Maine. The training and nutrition knowledge I have gained over the years has given me an appreciation for what many competitors of today go through to get into great shape. A love for bodybuilding is something that doesn't leave you and I am happy to be back promoting contests. Never say never!

A Product of Good Nutrition: a teenage Dan shows what a good diet and training program can do.

Chapter Fifteen:

Back, Although Never Really Gone

In a recently published article on myself, the author said something that I have to completely agree with: "He's never really been gone, nevertheless he is back, behind the scenes, and soon will be in the limelight," the article said of my return to bodybuilding promotion. And it is true, I have returned, and it feels like I am coming home to where I belong. Since retiring from bodybuilding contest promotion in 1980, and the publishing business in 1993, my life has been extremely full, but the urge to return to the bodybuilding business has always been there. It has been said that once you are in this business you can never really leave and that is also true. Once a bodybuilder always a bodybuilder and though my years have advanced, my passion for the sport is as strong as ever.

Since my retirement, bodybuilding has still played a major role in my life on many different levels. New opportunities presented themselves almost immediately, while other roles continued from my days in the iron game. Charity work is something that I have always enjoyed and my retirement allowed me to focus on more philanthropic goals, such as giving free seminars at schools. In 1987 I was appointed as Fitness Director of the National Kidney Foundation, a job that allowed me to do something that could benefit those less fortunate. My role here was to work closely with the Executive Director and President of the Foundation to develop fitness programs and coordinate sporting events with fitness and sporting personalities, which was no problem at all for me as I knew plenty of people in the sporting world, and would call on many of them to help me support this worthy cause. A background in checkers also served me well in this new role, as regular tournaments arranged by myself, working alongside the Nassau County Park's Department, would raise thousands of dollars annually for Kidney Foundation research.

As a bodybuilder, health was always my first priority. Building the body for health purposes was always number one for me, so the opportunity to help the National Kidney Foundation through developing public service programs aimed at educating the public on the needs of kidney patients and the need for organ donation, was a perfect way to continue my goal of health promotion. Not long after the National Kidney Foundation contacted me, I began raising money for them by issuing checkers challenges to whoever was game enough to take on "a checkers champion". For many of my checkers challenges, I would give my opponent two kings, leaving one for myself. I would then say, "You'll never beat me." Usually any good player who has two kings can beat one king, but there is a trick to it that not too many people know about. And no matter what your opponent does, it ends up as a draw.

What I usually did was get them all excited by having a warm up game, which didn't count. And of course I would lose this game. In the warm up game my opponent is counting their money already and I would usually say "Oh I should have gone to the other corner." I won't tell the whole secret here. Let's just say it involves forcing your opponent to line their two checkers up in one corner, while you, with your one checker, force a draw.

Another thing I would do is to give my opponent 12 checkers, keeping only two checkers for myself. Here I would tell them I would stop them from getting a king, giving up to ten to one odds – if they were willing to put up one thousand dollars I would put up ten thousand dollars and, needless to say, I would never lose. And, of course, all this money would go to the Kidney Foundation. Most people would put

Back, Although Never Really Gone

up a few hundred dollars, all sure that they were going to win. None ever won. I still run checkers tournaments to this day, the last ones being the Long Island Checkers Championships on June the 30th, 2007 and the 2008 New York State Checkers Championships held on July 13 at Jones Beach, South Park. All profits from the New York State Champs went to the United Cerebral Palsy Foundation.

Checkers Man: Dan in the early 1980s, moments prior to a checkers match to raise funds for cancer research.

If you have been blessed with so much and have had many opportunities for success, like I have, it is always nice to give something back. This is what I have done with the Kidney Foundation work in raising funds and helping those less fortunate, and also with the hundreds of appearances I have made at schools, mostly in the Long Island area. For the last 50 years, putting on shows in high schools where I discuss the dangers of steroids and other harmful practices such as smoking and drinking, has been some of my most important, and enjoyable work. Many times I would bring champion bodybuilders with me to give their honest views on drugs and to warn kids of these drugs' dangers. Often such people knew firsthand the dangers of performance enhancing drugs and their experience was valuable. These lectures would usually run for an hour and went over great. Many years after such talks I would meet up with kids who were there, to discover they had begun weight training and following a healthy way of living because of what I said during one of my appearances.

In the 1950s I would put on shows for sporting goods stores that handled my barbell equipment. Then I was asked to lecture at high schools across the county. It grew from there and I must have done close to 200 talks since it all began, reaching out to thousands of kids. These are still a regular part of my public service work and today I speak annually at three local Long Island schools: Hewlett-Woodmere Middle in Hewlett, Oceanside High and Shaw Elementary. My grandson Cary Epstein teaches in Hewlett H.S., my granddaughter Ilissa Epstein teaches at Shaw in Valley Stream. My strategy for each lecture is to do a couple of little magic tricks and mix it up so it sparks everyone's interest. Then hit them with the important stuff. In August 2007, I along with bodybuilding champion, Leon Brown, spoke to a large group at a Suffolk Y Jewish Community Center camp in Commack, Long Island. It is always a great pleasure reaching out and influencing people to make the right life choices and these engagements are the perfect way to do this.

Being inducted into the National Jewish Sports Hall of Fame in 2007 is one of the highlights of my life and was an incredible honor. You can attain no greater recognition than respect and acknowledgement from your peers and the National Jewish Sports Hall of Fame, established by organizers at the Suffolk Y Jewish Community Center 15 years ago, has given Jewish athletes from all corners of the U.S. the respect they deserve. The intention of the Jewish Sports Hall of Fame is to educate people about, and pay tribute to, Jewish sportspeople, much the same way the WBBG has, for decades, honored bodybuilding and fitness personalities. For me it felt great to be inducted into the class of 2007 along with such magnificent Jewish sporting personalities as sports broadcaster Howard Cosell and swimmer Mark Spitz, among many others. Director Alan Freedman, President Andrew S. Levy and executive director Joel A. Block are to be commended for making this event celebrating the sporting achievements of my people possible.

On receiving my official induction invitation my first thought was, "I am glad they are honoring me while I am still alive." After all, this is the kind of occasion you want your family and friends to share and when the day came I felt great happiness having mine there with me. My wife Thelma and children being there made it all the more special as, with their tremendous support, they made it possible for me to do what I did to achieve such recognition, and as a man proud of my heritage, I wanted them along with my 15 grandchildren and six great grandchildren to see that their culture carries a strong tradition of success. Of all the awards received over the years, being inducted into the National Jewish Sports Hall of Fame would be the most satisfying, as it is based on the degree of influence the inductee has had within the Jewish community, the level of respect to which they are held among their peers, along with the fact they had to overcome adversities, challenge stereotypes and set a path for others to follow to get to that point. It was also extra special for me as I was the first ever bodybuilder to be inducted, which can only have a positive impact on the sport I love.

As you advance in years, it is important that what you have worked so hard for has had a positive influence on the lives of other people, and receiving recognition for what you have done tells you it has. My bodybuilding work has always been done to advance the sport and two of my awards, the 1980 AAU Hall of Fame Award and the 1983 Champion award, are near to my heart for this very reason.

The AAU award came as a bit of a surprise as I had only competed as an amateur for three years, but over that time, and despite never winning the Mr. America, proved that I was among the very best. When I was contacted and told the award would be given in Atlantic City, and I would be sharing the stage with other top former AAU bodybuilding champions, I felt a sense of satisfaction that I was considered amongst the AAU's greatest ever bodybuilders.

The 1983 Champion Award was presented by New York's prestigious Downtown Athletic Club and was given to recognize my competitive bodybuilding achievements and overall influence on the bodybuilding industry. Since I had had involvement with the Downtown Athletic Club with the inducting of Ronald Reagan and Steve Reeves into the WBBG Hall of Fame the club was a special place for me and to receive one of their awards was fitting. What made receiving this award extra special was the fact that Steve Reeves and his lovely wife Aline had flown in especially to attend. Bodybuilding great Bill Pearl was also there.

Standing Proud: Dan receiving his Champion award, with Mrs Steve Reeves and Steve Reeves in attendance.

The Downtown Athletic Club, a 35-floor-building based in lower Manhattan, has enjoyed a long history as being one of the most celebrated sporting bastions in the U.S. It's probably best known for it's annual Heisman award given for college football excellence, but also became known for awarding bodybuilding and strength athletes after I inducted Steve Reeves in 1973. After I first inducted Reeves, the Downtown Athletic Club invited him to attend the Champion Award ceremony every year, which they had established after this time. The club closed in 2002, after experiencing major financial losses in the aftermath of the appalling tragedy that hit America on September the Eleventh, 2001.

Champion Award: It's Dan's turn to be honored as Steve Reeves congratulates him on his receiving the prestigious Champion Award at the Downtown Athletic Club.

Not long after retiring from contest promotion, and one year after I had been presented with the Downtown Athletic Club Champion Award, I was involved in a contest of another sort. As the scope of my Hall of Fame awards was broadened to include people from many different areas who best represented the health and fitness lifestyle, I made my way to the Whitehouse to induct President Ronald Reagan and with this meeting came the photo opportunity of a lifetime: Reagan and I arm wrestling on the Oval Office desk. This photo, published all around the world, resurfaced in 1996 at New York's Museum of Modern Art, as part of their 100th anniversary celebrations, where they featured the most interesting photos of the century. In this collection they also included a 1972 photo of me inducting then New York Mayor, Abe Beame along with Johnny Weismuller and Buster Crabbe into the WBBG Hall of Fame, a photo the New York Times picked as their best picture of the century. Because of this meeting, Mayor Beame presented Johnny Weismuller and Buster Crabbe with the keys to New York City. I had officially retired from the business, but my legacy to bodybuilding was living on through photos and this was good to see.

You might remember me mentioning the official Whitehouse lapel pins I was presented with during my historic meeting with President Ronald Reagan. I am often asked what happened to these. Well after receiving them I would wear these gold-plated, very ornate pieces - a little larger than a nickel and bearing the official Whitehouse seal - on my suit almost everywhere I went, and everyone would remark on how nice they looked. They were my pride and joy, a constant reminder of the time I spent with the President. I think now is a good time to discuss what happened to these pins.

I was going to the Concord Hotel with my family to run a bodybuilding contest one year and I put my luggage on top of the car roof, tying it down and securing it as best I could. I was told at the time that due to tremendous winds that were hitting, it might be unsafe to place my luggage - which included many valuable items including the lapel pins - on the roof of my car. But since I was staying at the Concord for over a week, and all my family were coming along for the ride, the rest of the car was packed to capacity so I figured I really had no choice. With great pride in my resourcefulness, I said to anyone within earshot, "This luggage will never fall off. It's all good and tight." Needless to say it fell off on the New York Thruway. With an almighty gust of wind it blew off the top of the roof and was scattered all over the road. By the time people told me what had happened, blowing their horns and signaling for me to turn around, it was too late. I couldn't really back-up because by the time they had reached me I was quarter of a mile ahead, doing about 60 to 70 miles per hour. By the time I circled around, someone had stopped and picked it up and I lost all of my clothes, along with those beautiful lapel pins. There might be someone out there with a rare set of presidential lapel pins that were not given to them personally. If so, they may now have the back-story on how they got them.

Writer: Art Buchwald, Washington Post Newspaper humorist writer, who wrote a story on Dan in the aftermath of the President Reagan arm-wrestling match.

Though I had retired, my reputation as a promoter and trainer was still alive and well, so much so that people from all over the world would - and still do - seek my advice on health and fitness matters. From 1993 through to the present day I have taken a background role in assisting people to achieve their training goals, and this has been a great way for me to stay connected to bodybuilding. In fact, right now I am training a 17-year-old kid from Russia who is poised for bodybuilding success. At six feet four inches and 190 pounds of solid muscle, Nikita, who has been training with me for six months through Internet and telephone conversations, started out with very little endurance, but he could press some reasonable weights and had worked his way up to 250 pounds for eight reps on the bench press. His body was quite solid but he did not have much definition. With my training methods, which included an emphasis on high reps and endurance, he is looking incredibly sharp these days. Like I said before, once you are in this business you can't get out. Besides, training people provides me with a tremendous thrill, just seeing them progress to achieve their physical fitness goals.

With Nikita it is the same deal Louie Ferrigno and I had back in the 1970s: no contract and a partnership based on friendship and faith. The only thing I asked from this kid is that he thanks me at the end and stays off any kind of bodybuilding drug. When we first spoke, I told him, "If you ever take steroids I want nothing to do with you, because you will end up living a short, sick life". He assured me he would never touch them and I am happy to have helped this young man on the fast track to permanent lifelong, natural bodybuilding progress as I am sure he will heed my advice and stay clean. His training is going so good and his progress has been so rapid that I predict he will be another Lou Ferrigno. Along with Nikita, I am secretly training several other bodybuilders and intend to publish their results, along with Nikita's, when the time is right.

Retired Champions: Dan with (left to right) 1980 Junior Mr. America, Ernie Santiago and 1957 AAU Mr. New York City and former WBBG champion, Kenny Hall, in 2005.

Back, Although Never Really Gone

Dan in 2005 with 1962 Mr. America winner, Joe Abbenda

My own training has never stopped. A while back I routinely trained in the gym attached to our North Woodmere home, but today it is 30 push-ups every morning along with various lighter weight movements. With the push-ups I go to failure, and for my curls I do 78 repetitions with around 35 pounds. Actually I do all my exercises in sets, starting with one with a few seconds rest, then two, climbing the ladder in add reps style: one rep, two reps, three reps, four reps and so on up to 12 which gives me a total of 77 reps. When I hit five reps, that's 15 reps total and I try to go up to at least 12 reps on each set. Sometimes I will do seven sets of ten, and on the last rep in my last set of ten I will do 16 extra reps just to get the pump. But I don't have to kill myself, as I'm not out to prove anything these days. Being America's Most Muscular Man is no longer a goal and you won't be seeing a bodybuilding comeback from me anytime soon. Remember I have had a heart condition all of my life and don't want to push too hard at my age only to end up with a heart attack. There are just too many people who push themselves too hard. So these days it is some light exercises like side laterals and curls for very high reps, just to feel good and to know that there is still some blood circulating in my body, and I do still aim for the pump, and most of the time I achieve it. Being superman is not my aim and I lift weights just to stay healthy and enjoy life. I recommend that most people do the same. It always pays to consult your doctor before attempting any form of training though, regardless of your age.

Still Pumping: Dan at age 78.

My daily routine these days also includes a very hot shower. Not uncommon you say? With my hot showers the water temperature is turned to ice cold shortly after hopping in. Much the same way I would plunge into the freezing cold outdoor pool back in North Woodmere, after sitting in the sauna for 10 minutes or so, standing under a cold shower after the setting has been on hot tends to revitalize me. It's like a shock treatment for my head and body. Sports people do this to a similar extent and they call it contrast showers and it is supposed to help with circulation and muscle recovery. This I don't recommend for anybody of any age. Remember I play by different rules and contrast showers may not be everyone's idea of a good time.

One thing I have been doing since age 18, and I have no proof that there is any real merit to it as I have only done it on myself, is to massage Vaseline hair tonic into my scalp for three minutes very vigorously directly after climbing out of my cold shower and before combing. I feel this is the secret to maintaining a full head of healthy hair, as my father was balding at age 60 and my older brother, Harry, was losing his hair at the same age. Neither of them did what I currently do. Since balding is thought to be genetic, maybe I am onto something. But who knows? When they stopped selling Vaseline hair tonic I switched to clear mineral oil and have been using this over the past five years instead. You might think me crazy but this process seems to keep my hair very healthy. My hair is shiny, full and thick with very little grey and in place all day long. My barber asks me what I put on my hair and I tell him, "Chicken fat." Along with keeping my body fit I have also always been a stickler for good hygiene and grooming. I feel that with advancing age we could all do well to maintain our appearance as I feel this markedly improves quality of life and adds years to it.

Looking Sharp at 80: belying their years, Dan and Thelma enjoying a night out.

Training partner: Rebbitzen Esther Jungries and her beloved husband Rabbi Theodore Jungreis. Rabbi Theodore trained with Dan in Dan's home gym.

Keeping fit and healthy has brought its share of advantages, not the least being a long and fulfilling life. Staying in shape also keeps me striving for greater heights and the resuming of the WBBG and MTI, which you will be hearing more of later in this chapter, is due in large part to my willingness to never say never on the health front. As anyone who has achieved great success in the promotion and publishing fields will tell you, publicity is the key. For someone in my position, with the aim of furthering bodybuilding, it is important that I present optimal health and vitality at all times.

Having a strong presence in the media is one way of keeping the publicity machine rolling. Since 1993 various media have profiled me. I have been featured in the New York Times many times and, of course, Long Island Newsday, my local paper, regularly keeps the public informed on what is happening in my life. One medium that reaches the widest possible audience is the Internet and I have to say I have become quite web savvy over the past five years. Maintaining contact with people from all over the world through e-mail has been a great blessing as this has allowed me to not only maintain closer ties to family and friends, but also to meet many tremendous people, many of which have helped me to re-enter the bodybuilding scene, at a faster rate than would otherwise have been possible. The wonders of the Internet never cease to amaze me; it truly is the future of business communications and a must for anyone involved in almost any kind of business practice.

My first real online involvement came in 2001 through bodybuilding history website musclememory.com run by computer programmer and bodybuilder, Tim Fogarty. Tim saw the need to comprehensively document bodybuilding's history in the most easily accessible way and what he has done with his site is remarkable. In over 100,000 entries Tim has provided a near complete database of bodybuilding magazine covers, contest results dating back to the early 1940s and profiles on past and present bodybuilding champions. Tim contacted me in 2001 asking for access to my magazine archives, including covers, articles and other historical information and I was very happy to oblige. To help him with his mission, I invited him over to my house to sort through my archives, most of which was in storage in a back room. Since then, all *MTI* covers have been placed on musclememory.com along with many articles and much historical information provided by myself. It feels good to have helped preserve bodybuilding's history in this way and Tim has done as good a job as anyone of allowing for this to happen, in the broadest possible way. Tim even developed my personal website - danlurie.com - which receives many daily hits and allows me to keep people informed on what is happening in my life, while providing a detailed background on my bodybuilding history.

Since having an online presence, a world of opportunities has come my way and many positive people have entered my life. In late 2005, a young writer, David Robson, contacted me requesting an interview. He told me he had followed my career and would like for readers of the website he continues to write for - bodybuilding.com - to learn more about my history. That first interview we did together was published in December 2005 and David and I quickly became good friends. So successful was that interview - which gave bodybuilding fans a good overview of my life - we did a part two, which was run on March 2006.

Since then we have kept in close contact, and have done two further bodybuilding.com interviews, making the total four, which must be some kind of record. As you will know, David is the co-writer of the book you are now holding.

Another close friend who is also an accomplished writer and respected bodybuilding historian, Randy Roach, came into my life through the web and since 2004 I have worked very closely with Randy on his book Muscle, Smoke and Mirrors, a two volume work that provides probably the most detailed history of bodybuilding and, in particular, its nutritional legacy of any book ever published. As part of his research into bodybuilding's origins, Randy contacted me and since then we have been in constant contact. When Randy first rang me he wasn't sure I was still alive. His first words were: "Dan I thought you were dead." He heard I had died, so now when we talk I tell him, "Randy, I am doing okay for a guy who has been dead for a long time. I hope you can hear me as I am now talking to you from my grave." Nevertheless, Randy has become a great friend.

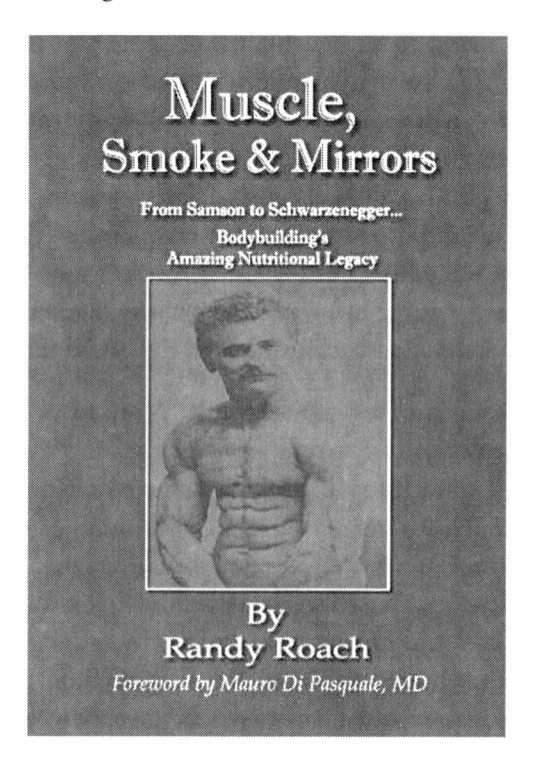

Back, Although Never Really Gone

Three men who have had a major influence on recent developments in my life are Greg Sushinsky, a respected writer and bodybuilding authority, Steve Speyrer, a gym owner, personal trainer and writer and Alan Palmieri, a former five term mayor of Jefferson County Tennessee, gym owner and businessman. The one thing that binds these men is the fact they are all bodybuilders, and some of the most knowledgeable spokespeople for bodybuilding I have ever met.

Steve Speyrer first contacted me back in 2002 for no other reason than to say hello and thank me for inspiring him to reach great heights in the bodybuilding field as a natural bodybuilding champion. He told me that I "blew all the other so called trainers and publishers away," which I thought was high praise from this very nice man. Since then we have been in regular contact and he has supported me wherever possible. Steve is one of the most passionate advocates of bodybuilding for health I have met. His Classic Anatomy Gym and Bodybuilding Hall of Fame are world famous and I had the pleasure of being inducted into this Hall of Fame in 2002. Steve told me that as a kid he badly wanted a copy of my Positrain book and saved hard until he could afford one. Years later he found my e-mail address on the Internet and we began talking. He quickly featured me on his website and to this day I credit him with bringing me back from the bodybuilding dead. Alan Palmieri has supported me in much the same way Steve has: with full commitment to preserving the history of bodybuilding through the promotion of my recent bodybuilding projects. Greg Sushinsky is the consummate professional writer. I met Greg through Steve Speyrer in 2005 and we have worked on several projects together over the past three years.

Since this chapter began I have been referring to the "several projects" I have been working on and I have often mentioned throughout this book my bodybuilding "comeback". As I have said, my goal has always been to elevate bodybuilding in an honest and dignified way. With the help of the five men I have just spoken of, this aim continues. At 85, I am back. The ultimate goal for me was to bring back *MTI*, but these things take time and we instead went with a bodybuilding first: a newspaper targeted at the bodybuilding community, which featured some of the best writers in the business today along with all the latest developments in the iron world. The first issue of *Muscle Training Illustrated News* came out in September of 2007 and had good reviews. Greg Sushinsky and his talented wife Marsha, who helped with her technical and troubleshooting expertise, are the people I can thank for making the newspaper possible. Greg's layout and editorial skills along with the ever-present eye of his dog Monique made it possible. I will make it known here in the pages of this book that I hired Greg's Dog Monique to spy on Greg, to make sure he did the paper properly. I sent Greg some money to buy Monique bones, but she was instead bought steak. I am told the dog slept with one eye open, watching to see if production was going well.

One man who has supported me is Arley Vest and one website I have always enjoyed is Arley's Natural Champion, which is devoted to natural bodybuilding and is probably the best publication of its kind on the Internet. In 2007 David Robson interviewed me on the issue of drugs in bodybuilding for Natural Champion. This interview was my way of supporting a man who has done as much for natural bodybuilding as probably anyone else. We need more like him. Like me, Arley has a background in competing and contest promotion.

Of course, another of my projects has been the book you are reading now. A book on my life has been planned for many years, but finding the right person to provide an accurate and detailed, yet entertaining account of my life in bodybuilding has not been easy. Tracing ones life without overlooking anything is a major process of information gathering and this is exactly what I have been doing for the past ten years: putting together many pages of information, charting all the major and not so major areas and events of my life. The timing had to be perfect. The next hardest thing was finding someone with a detailed knowledge of bodybuilding and a passion for the sport who could also write to a high standard. Once again I can thank the Internet for bringing me into contact with David Robson and now the book is part of bodybuilding history.

The biggest task I have faced over the past two years is re-starting the WBBG. Not that it was ever dead to begin with but, as I like to say, just taking a well deserved rest. The WBBG was still going strong back when I decided to retire for health reasons and to take on new

Back, Although Never Really Gone

projects. After a good rest it is again ready to become a force within the bodybuilding industry. Bringing back the WBBG was important to me for two main reasons: I dearly wished to see a return to the more desirable, balanced physique with less of an emphasis on drugs, and again felt it was time to start honoring those champions who have paved the way for bodybuilders of today, through its Hall of Fame. At one point bodybuilding was new, fresh and exciting and its athletes' physiques were, with hard work and discipline, largely attainable for the general population. Today they are totally unreal and loaded with all manner of drugs. The new WBBG has put in place guidelines to ensure this trend does not continue unabated.

Committed to Excellence: Dan with his WBBG 1978 Mr. And Ms. Pro Mr. America and Mr. Olympus judging panel. (Bottom row, left to right): Al Fives, Julie Levine, Andy Bostino, Chris Dickerson, Dan, Walter Podolak, Hy Schaeffer, Lenny Russell, unknown, Tony Schtinna. (Top row, left to right): unknown, Leo Murdock, Steve Michalik, unknown, Tony Pearson, unknown.

My past WBBG shows were always run fairly and open to all comers. This is something that will not be changed, as we will again welcome anyone from any federation, and politics will play no part in the outcome for any competitor. When describing my vision for the WBBG, I like to use a beauty pageant example. These pageants usually choose a tall, blond woman to win, the Ms. America being a good example. Well if you are five foot four and have red hair you don't have a chance. The same thing applies to men's professional bodybuilding today: if you do not have massive, unrealistic size you simply have no chance of winning. What the WBBG will emphasize is a physical ideal that best represents the classic physique, one with a smaller waistline, broader shoulders, good definition - though not the kind of ripped, monstrous appearance that can only be attained through extreme use of chemicals - and nice presentation. The Steve Reeves physique is an example of what we want.

When bodybuilders turn professional they often find themselves up against monsters and cannot compete on this level under the current judging criteria. The WBBG provides an alternative for these men and women. WBBG judging standards will radically depart from what is now in vogue and we will let the competitors and judges know exactly what we are looking for. Those competitors with massive waistlines, and who show obvious signs of synthol and excessive anabolic drug use will be scored down. Either these guys will get the message and clean up or they just won't come back. Many competitors have told me they are afraid to compete because their look - smaller with nice lines and better proportions - will not compare to the ultra-massiveness that is often rewarded today.

With these aims in mind, I along with Doug Going got to work organizing the first WBBG bodybuilding contest and International Fitness and Sports Hall of Fame awards in 27 years: the WBBG North America Bodybuilding and Figure and Fitness Championships, held on August 25 in South Portland, Maine. Well, as we know, good things take time and this event, though it was well down on anticipated numbers of competitors, and not up to the usual standard expected of WBBG contests, did signal the beginning of my comeback as a promoter. The nice thing about this event was that fact that we held the Hall of Fame ceremony on the same day as the bodybuilding event and the competitors had the opportunity to mix with many past champions and the legends themselves got to meet up with men they competed against and admired as fellow athletes.

Back, Although Never Really Gone

The Greats Meet Again: (left to right) Tony Atlas, John DeFendis, Harold Poole, Bob Gajda, Leon Brown, Warren Frederick, Anibal Lopez, Dan, Steve Michalik and Paul Bernstein at the 2007 WBBG Hall of Fame awards, held in Portland, Maine.

2007 WBBG Hall of Fame Awards: (left to right) Harold Poole, Leon Brown, Dan, Tony Atlas and Warren Frederick

Since retirement I have maintained contact with many of bodybuilding's greats - both WBBG and non-WBBG athletes - and in line with my philosophy on non-discrimination I have always respected the achievements of all bodybuilders and fitness personalities. The discipline it takes to get to the top is the same for all competitors. It was no surprise then that the list of inductees for my first Hall of Fame awards in a long while were selected for their contributions to bodybuilding, fitness and sports, not based on any federation to which they were affiliated or any political stance they took. And what champions we had. Of the 10 men who arrived in Maine to be honored, all had made amazing progress as pioneers for health and fitness and the sport of bodybuilding, and I was extremely proud as they accepted their awards. Steve Michalik, Harold Poole, Sergio Oliva, John DeFendis, Leon Brown, Bob Gajda, Tony Atlas, Warren Frederick, Anibal Lopez and Paul Bernstein all looked great, showing how good weight training has been to them, as they mingled with the crowd and reminisced about their competition days. Just seeing these champions all in the one place brought back many wonderful memories from my early contest promotion days and renewed my enthusiasm to continue. As part of the induction we featured a very nicely done two-minute video clip of each champion with audio commentary and pictures highlighting their achievements and providing an overview of their career.

A major reason for establishing the Hall of Fame awards back in 1968 was to not only give credit to top bodybuilders and fitness people but to allow the public to get closer to these men and women. Often bodybuilding fans only read about their idols, or occasionally saw them from a distance at an event of some sort. My Hall of Fame dinners were run to bring the fans closer to the athletes. Usually everyone being honored had a name badge and anyone in attendance had the freedom to talk to any of these champions. I feel honored to be the first man to make bodybuilders and other famous sporting personalities of the past accessible to the general public in this way, and this is something that will continue. I will continue to grow the WBBG, and will always aim to promote bodybuilding. I feel, based on the anticipated response to the 2007 event and the number of quality past-champions in attendance for the Hall of Fame ceremony, the WBBG will only continue to grow. Like I said, good things take time and with more promotion and publicity and with a few of the kinks ironed out, the WBBG will only become stronger.

The happiest moments in my life, other than spending time with my family, who remain my greatest joy, have come through bodybuilding and strength training. Setting those strength records all those years back, around the time of my most muscular title wins, still rank as special moments. Back then it was all trial and error and competitive bodybuilding was just beginning, so the gains I made and the strength feats I did were up there with the best. I remember first attempting that one-arm bent press with 100 pounds. It might sound funny but even this weight seemed an amazing achievement at the time. Then it jumped to 150, then to 200 at one of Sigmund Klein's shows. The following year I kept practicing until, in 1945, I topped out at 285 pounds at 168 pounds bodyweight. You don't see too many people doing this lift nowadays and I'm not surprised as it would be one of the harder weight training movements to master. Once you are under the weight you then need the strength to straighten the legs and press it while keeping the body fixed in the bent position. You need to keep the bar straight otherwise it will break your wrist if it is not properly balanced. One thing I discovered here - and this can be a lesson to all who wish to progress as either pure strength athletes or bodybuilders - is that technique is more important than brute strength. Using the muscles correctly will always overcome sheer physical exertion. With my one-arm bent press I remember having to get right under that weight, kind of twisting the body to the side away from the bar while pressing at the same time. And boy did you have to be flexible, and somewhat of a contortionist.

Diversifying into other types of lifting saw me pull 1810 pounds in the back lift and push 1230 pounds on the leg press. This kind of lifting - along with my 1225 parallel bar dips in ninety minutes and 1665 push-ups in the same space of time - are records that really laid the foundation for everything I have done since. Just knowing that I could achieve all of this and that I had the determination to succeed, really gave me the motivation to take chances to become successful in the business world. I urge anyone of any size, shape, nationality, sex or creed to take up weight training, as it will develop personal strength of character and a determined mindset faster than anything else. Remember, with weight training you are in total control of the outcome. If you fail, you fail. There is nobody else to blame. So you work extra hard and your mind becomes strong, your resolve strengthens and you become at one with the iron. There is you and the steel and you will do all that is humanly possible to move that load. If you can squat 400 pounds for reps, you can attempt any of life's challenges.

"You become at one with the iron". America's Most Muscular Man doing what he does best in an early photo by famed photographer Earl Forbes.

Of course, winning America 's Most Muscular Man title for three years running was another highlight of my career and boosted my confidence much the same way those early lifting years did. Coming so close to claiming the Mr. America title might seem a strange source of satisfaction, but it too is high on my list of greatest moments. The AAU Mr. America had, and still has, a special place in the hearts of all who captured it. In the early 1940s winning this title was my life and all else fitted around this aim. Coming so close under very controversial circumstances tested my resolve and developed within me an ability to accept setbacks and move ahead without looking back, except to outline these setbacks for posterity as I have done here. Besides, many do consider me an uncrowned Mr. America and that is just as good in my eyes. For me though, just getting in great shape and contesting such a big event is enough of an achievement. Knowing I was one of the best bodybuilders in the world at that time is something I will treasure always. Another lesson: competing in a bodybuilding contest is the biggest test of character I can think of. There are very few, if any, sports that consume you so much. You train, eat, sleep and breathe it. When you are up on that stage there is no hiding. If you mess up, everyone in attendance can see it, so you work hard to get it right, get it perfect. This too builds, and takes, amazing strength of mind and fortitude, which can be applied to all other areas of life. Bodybuilding, quite simply, creates well-rounded champions, those who are more likely to surmount any of life's obstacles.

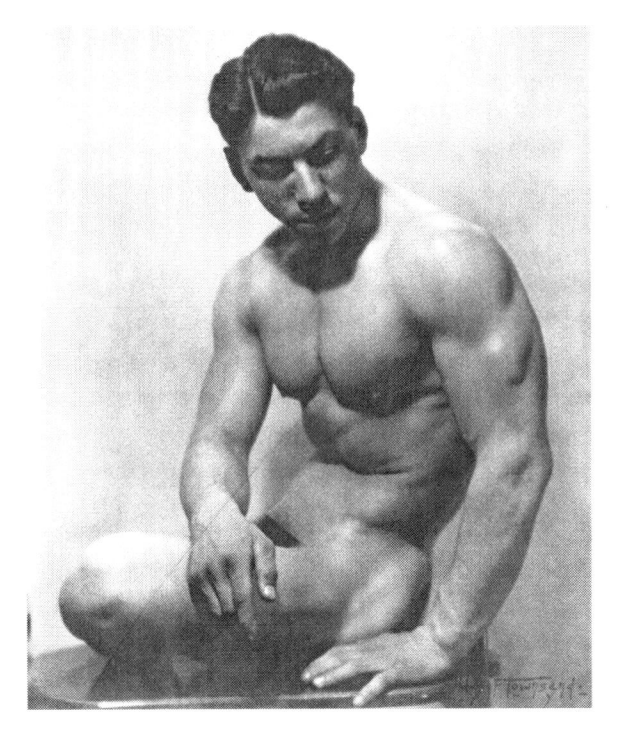

"You train, eat, sleep and breathe it". Dan showing the physique of a champion in this classic relaxed shot.

Most bodybuilders starting out will tell you that publicity is very important and I was lucky enough to have many great people help me in this area. During my years of vying for the Mr. America title, and even in the lead up to this, when I was skinny kid with some potential but little else, talented photographers Earle Forbes and Lon Hanagan would take, for free, many pictures of me posing. If you are to be successful in the bodybuilding magazines, good pictures are essential.

Lon Hanagan was a fine man who loved music, opera in particular, and would take some of best physique pictures in the world. Later I found he was the organ player for Radio City Music Hall. He would also play the piano for me at my shows where he would also double as a judge. Earle Forbes was the one who took most of my pictures from when I started as a skinny kid at age 17, through to when I became a bodybuilding champion. He spent a lot of money taking pictures of me and he always gave me copies. Earle liked to use props with many of the photos he took with his Kodak Brownie camera and I remember he would experiment with different angles, where I would pose in less than conventional ways giving each pose a dramatic and artistic look all of its own. He was certainly one of the more creative photographers I ever worked with. The "sword" photo on the cover of this book is one of the best he took of me.

To work with such talented people was a tremendous experience for a young man starting out in bodybuilding and I credit these men for helping me to become one of the best bodybuilders of my time. They say to succeed in life, you must stand on the shoulders of giants: these men, along with other influential people like my parents and good friends are truly giants and I would not have achieved my goals without them.

After my competition days the opportunity to act on the Sealtest Big Top Show presented itself. This stands out as being another great moment because it gave the Dan Lurie name nationwide appeal. Because of this the opportunities really came in the late 1950s and early '60s, after the show had ended. Being television's first strongman and involved with one of America's first television programs for children, the most popular children's show of its time and two-time Emmy nominee, was an experience of a lifetime. I still have my Sealtest cape and will often take it our from time to time to relive old memories of my time as Sealtest Dan, the Muscle Man.

Back, Although Never Really Gone

Talented Man: One of Dan's early photographers, Earle Forbes, in Coney Island, 1940.

Dramatic Shot: an inspired Earle Forbes picture, capturing Dan at his best.

Careful Dan: Sealtest Dan gets acquainted with one of his Big Top supporting cast.

Those Were the Days: Dan (left) with Sealtest ringmaster, Jack Sterling (holding Dan's Sealtest Dan cape).

Juggling all my barbell and gym business commitments while acting on the Big Top Show was a test in itself. But it certainly paid off and after my time in the circus things really got rolling on both these fronts. If this wasn't enough, my magazine publishing and contest promotion roles made me wish I had been born with ten arms and ten legs. But I managed.

I feel *MTI* and the WBBG played a major part in bridging the gap between crooked contests and those bodybuilders who wanted a fair deal. There were no frills with anything I did either in promotion or publishing and the only requirement I really stipulated was that everything that was done under the *MTI* of WBBG name had to be done first class, or I didn't bother at all. The WBBG Hall of Fame dinners were, I feel, an important way to give worldwide recognition to the many greats who were often forgotten about except within certain pockets of the bodybuilding community. It was, and is, my job to keep their legacies to the bodybuilding and fitness world alive. I have always believed we should honor those who, through their achievements, have made the world a richer place, and even though we will all eventually pass on it is nice to know that our contributions will not be forgotten. It is for this reason that I will present yearly awards to those who have given so much but who are no longer with us. Steve Reeves, John Grimek and Charles Atlas were honored in memoriam for their lasting legacy to bodybuilding and fitness, at the 2007 WBBG Hall of Fame induction ceremony. For them, as with those champions who were in attendance, we showed a two-minute tape celebrating their pioneering life. We showed pictures of Charles Atlas pulling a train and his now-famous comic book advertisement. Many there were surprised to know that Charles Atlas had achieved so much.

Running contests was a way for me to promote the achievements of bodybuilders and to reward their training efforts. I knew how hard it was to train for a contest and had experienced the agony of defeat enough to know that bodybuilders needed a fair shake. It was also very rewarding to learn that many of my contests provided bodybuilders with their first taste of competition success, which gave them a lifelong love for competing and training and the health and personal growth benefits that go with these disciplines.

Acknowledging the Best: Dan was a big supporter of the world's greatest physique champion, Sergio Oliva. With Dan and Sergio is Nautilus exercise equipment inventor Arthur Jones and his wife.

Along with *MTI*, WBBG contests would showcase many emerging champions, giving them their start in the industry. Bodybuilders on the East Coast, as good as they were, were often overlooked in the wider bodybuilding media since the West Coast – Venice Beach California in particular - was the place to be and those who chose to train there naturally received most of the exposure. I feel proud to have given the East Coast guys their time in the spotlight through the pages of *MTI* and on the WBBG stage. Seeing bodybuilders improve to where they are at the top of their game brings no greater joy.

Being in the bodybuilding business for me has always meant juggling a whole range of projects. Like I said, today things are considerably quieter but at one time if it were related to bodybuilding I would be in on it. People thought I was crazy doing so much, but I loved what

Back, Although Never Really Gone

I was doing so I figured, why stop? Along with a barbell business that went on to become the most successful of the 1960s and '70s, I ventured into the health food market and even the sauna business.

When I first came out with my protein supplements in 1965, the year *MTI* came into being, the market had very few such products and, capitalizing on consumer need for quality bodybuilding products, I sold truckloads. When researching who could produce the best products, to give my customers the biggest bang for their buck, I looked widely for the best, finally settling on a manufacturer in Long Island. At first, labelling was something I did not put too much emphasis into, opting instead for the simple black and white design – no frills. The quality was the thing I put most of my energies into, extensively researching the best ingredients and formulating a high class, top quality product. But this kind of backfired on me. It seemed labeling and presentation was as equally important as quality. Realizing this, I came out with four-color litho labels and then things really took off. An important business lesson: how you present and market your product is of fundamental importance to selling lots of it. It may be the best quality on the market but if it does not appear to be attractive, you can kiss sales goodbye.

Among the many supplements I sold, the big seven-pound cans Jet-707, which were originally marketed using Lou Ferrigno's image, and which were used by big Louie and other champions such as Sergio Oliva, flew off the shelves. The claims I made that it would pack on pounds of muscle really were valid and repeat business became the norm. When Sergio started endorsing these, sales skyrocketed.

Being a big lover of the health benefits saunas provided, it was only a matter of time before I expanded into this market. In the 1960s, when I first got into the sauna market, I had a large factory in Utica Avenue, Brooklyn, where my barbell business was based. In this building I had access to the types of resources needed to make a real success of this business, and so sprang the Dan Lurie Sauna Corporation. Like my bodybuilding equipment, the saunas would also be produced to a high standard, and while it lasted they sold extremely well. I even had several installed in my North Woodmere home. The saunas came in a variety of sizes: from three-by-four to 10-by-20. Most of these were sold privately, but a few were bought by department stores. Once again my son Mark was head of manufacturing and actually built the heating element units himself.

When I first retired from the publishing and contest promotion business, it happened earlier than I would have liked but it had to be done because I knew that if I kept going my health would suffer. Another lesson I learned was that no matter who you are, you cannot defeat nature and if you push your body day in and out with several stressful projects at once, you will eventually pay the price. You cannot balance 100 things in one hand and 100 in the other. I did and ended up with a silent heart attack at 65, which, thank God, was not fatal. I figured it was a warning from God. Slowing down was not a choice for me, but a must. I had built up a nice nest egg and that is what you save your money for when you look to retire. So retire I did and the best thing about it was that I got to enjoy more time my wife and family. And that is what I have been doing for almost 20 years now. I still get together with at least half a dozen of my family on Saturdays and Sundays and we go out to dinner and Grandpa Dan picks up the bill. Some things never change.

I did just mention that retirement from my once hectic schedule was needed, and this is true, but, as also discussed in this chapter, once hooked on bodybuilding, it is very hard to walk away completely. In 2007 the first WBBG show and Hall of Fame awards in 27 years, the North America Bodybuilding and Figure and Fitness Championships, marked my official comeback as a bodybuilding contest promoter. In 2008, bodybuilding promotion was taken a step further with the WBBG Mr. and Ms. Jones Beach USA contest, held on August 24, which raised funds to benefit the United Cerebral Palsy Foundation. At least 25,000 attended this free contest held right on the beachfront, a show that will probably go down in history as being one of the biggest bodybuilding events – spectator-

Back, Although Never Really Gone

wise – ever held. Head of the judging panel was none other than my good friend and former Mr. America, Mr. Universe and Mr. USA bodybuilding champion Steve Michalik, who along with his fellow judges made history by standing up and being counted and showing their respective scoring sheets: no more deception in bodybuilding! With national media coverage and a wonderful line-up of promising future bodybuilding talent, this contest, which has made Jones Beach a 'muscle beach of the East', will surely attract America's top amateur bodybuilders for many years to come. And, as well as giving me the tremendous satisfaction of seeing the sport of bodybuilding grow and prosper under the WBBG banner, the Jones Beach show will keep me involved in the sport I love.

The Mr and Ms Jones Beach USA promotional poster

Dan Lurie: Heart of Steel

Winners: Dan (immediate left) with the 2008 Jones Beach USA winners, and head judge Steve Michalik (immediate right).

Dan shows off his muscles to the crowd, at 85 year young!

Back, Although Never Really Gone

One thing that kept me going in the often-cutthroat bodybuilding industry is the wonderful sense of achievement I get helping people to achieve their goals, and the quality of life I have able to provide for my family. Anyone in the bodybuilding publishing and contest promotion business will probably tell you that it is no popularity contest and that people will stick the knife in at any given opportunity to gain a corporate advantage. Sure, if you have a genuine grievance against someone, you must act on this, but in the interests of simply stirring up animosity and creating falsehoods about a person, some people are relentless. I suppose it is the intensely competitive nature of the bodybuilding game with its few main players, and the fact publishers and promoters themselves were also often once bodybuilders, a group of people who will usually do whatever it takes to get to the top, that makes the bodybuilding business what it is. In the 1940s, '50s and '60s there was Weider, Hoffman and myself propping up the bodybuilding industry and as you will have read in this book, and elsewhere, relations between the three of us were not what you would call amiable.

Retirement? Dan in retirement mode as King Neptune: taking part in the annual Coney Island Parade in 1985.

His daughter, Sandy, is Queen of the Mermaids.

Many of my closest friends tell me today that, from their perspective, I was simply erased from bodybuilding history after my retirement. Looking back I guess this is true to a certain extent, as many bodybuilding history books do not give me any acknowledgement for what I had done to promote the sport at the highest level. It is my hope that the book you are reading will have filled you in on my life and you now have a broader understanding of bodybuilding's history and my contribution to it. What is interesting is that the public will often believe what they are fed and the truth is often hidden from view; history is changed as a result. A good friend recently described me as being warm and humble, dynamic, energetic, passionate, enthusiastic, sensitive even! This is the Dan Lurie those closest to me see, but unfortunately not the perception some people have of the kind of person I really am. As long as I continue to be the kind of person my friend described, I feel I have done my job here on earth and my real contributions to bodybuilding and fitness will stand for all time.

Back, Although Never Really Gone

Enjoying Good Company: Dan and Thelma (left) with swimming legend Mark Spitz (with dark hair, seated), Xavier Cuget and his wife Charo, and daughters (left to right) Andrea, Jill and Sandy - in Acapulco Mexico, 1973.

With all that has happened in my life, the successes, the failures, the good times and the bad, It is my family that remain my greatest joy as they continue to provide the love and support that I am so fortunate to receive. Not everyone can be so blessed and I never take any of my family for granted. I suppose I am lucky since all of my children live within three miles of each other and most my grandchildren – three from each of my children - are locally based too. My six great grandchildren are also a blessing from God. We regularly get together and enjoy each other's company, and talk about how our lives have unfolded and what is left to come. My wife is my constant companion and just a wonderful human being, who I am eternally thankful for.

If I were to summarize my philosophy on life it would have to be "to live healthy and happy always". To achieve this, a good start would be to treat people with respect, as in doing this you also gain respect. Always care for your family and loved ones and work to provide the best possible life for them. Live honestly and speak the truth always. Throughout my life I have learned many lessons, and grown from these lessons, and have been influenced by many great people, many of which are mentioned in this book and many others who know who they are. I dearly love them all for helping me to become the person I am today. Bodybuilding has been my life and I hope my role in its continued promotion will help it to become the sport I know from experience can benefit people in so many ways. Keep pumping iron, respect yourself and others, be strong and remember: "health is your greatest wealth."

Dan with Family in 1960 (from left to right): Mark, Sandy, Thelma, Andrea, Shelly and Jill. Photo taken at a 13-year-old Mark's Bar Mitzvah party.

Back, Although Never Really Gone

The Reason: Dan and the secret to his success, his family, in 1990. Wife Thelma is to Dan's immediate right.

"The Lurie Clan" - Just a portion of Dan's close-knit family on their annual apple picking adventure in Connecticut, 2008.

Dan and Thelma's 15 Grandchildren

Back, Although Never Really Gone

Dan, his wife Thelma and their 5 kids pictured in 2008. From left to right, Mark, Dan, Sandy, Shelly, Thelma, Andrea and Jill.

Index

A

AAU (Amateur Athletic Union) 29
AAU Hall of Fame 371
AAU Mr. America magazine 136
add reps 353, 356, 358, 377
Adonis Health Club 25, 26, 28, 30, 33, 220
aerobics 349
America's Most Muscular Man 1, 3, 29, 34, 36, 39, 40, 41, 42, 48, 51, 53, 54, 71, 75, 76, 77, 78, 79, 87, 90, 174, 234, 274, 292, 353
anabolic steroids 322, 332
Anzio Beach 7
athletes 37, 50, 51, 63, 66, 67, 68, 112, 117, 118, 120, 121, 122, 136, 137, 141, 206, 211, 228, 274, 287, 288, 296, 308, 321, 322, 325, 328, 329, 330, 332, 340, 356, 361, 365, 370, 373, 386, 387, 388, 389

B

Ballet Squats 360
bodybuilders 25, 30, 33, 36, 39, 41, 67, 72, 77, 80, 108, 122, 124, 125, 136, 138, 139, 144, 150, 160, 162, 164, 165, 166, 167, 206, 214, 217, 223, 232, 234, 239, 240, 244, 274, 287, 288, 300, 308, 310, 315, 317, 319, 321, 324, 325, 326, 330, 340, 344, 345, 353, 364, 370, 371, 376, 383, 385, 386, 387, 388, 389, 391, 392, 395, 396, 399, 401
bodybuilding 1, 4, 23, 24, 25, 26, 28, 29, 30, 33, 36, 37, 39, 41, 43, 44, 45, 46, 47, 48, 50, 51, 52, 53, 61, 62, 63, 64, 65, 66, 67, 68, 69, 70, 72, 73, 74, 75, 77, 79, 83, 84, 85, 86, 87, 88, 89, 91, 101, 102, 105, 106, 107, 108, 109, 112, 113, 114, 115, 116, 117, 118, 119, 120, 123, 124, 125, 126, 128, 130, 133, 134, 135, 136, 137, 138, 139, 140, 141, 142, 143, 144, 146, 147, 149, 150, 151, 154, 158, 159, 160, 161, 162, 163, 164, 165, 167, 168, 169, 171, 172, 173, 179, 185, 187, 189, 201, 202, 203, 207, 208, 211, 212, 213, 214, 215, 216, 219, 223, 224, 225, 226, 227, 230, 232, 234, 236, 238, 244, 246, 251, 253, 265, 268, 269, 274, 277, 287, 288, 289, 292, 293, 295, 297, 299, 300, 301, 302, 303, 304, 305, 307, 308, 309, 310, 311, 312, 313, 314, 315, 316, 317, 319, 320, 321, 322, 323, 324, 325, 328, 331, 332, 333, 335, 336, 338, 339, 341, 343, 345, 347, 349, 350, 351, 355, 356, 361, 365, 366, 367, 370, 371, 372, 374, 375, 376, 377, 380, 381, 382, 383, 384, 385, 386, 387, 388, 389, 391, 392, 395, 396, 397, 398, 399, 401, 402
Boxing Training Illustrated 135, 238
Brownsville 21, 104, 175, 176, 235
Bungalow Bar 12

C

Canarsie, Brooklyn 16
carbohydrates 319, 362, 363, 364
Century Plaza health club 227
Champion Award 372, 373
checkers champion 108, 368
Club Elegante 174
Concord Hotel 69, 194, 199, 224,

230, 271, 374
Coney Island 21, 110, 202, 212, 393, 401

D

Dan Lurie Barbell Company 1, 41, 51, 58, 59, 61, 62, 69, 70, 72
Death in the Locker Room 328
Dianabol 318
Downtown Athletic Club 270, 271, 274, 372, 373
Drop-sets 337, 354, 359
Dynamic Tension 64, 213, 214, 215, 216

E

endurance 31, 189, 268, 270, 283, 284, 344, 345, 349, 353, 354, 356, 357, 359, 360, 376

F

Ferkie's Gym 21, 104

G

George F. Wingate medal 15, 17
Growth Hormone 321

H

Heisman award 372
Hercules movies 149, 290
Hot Rock Magazine 136, 208
Hunter College 126, 263, 288, 289, 290, 314

I

IFBB Mr. Universe 124
Instant Action Postitrain 342
Insulin 321
intensity techniques 353

J

Joe Franklin Show 109, 223, 224, 288, 290, 292, 296
John F. Kennedy International Airport 158, 281, 288

Junior Mr. America 35, 36, 47, 50, 64, 151, 376

K

Karate Training Illustrated 135

M

Madison Square Garden 4, 21, 207, 215, 253, 290
magic rope 349
meat and water diet 147
Monte Carlo 258, 267
Mr. America 24, 29, 30, 33, 35, 36, 37, 39, 40, 41, 42, 43, 46, 47, 48, 49, 50, 51, 54, 64, 65, 67, 68, 75, 76, 83, 86, 109, 115, 123, 124, 125, 126, 131, 132, 136, 143, 145, 146, 147, 148, 151, 154, 161, 162, 164, 165, 168, 169, 197, 206, 208, 210, 217, 219, 268, 288, 290, 292, 295, 296, 297, 298, 299, 300, 302, 304, 305, 307, 310, 311, 319, 321, 323, 327, 331, 332, 333, 337, 341, 346, 347, 348, 350, 354, 371, 376, 377, 385, 390, 391, 399
Mr. Olympia 108, 119, 120, 124, 125, 128, 144, 146, 151, 162, 163, 164, 167, 295, 296, 299, 302
muscle 3, 16, 20, 25, 28, 29, 31, 36, 43, 48, 63, 75, 76, 77, 87, 88, 89, 91, 105, 130, 135, 138, 144, 147, 168, 203, 206, 213, 220, 258, 274, 305, 306, 314, 316, 319, 321, 323, 325, 328, 337, 339, 340, 342, 347, 349, 351, 352, 353, 354, 358, 360, 361, 363, 364, 375, 378, 397, 399
muscle magazine 3, 314
Muscle Training Illustrated magazine 308, 312, 332

N

NABBA Mr. Universe 149, 151, 160,

162, 304, 309, 332
National Jewish Sports Hall of Fame 207, 370, 371
National Kidney Foundation 367, 368
New York Daily Sun Diamond Belt Boxing Championships 21
nutrition 116, 118, 288, 301, 308, 319, 347, 361, 365, 366

O

Oval Office 1, 272, 273, 278, 279, 281, 284, 374

P

power 14, 25, 29, 30, 31, 48, 57, 104, 158, 203, 206, 253, 324, 353, 360
Prince Rainier III 258, 259, 267
progressive resistance 339, 345
protein 128, 144, 147, 151, 154, 295, 319, 361, 363, 364, 397
push-ups 15, 18, 31, 32, 33, 35, 44, 91, 95, 213, 232, 274, 329, 347, 360, 377, 389

R

records 59, 68, 116, 130, 165, 232, 328, 359, 389
Aline Reeves 3
Rockaway Beach 9, 10, 11, 174

S

Sealtest 11, 89, 90, 91, 92, 93, 94, 95, 96, 97, 98, 102, 103, 104, 107, 194, 225, 229, 230, 290, 310, 323, 362, 392, 394
Sealtest Dan 89, 90, 91, 93, 95, 96, 97, 98, 102, 103, 104, 107, 194, 229, 230, 323, 392, 394
steroids 34, 148, 149, 317, 318, 319, 320, 321, 322, 323, 324, 325, 326, 327, 328, 329, 330, 331, 332, 334, 369, 376
strength 4, 7, 8, 14, 15, 16, 17, 20, 25, 26, 30, 31, 33, 34, 43, 45, 47, 81, 88, 89, 90, 91, 95, 104, 105, 106, 116, 130, 131, 132, 138, 201, 202, 203, 204, 205, 206, 211, 213, 214, 232, 254, 255, 268, 270, 277, 280, 284, 285, 287, 295, 301, 306, 311, 318, 319, 321, 323, 329, 335, 336, 341, 345, 353, 357, 360, 372, 389, 391
Strength and Health Magazine 42
Suffolk Y Jewish Community Center 370
Super-sets 353

T

Tarzan 14, 134, 220, 230
testosterone 171, 317, 318, 319, 324, 325
Tilden High School 15, 16, 17, 18, 175, 229
Time Magazine 44

U

United Cerebral Palsy Foundation 369, 398

W

Warren Lincoln Travers 21
WBBG Man of the Year 300
WBBG Physical Fitness Hall of Fame 214, 234
weightlifting 26, 27, 29, 34, 47, 67, 217, 219, 220, 312, 316, 318, 327, 335, 336, 337, 345

Y

Your Physique Magazine 3